THE BEST OF
ROWAN

50 DESIGNER KNITTING PATTERNS

STEPHEN SHEARD, EDITOR

INTRODUCTION BY KAFFE FASSETT

INTERWEAVE PRESS

Cover design, Elizabeth R. Mrofka

Production editors, Kathleen Hargreaves and Judith Durant

Production, Dean Howes

Printed in the United States by R.R. Donnelley & Sons Company

Library of Congress Cataloging-in-Publication Data

The best of Rowan: 50 designer knitting patterns/Stephen Sheard,
  editor.
     p.   cm.
  Includes index.
  ISBN 1-883010-57-8 (pbk.)
  1. Knitting—Patterns. 2. Rowan Yarns. I. Sheard, Stephen.
TT820.B59 1998
746.43'2043—dc21   98–33709
                                    CIP

First Printing: IWP—10M:897:DON

Publisher

Interweave Press, Inc.
201 East Fourth Street
Loveland, Colorado 80537
USA

THE BEST OF ROWAN
50 DESIGNER KNITTING PATTERNS
CONTENTS

INTRODUCTION

I love the whole Rowan story. Born of the bony and rugged Yorkshire landscape, Rowan yarns reflect the colours of their surroundings. The blackberry, lichen, and moss in the valleys, the subtle shades of the stones and granite in the hillsides around the mill—all meet and blend in the Rowan tweeds, chenilles, and wools.

I first met Rowan's founder Stephen Sheard at a weekend workshop in Roehampton in 1983, where he was selling weaving yarns, and I was teaching a workshop on colour. I spotted a gorgeous, ecru chunky chenille, longing to know if he had other colours. When he asked if I would design a range of colours for him, I was amazed but delighted. It was a momentous meeting for us both, and thus began a creative partnership that has spanned fifteen years.

Those initial Rowan yarns met with an enthusiastic but puzzled response from knitters. Where were the patterns? There were no existing designs that could do justice to them, so I agreed to design a range of kits using up to twelve colours each. Again, response was disappointing. I had been told many times by yarn spinners that knitters didn't want anything out of the ordinary. 'The British don't want to look distinctive', they insisted. Stephen and I did not agree. I have always spotted the gypsy under the patina of taste that overlies British fashion, an element that the French and the Italians have never managed to imitate for all their wonderful chic.

So we decided to push our luck, and to find someone who shared our vision. I contacted Mary Eddy, fashion editor of *Woman and Home* magazine, and offered to

Photograph by Steve Hanson

Rowan yarns reflect the colours of their Yorkshire surroundings

design a jacket for their front cover. Mary's feel for the innovative gave her the same intuition as ours that the British knitting public was only waiting for a little inspiration to break out into glorious colour. So 'Super Triangles' jacket appeared on the front cover of the magazine in spring 1984, to a tumultuous welcome from knitters. Although the design comprised more colours in one garment than had ever been used before, each row used only two, so anyone who could knit simple Fair Isle could tackle it. The kit sold over 7,000 in the first few months, outrageously exceeding all previous sales. Stephen and I knew our hunch was correct.

With the kick start we needed, we had the confidence to move ahead with even more luscious and unique patterns. Designers like Sasha Kagan, Susan Duckworth and Jamie and Jessie Seaton started producing deliciously ornate and richly patterned designs in many, many colours. It was a thrilling and wonderful time for us all and proved that there is no challenge that knitters will not rise to once they have been inspired.

Today knitting has taken a new place in the textile arts. Emerging from the extraordinarily creative phase of the last fifteen years, the craft is now taken seriously. No longer is it dismissed as a 'granny pastime'. Knitters are esteemed for their skill and dedication, their work properly valued for its creative input. Together we have taken a traditional craft, once essential for survival, and transformed it into a life-enhancing medium, with the potential to create magic in our lives.

Kaffe Fassett

5

A HISTORY OF ROWAN YARNS

In the corner of Stephen Sheard's rambling garden in the Yorkshire countryside is a tree that he watches with special interest. It is a rowan tree. It was given to him by Steve, the partner of knitwear designer Sasha Kagan, and he has watched it progress from a tiny sapling to a flourishing young tree.

It was an inspired gift, the namesake of the remarkable company that Stephen has run for almost twenty years. Let's be clear about one thing from the start: Rowan, the creative force that took the hand-knitting world by storm in the 1980s, is a mere pip-squeak of a firm. In the global scheme of things, where success in fashion and textiles is measured not in millions but billions, Rowan's sales barely register.

Yet Rowan is special. The company has a worldwide reputation for its knitting yarns, patterns, and range of complementary products that is constantly developed and updated. Its name is linked to some of the best knitwear designers around. Remaining loyal to the designers who grew up with it, Rowan is also assiduous in nurturing up-and-coming talent. Its garment collections are a subtle mix of naiveté and sophistication. Its designs draw on tradition while being true to the moment. Above all, Rowan is colour, wonderful colour, in all its contrasting moods and hues. It was through colour that Rowan first made its mark, and it is Rowan's magical sense of colour that continues to delight its customers. If the company has few real competitors, it is because Rowan is unique. Its colours are not borrowed from elsewhere, poached from other collections, or bought from lavishly-paid consultants: they are Rowan's own.

The naming of Rowan goes back to a weekend in the summer of 1978, when Stephen Sheard and his business colleague Simon Cockin spent several hours experimenting with words to represent the yarn company they were in the process of forming in an old mill, a mile outside the small town of Holmfirth. After much deliberation they came up with Rowan. 'We wanted a word that captured a feeling of good design and natural materials,' says Stephen. 'We both thought the name Rowan was evocative of nature without being too quaint or twee.'

Also known as mountain ash, rowan grows profusely on the banks of the small river that rushes down from the moors past the Yorkshire mill that is Rowan's home. Each autumn heads of rowan berries, which turn from bright orange to rich red, enliven the more muted colours of the rugged hillside. One of England's few native trees, the rowan is a hardy species. Perfectly adapted to the unforgiving weather of its moorland environment, it sends tough roots into the thinnest, poorest soil. In times gone by, the rowan wood was prized by wheelwrights and fletchers. Its brightly-coloured berries, too, were once gathered to make a drink rich in vitamin C.

It was right that Rowan should take its name from the natural world. Not only does its production focus entirely on fibres from natural, renewable resources, but the company's inspiration lies in the Yorkshire countryside. The word 'mill' conjures up a picture of William Blake's 'dark satanic mills', blackened with soot and exuding plumes of smoke. But imagine instead a narrow country lane, flanked on either side by high stone walls, winding down to a tiny hamlet. A scattering of weavers' cottages dating from pre-industrial times cluster round a tall sandstone building tucked into the hillside. This is Rowan's Green Lane Mill.

Erika Knight, a knitwear designer who bought yarn from Rowan in the early days, recalls being collected with another designer from Wakefield station and driven back to the mill. 'As we turned down this tiny lane, I remember thinking, "it just can't be down here",' she says, 'But there it was: a wonderful mill. Immediately you went in, the feeling was of coming home.'

Built around 1830, the four-storey mill produced wool gabardine cloth destined for the sturdy overcoats worn during the heyday of the British Empire. Before the advent of steam, the mill's noisy shuttle looms were powered by a water wheel turned by the River Ribble, which fed five other mills farther downstream. The water wheel was made redundant by a steam boiler, which exploded one fateful day in 1913. According to a local man who, as a small boy, witnessed this calamitous event, the mill 'never wove another pick.'

When Stephen Sheard and Simon Cockin bought Green Lane Mill in 1979, the building had suffered some fifty years of neglect. The roof had caved in at several places, and a pair of owls was nesting in what is now the

Photograph by Steve Hanson

Tucked into a Yorkshire hillside, Green Lane Mill is home to Rowan Yarns

kit-making room. Once their young had flown, these particular residents were gently encouraged to find alternative accommodation.

Stephen's own roots are firmly embedded in West Yorkshire. He was brought up in the village of Almondbury, now a suburb of Huddersfield. His father, who came from farming stock, was an embodiment of the work ethic instilled in families who had never had things easy. Starting off by selling footwear, he opened a draper's shop, eventually expanding to three stores. Each proudly bearing the legend 'J E Sheard High Class Family Draper' in gold letters, the shops stocked everything needed for the family—from white cotton vests and long grey socks to working boots and warm winter jackets. The linoleum floors were polished to a glassy sheen. The merchandise lay neatly stacked in the glass-fronted drawers of oak cabinets.

The eldest of four children, Stephen was involved in the business from an early age. Early in his teens, it was his duty to do the 'rounds' on Saturday mornings, travelling to outlying cottages to collect the weekly installments of money owed to his father's business. Saturday mornings were savoured rather than resented as the rounds gave Stephen ample excuse to ride his scooter up and down the muddy lanes.

Stephen was a natural entrepreneur and craftsman. 'I was always involved in a project of some kind, whether it was collecting conkers, weaving wicker trays or building a canoe,' says Stephen. 'I liked working with my hands and making things to sell. I hated lessons, most of which seemed to have little point.'

On leaving school, Stephen joined his father's firm to get a taste of business. It was a disaster. Father and son, alike in their single-mindedness, clashed, and, after an unhappy six months, Sheard senior wisely called it a day. At age seventeen, without a job, and with no qualifications, Stephen faced a bleak future. This all proved a turning point. Deciding to enter the textile industry, which surrounded him in its multifarious forms, Stephen went to Huddersfield Polytechnic to learn textile design. Here he proved himself to be a highly-motivated student, and in his final year he won a nationwide competition for woven design.

After college, Stephen worked for a number of local companies, building up valuable experience in textiles. In 1971 he joined a Lancashire firm owned by the Cockcroft family, a name made internationally famous by Sir John Cockcroft, the Nobel-prize winning nuclear physicist. Stephen was asked to design a collection of tweed upholstery fabrics, working alongside a Swedish designer who had been hired to inject the sought-after 'Scandinavian' look. Before long, Stephen was invited to Sweden to see for himself the modern approach to design.

This brief trip proved pivotal. The Swedish textile industry had none of the inheritance that was traditionally the strength, but ultimately proved the downfall, of the Yorkshire textile industry. In Sweden, Stephen saw that designers, who in Yorkshire came lower down the pecking order than sales and technical people, were running their own companies. The revelation that a company could be design-led came at exactly the right time, for Stephen had already begun to buy up old hand dobby looms for just a few pounds each, installing them in the loft of a former cooperative building next to the thirteenth-century church in Almondbury.

In the evenings and weekends, Stephen experimented with weaving. Using the thick selvages cut from fabric woven on modern rapier looms (which were sold to waste merchants) on a linen warp, he produced thick chenille-like rag rugs to sell through craft retailers.

Leaving his secure job with the Cockcrofts, who berated him for throwing his career away, Stephen established a second enterprise to cater to the growing market for craft activities. His hand-weaving kits, which came complete with a frame loom, materials, and instructions, sold in thousands to craft shops up and down the country.

At this point Stephen was joined by a friend, Simon Cockin, a civil engineer who had recently returned from Australia, where he had been on a bridge-building job in Hobart, Tasmania. Bursting out of their cramped premises in the co-op loft, Stephen and Simon leaped at the chance to buy Green Lane Mill for the handsome price of £8,000 (US $12,000). Patching up the holes in the roof and installing a wood-burning stove to stave off the worst of the cold, they set to work weaving rugs and making up kits.

The move into knitting yarns came about more by accident than design. In sourcing yarns for the weaving kits, Stephen and Simon had built up a portfolio of high-quality pure wool yarns. These they sold to handloom weavers at craft shows. Soon they were also supplying the first generation of designer knitters, whose creativity was making fashion headlines. These young knitters, many of whom had only recently left art school, were struggling to find suppliers willing to provide small quantities of yarns in a good range of colours. In their relaxed, colourful clothes, they got short shrift from the besuited sales representatives of the Yorkshire spinning mills, whose production was geared to customers ordering not pounds but tons of yarn.

Stephen was immediately impressed by the ability and integrity of these small-scale knitters. They included such well-known designers as Sasha Kagan, Erika Knight, Susan Duckworth, and Jean Moss. It was through working closely with such highly creative designers, and responding to their needs for a 'paintbox of colours', that Stephen began to develop Rowan's own style.

'It was just wonderful to come across Rowan,' says Erika Knight. 'I'd had tremendous problems trying to source yarns, both in the UK and abroad. You kept hearing these spinners saying, "Look, darling, don't you understand? The minimum order is ten kilos." Stephen's attitude was so different. He actually listened.'

Sasha Kagan, a designer with a series of creative knitting books to her name, remembers Stephen coming to see her in her studio in mid-Wales during a tour of knitwear designers. 'No other yarn supplier had ever come to visit us. Stephen wanted to get to know designers and learn what our needs were,' she says. 'My partner Steve, who grows trees, gave Stephen a rowan tree to plant in his garden. When my fourth child was born I called him Rowan, inspired by the red berries of the rowan tree. I thought his hair might be red like mine.'

In order to dye up the small quantities required by small producers, Stephen and Simon offered work to a local dyer, Mike Barraclough, whose employer's business was closing down. Mike, whose premises are four miles down the road from Rowan's Green Lane Mill, calls his small enterprise Mammoth Dyers. 'Mike likes to say that he's the second best dyer in the

Photograph by Steve Hanson

Stephen Sheard, co-founder and general manager of Rowan Yarns

country. We've never found out who's the best. His shades are always spot on,' says Stephen.

A major breakthrough came in 1982, when an American-born artist, dressed in battered jeans, wandered into the Rowan stand at a craft fair. This was Kaffe Fassett, who was later to become a knitting legend. The brief and non-committal conversation that followed was to change the course of both their careers.

In typically laid-back manner, Kaffe asked Stephen if he had any colours in the white spun chenille yarn that Rowan was showing for the first time. Stephen replied that he didn't. Matters could have rested there, but Stephen returned to Holmfirth with the feeling that he had met someone very special indeed. Guided by his intuition, Stephen asked Kaffe to colour up some yarn for a range of dyed chenille yarn. Within the space of a few weeks, Kaffe was working regularly with Rowan, contributing design ideas.

'It was Kaffe who persuaded us that it was worth sticking with the creative end of the market. Acrylic hand knitting yarns were very big in the 1980s, and it would have been easy to go down that road,' says Stephen. 'It was Kaffe, too, who defied those who said that hand knitters would never knit up multicoloured patterns in fine yarns.'

It was a logical progression for Rowan, with its experience in weaving kits, to develop Kaffe Fassett knitting packs. Each kit, containing detailed instructions and as many as fifteen different colours, was quite literally a 'wool shop in a box', allowing amateur knitters to create a Kaffe Fassett garment with little wastage.

From the mid-1980s onwards, Rowan staged regular workshops for knitters, inviting knitwear designers to give inspirational talks and hands-on encouragement. Many took place at Green Lane Mill, others in London. One tour, set up for a group of American knitters, involved a visit to the Outer Hebrides to meet women knitting the traditional Fair Isle patterns.

'The workshops brought all these fabulous people together to create things in a lovely atmosphere. There were doctors, students, mothers, and daughters,' says Erika Knight. 'Lots of knitwear designers got to know each other through working with Rowan. There was a tremendous feeling of solidarity. We were like a great big family. Yet for all Stephen's approachability, he has never dropped his professional standards.'

The next move was into retailing. Rowan's design team could see that, as the long-established tradition of passing skills down between generations began to falter, the craft of hand knitting was in danger of disappearing. Knitting was no longer taught at school. The department stores, too, were closing their knitting sections, faced by mounting pressure to maximise turnover.

Rowan's 'shop-within-shops', with their strong design emphasis, were developed to step into this breach. Staffed by young textile design graduates fired with boundless enthusiasm for creative knitting, they made an immediate impact. The first Rowan shop opened at Liberty's of London in Regent Street in 1988. Ten more Rowan departments quickly followed in other stores. A concession in Paris was launched as recently as 1997.

Today Rowan has fifteen partner enterprises around the world, from Australia to Iceland. 'These businesses, most of which are run by women, are Rowan in their particular markets, doing everything that we do,' says Stephen. 'The enthusiasm and commitment of our overseas distributors is tremendously important to us.'

To say that the Rowan Magazine 'just happened' is, perhaps, misleading. But the magazine, which has become the mainstay of Rowan's operations, grew out of the company's need to tell a story with its products. Each season, it brings together the company's new colours, yarns and patterns, using both its in-house designers and independent designer knitters commissioned to contribute their own approach.

The first edition of the Rowan Magazine came out in 1985. It was an instant hit. Today, the Rowan Magazine is published twice a year, each with 120 pages of fashion and editorial. In between the main issues come slimmer editions, focusing on particular themes such as denim or tweed. All Rowan's publications aim to inform, guide, and, above all, inspire. Its market research has shown that, although most of the consumers who purchase the magazine buy it to make use of the patterns, some people buy it purely to build up a collection of contemporary knitting designs.

Rowan is justifiably proud of the creativity it has nurtured from within the company. The most glowing examples of this homegrown talent are Kathleen Hargreaves and her two daughters Kim and Lindsay, all of whom work for the company and live just ten minutes walk away from the mill. With no formal qualification in design, Kathleen joined Rowan to work in the warehouse, packing and dispatching kits. But it was not long before her expertise with knitting needles was discovered. In growing demand for pattern writing, Kathleen found herself making a valuable contribution to the creative direction of the company. Now the design and publication manager, she is responsible for planning every aspect of the magazines.

Kim, the eldest of Kathleen's daughters, first worked for Rowan during school holidays, helping to pack orders and fill shelves. Stimulated by the sumptuous colour combinations she saw used in the first Kaffe Fasset knitting kits, Kim began developing ideas of her own. Stephen, who had already noticed Kim's natural style in the way she dressed, was quick to spot that she was someone well worth encouraging. Today, Kim designs about a third of the garments in each Rowan Magazine. Her knitting designs have won widespread acclaim for their wearability and clever use of colour.

Kathleen's younger daughter Lindsay runs Rowan's UK sales office. Her vital job is to keep the company's many customers happy.

When the great designer knitting fever of the 1980s abated, leaving many spinners in the lurch, Rowan responded by clarifying its approach to both its knitting patterns and yarn collections. The elaborate, multicoloured patterns of the past were replaced by plain colours interpreted in simple, well-designed shapes, with the interest provided by subtle details.

The current Rowan yarn range is divided across seventeen qualities, offered in a staggering total of four hundred colours. These yarns are all produced exclusively for Rowan by a number of specialist spinners, each with a long history.

Multicoloured tweed yarns are spun by a nearby family firm called Samuel Lumb. The name of its six-storey building, Perseverance Mills, reflects the company's low church origins. Rowan's Kim Hargreaves works closely with Lumb's own designers to develop colour-blended yarns with exactly the right combination and proportion of colours.

Each spring, the rowan that Stephen Sheard planted so carefully in his garden puts out new branches. Sasha Kagan's son Rowan has also grown up strong and vigorous in the Welsh hills, although there's only a hint of red in his hair. As for Rowan, the small enterprise founded by Stephen Sheard and Simon Cockin in 1978, in all its development it has never lost its commitment to good design—and each year it, too, embarks on fresh ventures.

Alexandra Buxton

THE BEST OF ROWAN
50 DESIGNER KNITTING PATTERNS

THE DESIGNS

Sugar Plum
LOUISA HARDING

YARN
Rowan Designer D.K.

Sweater

A	D.D.K	Apple	635	4	x	50gm
B	D.D.K	Turquoise	609	3	x	50gm
C	D.D.K	Midnight	607	5	x	50gm
D	D.D.K	Plum	659	5	x	50gm
E	D.D.K.	Chestnut	663	3	x	50gm
F	D.D.K.	Raspberry	70	4	x	50gm

Cardigan

D.D.K			18	x		50gm

(photographed in Ecru 649)

NEEDLES
1 pair 3¼mm (no 10) (US 3)
1 pair 4mm (no 8) (US 6)
Cable needle

BUTTONS
6

TENSION
22 sts and 30 rows to 10cm measured over stocking stitch and 30 sts and 30 rows to 10cm measured over cable and bobble panel using 4mm (US 6) needles

MULTICOLOURED SWEATER
This garment is knitted in 6 panels each in a different colour and each with a central cable pattern. Use the INTARSIA technique described on the information page for the panels. The shaping is worked internally either side of the 20 st cable pattern

SELF-COLOURED SWEATER OR CARDIGAN
Worked in the same way as multicoloured sweater, but using same yarn throughout.

STITCH NOTE
Cable and Bobble Panel (worked over 20 sts)
Row 1: P1, (K2, P2) 4 times, K2, P1.
Row 2: K1, (P2, K2) 4 times, P2, K1.
Row 3: P1, (T3F, P1) twice, LT, (P1, T3B) twice, P1.
Rows 4 and 14: (K2, P2) twice, K1, P2, K1, (P2, K2) twice.
Row 5: P2, T3F, P1, T3F, K2, T3B, P1, T3B, P2.
Rows 6 and 12: K3, P2, K2, P6, K2, P2, K3.
Row 7: P3, T3F, P1, T3F, T3B, P1, T3B, P3.
Rows 8 and 10: K4, P2, K2, P4, K2, P2, K4.
Row 9: P2, MB, P1, K2, P2, C4F, P2, K2, P1, MB, P2.
Row 11: P3, T3B, P1, T3B, T3F, P1, T3F, P3.
Row 13: P2, T3B, P1, T3B, K2, T3F, P1, T3F, P2.
Row 15: P1, (T3B, P1) twice, LT, (P1, T3F) twice, P1.
Row 16: K1, (P2, K2) 4 times, P2, K1.

Sweater
BACK
Cast on 240 sts using 3 ¼mm (US 3) needles in the following colour sequence: 40 sts E, 40 sts C, 40 sts D, 40 sts B, 40 sts F and 40 sts A.
Work 11 rows in garter st, ie knit every row, keeping the 40 st colour panels as set.
Next row (inc): (K18, M1, K4, M1, K18) rep this across each colour panel. (252sts)
Next row: Change to 4mm needles and knit across row changing colours as folls: 42 sts F, 42 sts B, 42 sts D, 42 sts C, 42 sts E and 42 sts A.
Keeping colours correct purl 1 row. Keeping colours correct work in cable patt setting sts as folls:
Row 1: (K11, work row 1 of cable panel, K11) rep to end.
Row 2: (P11, work row 2 of cable panel, P11) rep to end.
Cont in patt until row 16 of cable panel completed.
Row 17 (dec): (K9, sl 1, K1, psso, work row 1 of 20 sts cable panel, K2tog, K9) rep across each panel. (240sts)
Cont working 16 row patt rep, dec 1 st at each side of 20 st cable panel on every first patt row as given until there are 156 sts, mark each end of row 122 for position of sleeve. **
Cont without further shaping until 12 full cable patts completed, then rep first 3 cable patt rows again.
Next row (WS)(dec): * P3, (K2, P2tog) twice, K1, P2, K1, (P2tog, K2) twice, P3, rep from * 6 times across row. (132sts)
Cast off all rem sts.

FRONT
Work as for back to **.
Cont without further shaping until 8 full cable patterns completed and then rep first 6 patt rows again.
Cont in patt taking centre sts into different colours to form collar as folls:
Next row (135): Patt 77 sts, join in yarn A, K1 in A, join in yarn F, K1 in F, patt across rem 77 sts.
Row 136: Patt 77 sts, P1 F, P1 A, patt to end.
Work 4 more rows taking the extra sts into yarn A and F as indicated on chart.
Split for neck and collar
Row 141 (inc): Patt 74 sts, using yarn A, K2, knit into front, back and front of next st, K1 turn and leave rem sts on a holder, work each side of neck separately. (80sts)
Row 142: Using yarn A, K2, P4, work 74 sts in patt as set.
Row 143 (inc): Patt 73, using yarn A, K3, knit into front, back and front of next st, K1, P2. (82sts)
Row 144: Using yarn A, K2, P2, K2, P3, patt across 73 sts.
Row 145: Patt 72, using yarn A, K4, P2, K2, P2.
Row 146: Using yarn A, K2, P2, K2, P4, patt across 72 sts.
Cont working from chart, taking 1 extra stitch into yarn A on each RS row as indicated, working first 3 sts in st st and rem sts in K2, P2 rib as set.
Cont from chart until chart row 195 completed.

Shape shoulder and collar
Next row (WS)(dec): Keeping colours as set rib 30 sts, * P3, (K2, P2tog) twice, K1, P2, K1, (P2tog, K2) twice, P3, rep from * once more. (74sts)
Next row: Cast off 44 sts, rib to end. (30sts)
Using yarn A only, cont in K2, P2 rib, until collar measures 12cm from shoulder.
Cast off evenly in rib.
With RS facing patt across sts on holder.
Complete to match first side, reversing all shaping and working collar in yarn F.

LEFT SLEEVE
Cast on 50 sts using 3 ¼mm (US 3) needles and yarn F.
Work 11 rows in garter st.
Next row (inc): K23, M1, K4, M1, K23. (52sts)
Change to 4mm (US 6) needles and yarn C.
Work 2 rows in st st beg with a K row.
Set cable panel as folls
Next row: K16, work row 1 of cable panel, K16.
Next row: P16, work row 2 of cable panel, P16.
Cont in patt as set working 16 row rep 9 times and then the first 6 rows again (150 rows) and AT THE SAME TIME, shape sides by inc 1 st at each end of 3rd and every foll 4th row to 116 sts.
Cast off loosely and evenly.

RIGHT SLEEVE
Work as for left sleeve but replacing yarn F with A and yarn C with yarn D.

Cardigan (self-coloured)
BACK
Work as for sweater using same colour yarn throughout.

SLEEVES (both alike)
Work as for sweater using same colour yarn throughout.

LEFT FRONT
Using 3 ¼mm (US 3) needles cast on 114 sts.
Work 11 rows in garter st.
Next row (inc): K18, (M1, K4, M1, K36) twice, M1, K4, M1, knit to end. (120sts)
Next row: Change to 4mm (US 6) needles, knit across all sts.
Next row: Knit 5 sts, purl to end.
Now set cable panels as folls:
Next row: (K11, work row 1 of cable panel, K11) twice, K11, work row 1 of cable panel, K5 sts.
Next row: Knit 5 sts, work row 2 of cable panel, K11, (K11, work row 2 of cable panel, K11) twice.
Cont on sts as set until row 16 of cable panel completed.
Row 17 (dec): K9, (sl 1, K1, psso, work 20 st cable panel, K2tog, K18) twice, sl 1, K1, psso, work 20 st cable panel, K5. (115sts)
Keeping garter st band correct cont working 16 row patt rep, dec 1 st at each side of 20 st cable panel on two outside panels but only on the one side of centre front panel, on every first patt row

until there are 80 sts. Mark the side edge of row 122 for position of sleeve.

Cont without further shaping until 8 full cable patterns completed then rep first 14 patt rows again.

Start forming collar

Row 143: Patt 73, K3, knit into front, back and front of next st, K1, P2. (82sts)

Row 144: K2, P2, K3, patt to end.

Row 145: Patt 72, K4, P2, K2, P2.

Row 146: K2, P2, K2, P4, patt to end.

Cont working from chart, until chart row 195 completed.

Shape shoulder and collar

Next row (WS)(dec): Rib 30 sts, *P3, (K2, P2tog) twice, K1, P2, K1, (P2tog, K2) twice, P3, rep from * once more. (74sts)

Next row: Cast off 44 sts, rib to end. (30 sts)

Cont in K2, P2 rib until collar measures 12cm from shoulder.

Cast off evenly in rib.

Mark position of 6 buttons the first to come 10cm from cast on edge the last to come 1.5cm from start of collar.

RIGHT FRONT

Using 3¼mm (US 3) needles cast on 114 sts.

Work 11 rows in garter st.

Next row (inc): K12, (M1, K4, M1, K36) twice, M1, K4, M1, K18. (120sts)

Next row: Change to 4mm (US 6) needles, knit across all sts.

Next row: Purl to last five sts, K5.

This sets the sts for the front.

Work as for left front reversing all shaping and making buttonholes to correspond with markers on left front.

Work buttonholes as folls:

Buttonhole row: K2, yon, K2tog, K1, patt to end:

MAKING UP

Press all pieces as decribed on the information page.

Join shoulder seams matching patt and using a firm backstitch.

Join cast off edges of collar.

Sew collar to back neck.

See information page for finishing instructions.

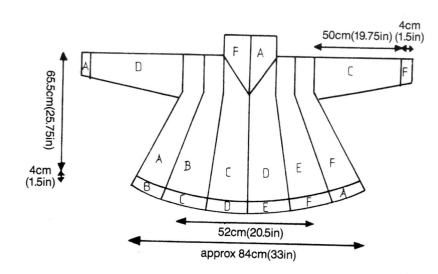

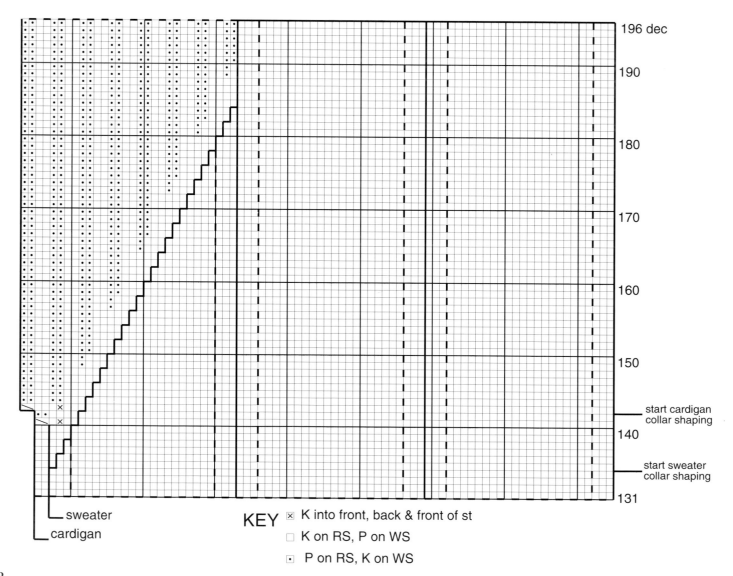

KEY   ⊠ K into front, back & front of st

☐ K on RS, P on WS

⊡ P on RS, K on WS

Pinwheel

KAFFE FASSETT

YARNS

Rowan Cotton Glace

		s	m	l		
A	Nightshade 746	2	2	2	x	50gm
B	Terracotta 786	2	2	2	x	50gm
C	Blood Orange 445	2	2	2	x	50gm
D	Shrimp 783	1	1	1	x	50gm
E	Delft 782	1	1	1	x	50gm
F	Sky 749	1	1	1	x	50gm
G	Pear 780	2	2	2	x	50gm
H	Hyacinth 787	1	1	1	x	50gm
J	Kiwi 443	2	2	2	x	50gm
L	Dusk 439	2	2	2	x	50gm
M	Swimming Pool 438	2	2	2	x	50gm
N	Petunia 789	1	1	1	x	50gm
P	Dijon 739	2	2	2	x	50gm
R	Lilac Wine 440	1	1	1	x	50gm
S	Gentian 743	1	1	1	x	50gm
T	Provence 744	1	1	1	x	50gm
U	Bloom 784	1	1	1	x	50gm
V	Mint 748	1	1	1	x	50gm

NEEDLES

1 pair 2¾mm (no 12) (US 2)
1 pair 3¼mm (no 10) (US 3)

TENSION

23 sts and 32 rows to 10cm measured over patterned stocking stitch using 3¼mm (US 3) needles

BACK

Cast on 130(134:140) sts using 2 3/4mm (US 2) needles and yarn L.
Work 17 rows in K1, P1 rib in the foll colour sequence:
2 rows P, 2 rows B, 2 rows J, 3 rows R, 2 rows L, 3 rows P, 2 rows R, 1 row S
Next row (WS)(inc): Using yarn S, rib 5(10:7), [M1, rib 7(6:6)] 17(19:21) times, M1, rib 6(10:7). (148(154:162)sts)
Change to 3¼mm (US 3) needles and joining in and breaking off colours as required work 118(128:138) rows in patt from chart for back using the intarsia technique described on the information page which is worked entirely in st st beg with a K row, end with a WS row.

Shape armholes

Cast off 6 sts at beg next 2 rows. (136(142:150)sts)
Cont until chart row 200(210:220) completed ending with a WS row.

Shape shoulders and back neck

Cast off 15(16:17) sts at beg next 2 rows.
Cast off 15(16:17) sts, patt 19(20:22), turn and leave rem sts on a holder.
Work each side of neck separately.
Cast off 4 sts, patt to end.
Cast off rem 15(16:18) sts.
With RS facing rejoin yarns to rem sts, cast off centre 38 sts, patt to end.
Complete to match first side reversing shaping.

FRONT

Work as given for back until chart row 178(188:198) completed ending with a WS row.

Shape front neck

Patt 60(63:67) sts, turn and leave rem sts on a holder.
Work each side of neck separately.
Cast off 4 sts, patt to end.
Dec 1 st at neck edge on next 8 rows and 2 foll alt rows.
Work 3 rows.
Dec 1 st at neck edge on next row. (45(48:52)sts)

Cont from chart until front matches back to shoulder shaping ending with a WS row.

Shape shoulder

Cast off 15(16:17) sts at beg next row and foll alt row.
Work 1 row.
Cast off rem 15(16:18) sts.
With RS facing rejoin yarn to rem sts, cast off centre 16 sts, patt to end.
Complete to match first side reversing shaping.

SLEEVES (both alike)

Cast on 60 sts using 2¾mm (US 2) needles and yarn L.
Work 18 rows in K1, P1 rib in colour sequence as given for back.
Change to 3¼mm (US 3) needles and cont in patt from chart for sleeve until chart row 145 completed and AT THE SAME TIME shape sides by inc 1 st at each end of 3rd row and every foll 4th row to 96 sts and then every foll 6th row to 116 sts, ending with a RS row.
Cast off loosely and evenly purlwise.

MAKING UP

PRESS all pieces as described on the information page.
Join right shoulder seam using back stitch.

Neckband

With RS facing using 2¾mm (US 2) needles and yarn S, pick up and K 29 sts down left front neck, 16 sts across centre, 29 sts up right front neck and 46 sts across back neck. (120sts)
Work 7 rows in K1, P1 rib in the foll colour sequence:
1 row S, 3 rows R, 1 row B and 2 rows P.
Cast off in rib using yarn P.
See information page for finishing instructions.

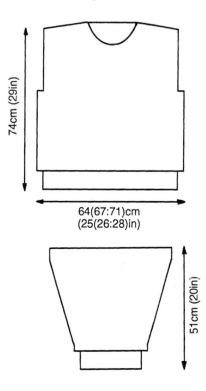

74cm (29in)

64(67:71)cm
(25(26:28)in)

51cm (20in)

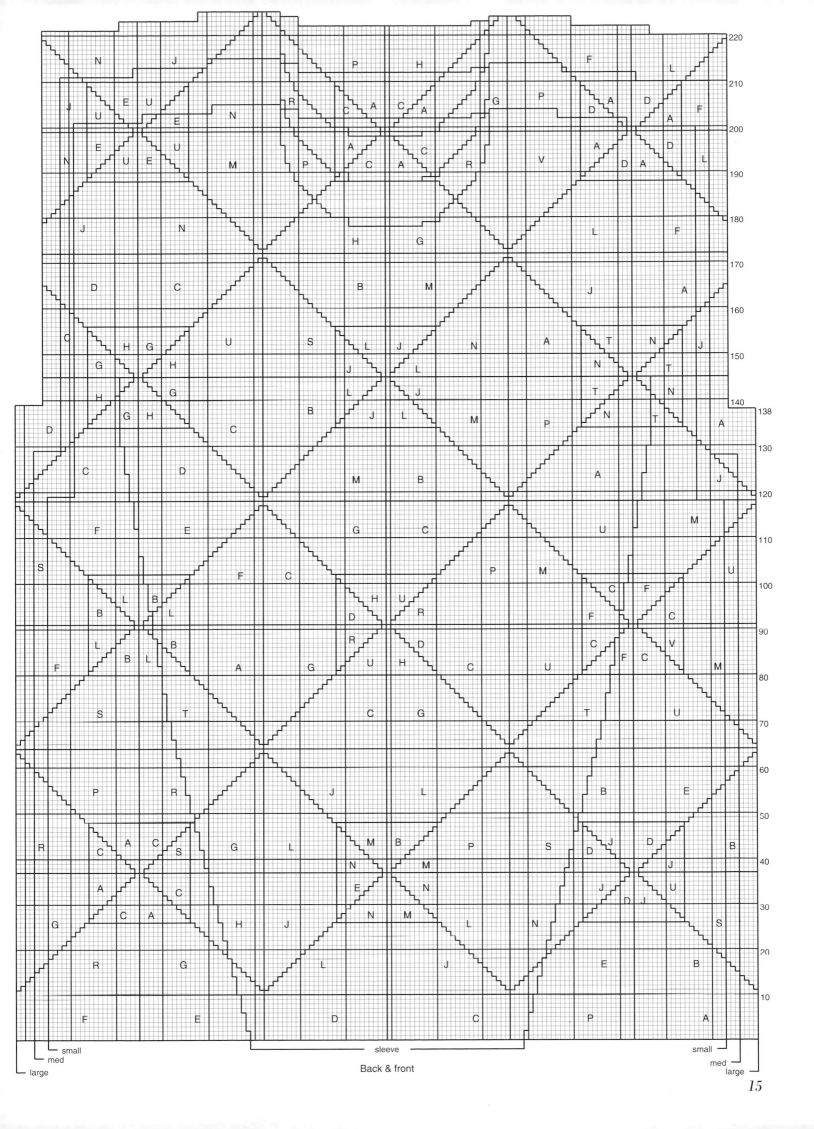

small
med
large

sleeve

Back & front

small
med
large

15

Heraldic Dogs

KAFFE FASSETT

YARN

Rowan Handknit D.K. Cotton

A	Port	245	5	x	50gm
B	True Navy	244	8	x	50gm
C	Evergreen	238	2	x	50gm
D	Sea Green	237	2	x	50gm
E	Tope	253	1	x	50gm
F	Pecan	213	2	x	50gm
G	Gerba	223	2	x	50gm
H	Black	252	1	x	50gm
J	Diana	287	2	x	50gm
K	Scarlet	255	2	x	50gm
L	Olive	247	2	x	50gm

NEEDLES

1 pair 3¼mm (no 10) (US 3)
1 pair 4mm (no 8) (US 6)
Circular needle 3¼mm (no 10) (US 3) 40cm long

TENSION

20 sts and 27 rows to 10cm measured over patterned stocking stitch using 4mm (US 6) needles

BACK AND FRONT (one piece)

Beg at lower back edge, cast on 102 sts using 3mm (US 3) needles and yarn B.
Work 21 rows in K1, P1 rib in foll colour sequence:
1 row B, 2 rows A, 2 rows G, 2 rows A, 2 rows G, 2 rows A, 2 rows B, 2 rows A, 2 rows G, 2 rows B, 2 rows A.
Next row (WS)(inc): Using yarn A, P4, (M1, P3, M1, P4) 14 times. (130sts)
Change to 4mm (US 6) needles and using the INTARSIA technique described on the information page work in patt from chart for back which is worked entirely in st st beg with a K row.
Work 166 rows in patt.

Divide for neck

Next row: Patt 50 sts, turn and leave rem sts on a holder.
Work each side of neck separately.
Cast off 6 sts at beg of next row, patt to end.
Work 2 rows without shaping. (170 rows completed)
This point marks the shoulder line.
Work 10 rows more without shaping.

Shape front neck

Inc 1 st at neck edge on next row and 2 foll alt rows.
Work one row.
Cast on at end (neck edge) of next row and foll 2 alt rows, 2 sts once, 4 sts once and 5 sts once. (58sts)
Work one row.
Leave sts on a spare needle for right side front neck.
With RS facing rejoin yarn to rem sts, cast off centre 30 sts, patt to end.
Work one row, then complete second side to match first side reversing all shaping.
Leave sts on a spare needle for left side front neck.
Next row (dec): Return to sts left on needle for right side front neck, rejoin yarn, patt across 58 sts, turn and cast on 14 sts, patt across 58 sts, left on holder for left side front neck. (130 sts)
Cont without further shaping until chart row 131 completed. Then complete the front by cont to follow the back chart down through rows 130 to row 1.
Change to 3mm (US 3) needles and work as folls:
Next row (dec): Using yarn A, P4, (P2tog, P2, P2tog, P3) 14 times. (102 sts)
Cont to work in K1, P1 rib reversing colour sequence as given for back.
Cast off evenly in rib using yarn B.

SLEEVES (both alike)

Cast on 42 sts using 3mm (US 3) needles and yarn B.
Work 21 rows in K1, P1 rib in colour sequence as given for back.
Next row (WS)(inc): Using yarn A, P3, (M1, P5) 7 times, M1, P4. (50sts)
Change to 4mm (US 6) needles and joining in and breaking off colours as required work 110 rows in patt from chart for sleeves and AT THE SAME TIME, shape sides by inc 1 st at each end of 3rd row and every foll alt row until there are 84 sts, then every foll 4th row until there are 110 sts. Take extra sts into patt as they occur.
Cast off loosely and evenly.

MAKING UP

Press all pieces as described on the information page.

Neckband

With RS facing, 3mm (US 3) circular needle and yarn A, beg at left shoulder, pick up and K 23 sts down left side front neck, 14 sts across centre front, 23 sts up right side front neck, 11 sts down right side back neck, 30 sts across centre back and 11 sts up left side back neck. (112 sts)
Work 9 rounds in K1, P1 rib in foll colour sequenc:
2 rounds A, 2 rounds B, 2 rounds G, 2 rounds A and 1 round B.
Cast off evenly in rib using yarn B.
Place markers 27.5cm below shoulder seam on back and front.
Set in sleeves between markers using back stitch.
Join side and sleeve seams using back stitch on main knitting and an edge to edge stitch on ribbing.
Press seams.

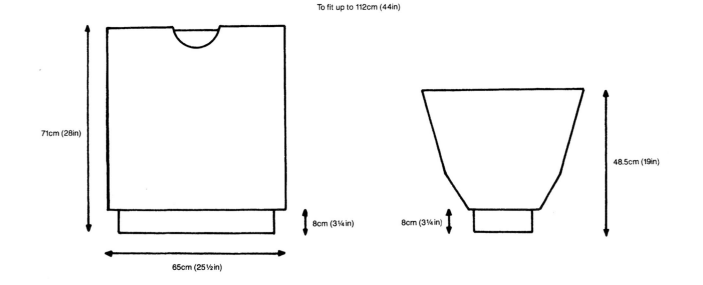

To fit up to 112cm (44in)

71cm (28in)

48.5cm (19in)

8cm (3¼in)

8cm (3¼in)

65cm (25½in)

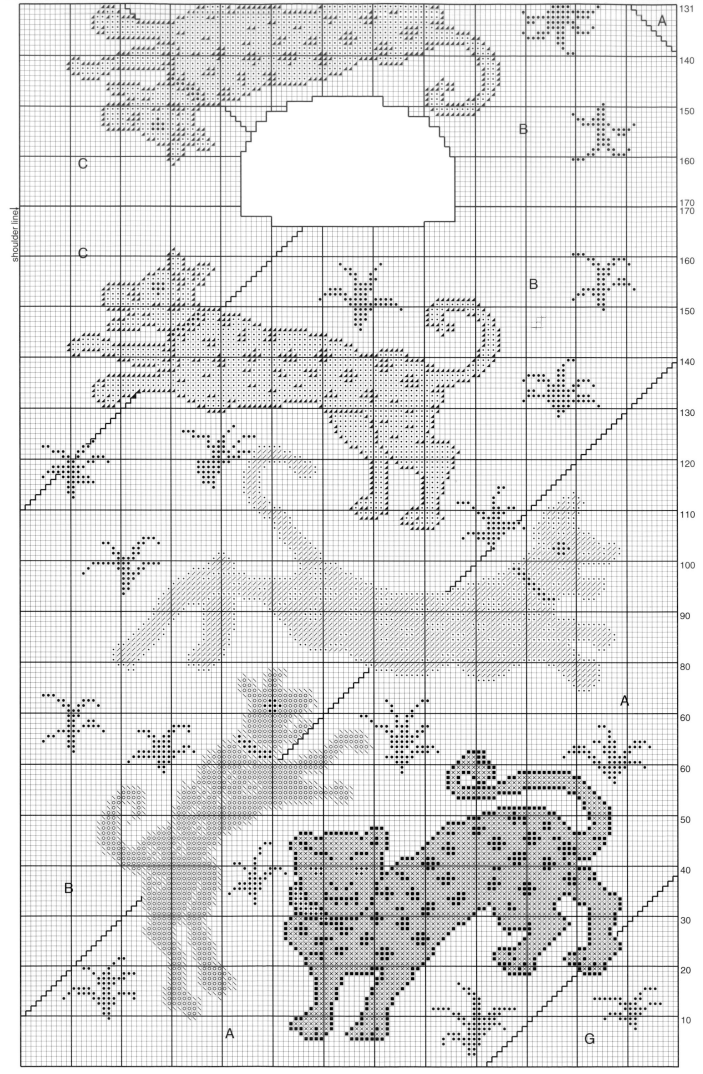

shoulder line

A 131
140
150
B
160
C
170
170
C 160
B
150
140
130
120
110
100
90
A
80
60
60
50
B 40
30
20
A G 10

18

back & front

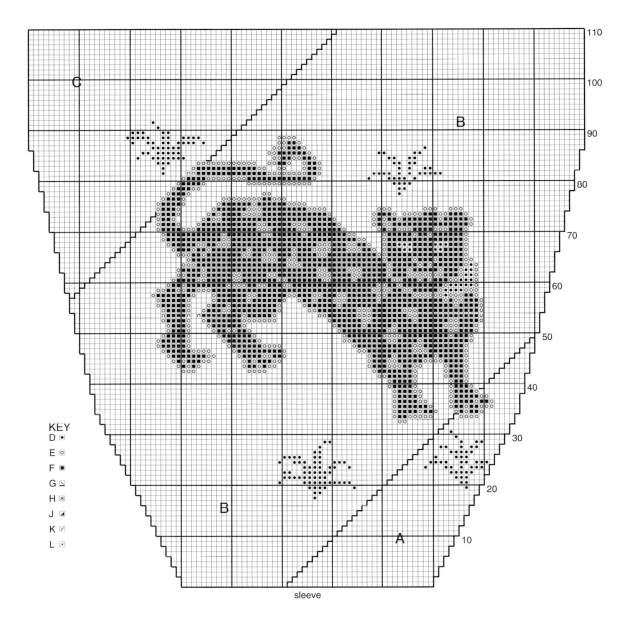

KEY
D ⊡
E ◉
F ▣
G ◨
H ⊠
J ◪
K ▨
L ⊡

sleeve

Miss Christie
KIM HARGREAVES

YARN

Rowan True 4-ply Botany and Donegal Lambswool Tweed

A D.L.T. Oatmeal 469 10 10 11 x 25gm
B Botany Jet 546 4 5 5 x 50gm

NEEDLES

1 pair 2³⁄₄mm (no 12) (US 2)
1 pair 3¹⁄₄mm (no 10) (US 3)

BUTTONS

9

TENSION

30 sts and 30 rows to 10cm measured over Fair Isle patt using
3¹⁄₄mm (US 3) needles.

BACK

Cast on 132(140:148) sts using 2³⁄₄mm (US 2) needles and yarn A and work moss st edging as folls:

* **Row 1 (RS):** (K1, P1) to end.
Row 2: (P1, K1) to end.
Row 3: Work as row 1.
Row 4 (WS): Join in yarn B, (P1A, P1B) to end, break yarn B.
Rep rows 1 to 3 once.
Row 8: Purl. *

Change to 3¹⁄₄mm (US 3) needles and joining in yarn B work 4 rows in fairisle patt from chart, working between appropriate markers and rep the 4 sts patt 33(35:37) times across row.
Keeping patt correct throughout, inc 1 st at each end of next row and 5 foll 12th rows, taking extra sts into patt as they occur. (144(152:160)sts)
Cont without further shaping until work measures 29.5(32:34)cm from cast on edge ending with a WS row.

Shape armhole

Cast off 5 sts at beg next 2 rows.
Dec 1 st at each end of next 7 rows and 2(4:6) foll alt rows. (116(120:124)sts)
Cont without further shaping until work measures 20cm from beg armhole shaping ending with a WS row.

Shape shoulders

Cast off 12(12:13) sts at beg next 2 rows.
Cast off 12(13:13) sts, patt 16(17:18) turn, leaving rem sts on a holder.
Work each side of neck separately.
Cast off 4 sts, patt to end.
Cast off rem 12(13:14) sts.
With RS facing rejoin yarn to rem sts, cast off centre 36 sts, patt to end.
Complete as for first side reversing shaping.

POCKET (make two)

Cast on 33 sts using 3¹⁄₄mm (US 3) needles and yarn A, work 30 rows in st st beg with a knit row.
Leave sts on a holder.

LEFT FRONT

Cast on 72(76:80) sts using 2³⁄₄mm (US 2) needles and yarn A and work moss st edging as folls:

Row 1 (RS): (P1, K1) to end.
Row 2: (K1, P1) to end.
Row 3: Work as row 1.
Row 4 (WS): (K1, P1) 3 times, join in yarn B, (P1A, P1B) to end, break yarn B.
Rep rows 1 to 3 once.
Row 8 (WS): (K1, P1) 3 times and leave these 6 sts on a holder for front band, purl to end. (66(70:74)sts)

Change to 3¹⁄₄mm (US 3) needles, join in yarn B and working between appropriate markers work 4 rows in fairisle pattern from chart for left front, rep the 4 sts patt 16(17:18) times across row.
Inc 1 st at side edge on next row and 5 foll 12th rows to 72(76:80) sts and AT THE SAME TIME when 30 rows of fairisle pattern have been completed place pocket lining as folls:

Place pocket lining

Row 31 (RS): Patt 17(21:25) sts, slip next 33 sts onto a holder and replace with 33 sts of pocket lining, patt to end.
Cont without further shaping until front matches back to armhole shaping ending with a WS row.

Shape armhole

Cast off 5 sts at beg next row.
Work 1 row.
Dec 1 st at armhole on next 7 rows and 2(4:6) foll alt rows. (58(60:62)sts)
Cont without further shaping until front is 17 rows shorter than back to shape shoulder ending with a RS row.

Shape front neck

Cast off 8 sts at beg next row and 4 sts beg foll 2 alt rows.
Dec 1 st at neck edge on next 3 rows and 3 foll alt rows. (36(38:40)sts)
Cont without further shaping until front matches back to shoulder shaping ending with a WS row.

Shape shoulder

Cast off 12(12:13) sts at beg next row and 12(13:13) sts beg foll alt row.
Work 1 row.
Cast off rem 12(13:14) sts.

RIGHT FRONT

Cast on 72(76:80) sts using 2³⁄₄mm (US 2) needles and yarn A and work moss st edging as folls:

Row 1 (RS): (K1, P1) to end.
Row 2: (P1, K1) to end.

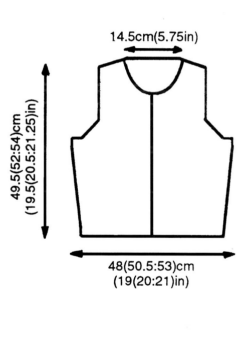

14.5cm(5.75in)

49.5(52:54)cm
(19.5(20.5:21.25)in)

48(50.5:53)cm
(19(20:21)in)

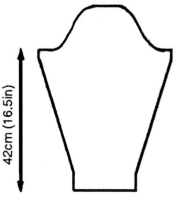

42cm (16.5in)

Row 3: Work as row 1.

Row 4 (WS): Join in yarn B, (P1A, P1B) to last 6 sts, break yarn B, (P1, K1) to end.

Row 5 (RS)(buttonhole): K1, P2tog, (yon) twice, P2tog, moss st to end.

Row 6: Moss st across row working into back of loops made on previous row.

Row 7: Work as row 1.

Row 8 (WS): Purl to last 6 sts, turn and leave rem sts on a holder for front band. (66(70:74)sts) Change to 3¼mm (US 3) needles, join in yarn B and working between appropriate markers on chart for right front complete as given for left front reversing all shaping and placing of pocket.

SLEEVES (both alike)

Cast on 62 sts using 2¾mm (US 2) needles and yarn A.

Work as given for back from * to *.

Change to 3¼mm (US 3) needles and joining in yarn B, work 2 rows in patt from chart, working between appropriate markers and rep the 4 st patt 15 times across row.

Inc 1 st at each end of next row and every foll 6th row to 100 sts, taking extra sts into patt as they occur.

Cont without further shaping until work measures 42cm from cast on edge ending with a WS row.

Shape sleeve head

Cast off 5 sts at beg next 2 rows.

Dec 1 st at each end of next 7 rows and 14 foll alt rows. (48sts)

Work 1 row.

Dec 1 st at each end of next 6 rows.

Cast off 4 sts at beg next 4 rows.

Cast off rem 20 sts.

MAKING UP

PRESS all pieces as described on the information page.

Join both shoulder seams using back stitch.

Button band

With RS of left front facing slip stitches from holder onto a 2¾mm (US 2) needle and keeping moss st patt correct work until band fits up front to beg neck shaping when slightly stretched. Slip st into place, cast off.

Mark position of 9 buttons, the first to come opposite buttonhole on right front, the last to come 1cm down from neck shaping and others spaced evenly between.

Buttonhole band

Work as for button band with the addition of 8 buttonholes worked as before to correspond with markers.

Collar

Cast on 109 sts using 2¾mm (US 2) needles.

Row 1 (RS): (K1, P1) twice, K to last 4 sts, (P1, K1) twice.

Row 2: (K1, P1) twice, P to last 4 sts, (P1, K1) twice.

Row 3: (K1, P1) twice, K1, M1, K to last 5 sts, M1, K1, (P1, K1) twice.

Row 4: Work as row 2.

Row 5: Work as row 1.

Row 6: (K1, P1) twice, P1, M1 purlwise, P to last 5 sts, M1 purlwise, P1, (P1, K1) twice.

Rep these 6 rows until work measures 5.5cm from cast on edge ending with a WS row.

Next row (RS): (K1, P1) to last st, K1.

Rep last row once.

Next row (RS): (K1, P1) twice, join in yarn B, (K1A, K1B) to last 5 sts, break off yarn B, K1, (P1, K1) twice.

Work 3 rows in moss st.

Cast off in moss st.

Pocket tops

With WS work facing slip sts from holder onto a 2¾mm (US 2) needle and using yarn A purl 1 row and AT THE SAME TIME dec 4 sts evenly across row. (29sts)

Next row (RS): K1, (P1, K1) to end.

Rep last row once.

Next row (RS): Join in yarn B, K1A, (K1B, K1A) to end, break off yarn B.

Work 3 rows in moss st.

Cast off in moss st.

Beg and ending halfway across front bands and matching centre of cast on edge of collar to centre back neck slip stitch collar into place.

See information page for finishing instructions.

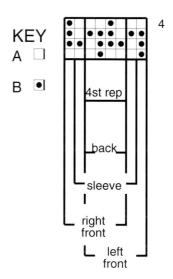

Russian Jacket
LOUISA HARDING

YARN
Rowan D.K.Tweed, Kid Silk, Designer D.K and Lt Wt. DK.

Black colourway

A D.K.Twd	Penguin	854	17	17	18	x 50gm
B D.D.K.	Pillar Box	632	1	1	1	x 50gm
C K.Silk	Old Gold	989	1	1	1	x 25gm
D Lt Wt. DK	Green	404	2	2	2	x 25gm
E Lt Wt .DK	Cinnamon	72	2	2	2	x 25gm

Natural colourway

A D.K.Twd	Wren	850	17	17	18	x 50gm
B K.Silk	Steel Blue	991	1	1	1	x 25gm
C D.D.K.	Airforce	65	1	1	1	x 50gm
D K.Silk	Holly	990	1	1	1	x 25gm
E K.Silk	Opal	976	1	1	1	x 25gm

NEEDLES
1 pair 3¼mm (no 10) (US 3)
1 pair 4mm (no 8) (US 6)
1 pair 5½mm (no 5) (US 9)
1 pair 6½mm (no 3) (US 10½)

BUTTONS
4

TENSION
Body of jacket
13 sts and 19 rows to 10cm measured over stocking stitch using 6½mm (US 10½) needles and 2 strands of yarn A
Collar and cuffs
21 sts and 28 rows to 10cm measured over patterned stocking stitch using 4mm (US 6) needles and single strands of yarn

Special abbreviation
Wrap st: slip next st, bring yarn forward between needles, slip sl st back onto LH needle, turn. (when working back across the wrapped sts take loop made and stitch together as one)

BACK
Cast on 64(68:72) sts using 5½mm (US 9) needles and **2 strands** of yarn A, and work 6 rows in moss st as folls:
Row 1: (K1, P1) to end.
Row 2: (P1, K1) to end.
Change to 6½mm (US 10½) needles and work in st st, inc 1 st at each end of 3rd row and every foll 10th row to 74(78:82) sts.
Cont without further shaping until work measures 25(27.5:30)cm from cast on edge ending with a WS row.
Shape armholes
Cast off 5 sts at beg next 2 rows. (64(68:72)sts)
Cont without further shaping until work measures 26cm from beg armhole shaping ending with a WS row.
Shape shoulders and back neck
Cast off 6(7:8) sts at beg next 2 rows.
Cast off 6(7:8) sts, patt 11, turn and leave rem

sts on a holder.
Work each side of neck separately.
Cast off 2 sts, patt to end.
Cast off rem 9 sts.
With RS facing rejoin yarn to rem sts, cast off centre 18 sts, patt to end.
Complete to match first side reversing all shaping.

LEFT FRONT
Cast on 32(34:36) sts using 5½mm (US 9) needles and **2 strands** yarn A.
Work 6 rows in moss st as for back.
Change to 6½mm (US 10½) needles and work in st st beg with a K row, inc 1 st at beg 3rd row and every foll 10th rows to 37(39:41) sts.
Cont without further shaping until front matches back to beg armhole shaping ending with a WS row.
Shape armhole and front neck
Cast off 5 sts at beg next row, knit to last 2 sts, K2tog.
Work 3 rows.
Dec 1 st at neck edge on next row and every foll 4th row to 21(23:25) sts.
Cont without further shaping until front matches back to beg shoulder shaping ending with a WS row.
Shape shoulder
Cast off 6(7:8) sts at beg next row and foll alt row.
Work 1 row.
Cast off rem 9 sts.

RIGHT FRONT
Work as given for left front reversing all shaping.
SLEEVES (both alike)
Cast on 30 sts using 6½mm (US 10½) needles and **2 strands** of yarn A.
Work in st st beg with a K row and AT THE SAME TIME, shape sides by inc 1 st at each end of 7th row and every foll 4th row to 68 sts.
Cont without further shaping until work measures 47cm or length required from cast on edge.
Cast off loosely and evenly.

COLLAR
Cast on 76 sts using 4 mm (US 6) needles and **1 strand** of yarn A.
Using the INTARSIA technique described on the information page, cont in patt from chart for collar, which is worked in st st beg with a knit row.
Work shaping from chart as folls:
Chart row 1: Patt to end, cast on 3 sts.
Work row one 5 times more. (94sts)

Keeping patt correct inc 1 st at each end of next row and every foll row until 170 sts and 45 chart rows completed.
Row 46 (WS): Work 162 sts, leaving 8 sts on LH needle, wrap next st, turn.
Row 47: Work 154 sts, leaving 8 sts on LH needle, wrap next st, turn.
Row 48: Work 148 sts, leaving 6 sts on LH needle, wrap next st, turn.
Cont to turn in this way following chart for pattern and shaping until row 61 complete. (86 sts)
Row 62 (WS): Using yarn A only, turn and purl 128 sts from LH needle.
Row 63 (RS): Work a purl row to form a foldline, purling the 42 sts held on other side of needle. (170 sts)
Row 64 (WS): Purl 128 sts, turn, K 86, wrap next st.
Turn, P90, wrap next st.
Turn K94 sts, wrap next st.
Turn and using 1 strand of yarn A only cont in st st, reversing collar shaping until 170 sts.
Change to 3¼mm (US 3) needles.
Dec 1 st at each end of every foll row to 94 sts.
Cast off 3 sts at beg next 6 rows.
Cast off rem 76 sts.

CUFFS (both alike)
Cast on 56 sts using 4mm (US 6) needles and **1 strand** yarn A.
Beg at row 17 on collar chart, work 28 rows in patt from chart working between markers for cuff and AT THE SAME TIME shape sides by inc 1 st at each end of 3rd row and every foll 5th row to 66 sts.
Row 29: Knit across row using yarn A only.
Row 30 (WS): Knit to form foldline.
Change to 3¼mm (US 3) needles and work entirely in st st, using yarn A, dec 1 st at each end of 6th row and every foll 5th row to 56 sts.
Cast off loosely and evenly.

MAKING UP
Press all pieces as described on the information page.
Button band
Cast on 6 sts using 5½mm (US 9) needles and **2 strands** of yarn A.
Work in moss stitch until band fits up left front to 10 rows below neck shaping ending with a WS row.
Dec 1 st at neck edge on next row and every foll alt row to 2 sts, cast off.
Slip st into place.

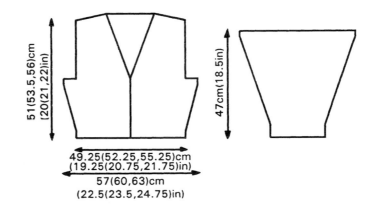

Mark position of 4 buttons, the first to come 4.5cm from cast on edge, the fourth to come 1cm below shaping on band, the others spaced evenly between.

Buttonhole band

Work as for button band with the addition of 4 buttonholes work to correspond with markers, as folls:

Buttonhole row: Patt 2, cast off 2, patt 2.
Next row: Patt across row casting on 2 sts over those cast off on previous row.
Slip st band into place.
With RS facing fold cuffs in half and stitch the row ends together.
Press seam.
With WS together fold cuffs in half and with the

seams matching slip st cast on and cast off edges to bottom of sleeves.
Sew collar neatly into place having centre of collar to centre back neck.
Fold in half and slip st into place on WS.
See information page for finishing instructions.

KEY

A ☐ K on RS,
    P on WS
B ⊡
C ☒
D ▾
E ·

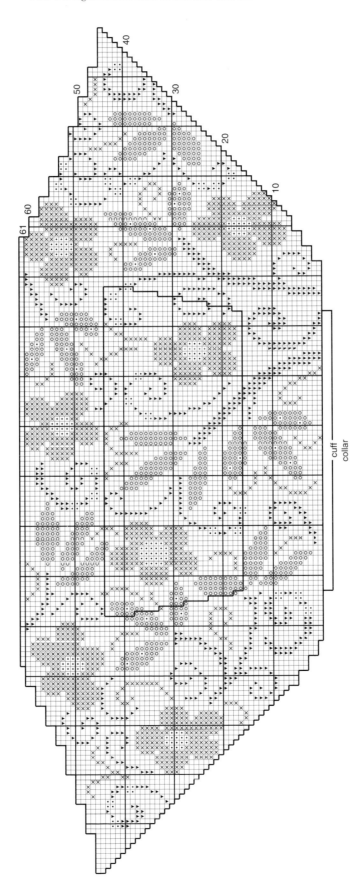

Chevron

ANNABEL FOX

YARN

Rowan Magpie Aran or Magpie Tweed

	short	long	
A	7	8	x 100gms
B	4	4	x 100gms

NEEDLES

1 pair 3¼mm (no 10) (US 3)
1 pair 4½mm (no 7) (US 7)

TENSION

18 sts and 23 rows to 10cm measured over patterned stocking stitch using 4½mm (US 7) needles

CHART NOTE: Read odd rows (K) from right to left, and even rows (P) from left to right.

BACK

Cast on 100 sts using 3¼mm (US 3) needles and yarn A.

Work 8cm in K1, P1 rib.

Change to 4½mm (US 7) needles, and cont in patt from chart for back which is worked entirely in st st beg with a K row. Rep the 30-row patt throughout and AT THE SAME TIME, shape sides by inc 1 st at each end of 3rd row and every foll 6th row for shorter length and every foll 7th row for longer length until there are 126 sts. Take extra sts into patt as they occur.

Shorter length: Work 5 rows without further shaping (80 patt rows).

Longer length: Work 9 rows without further shaping (96 patt rows).

***Shape armhole

Keeping patt correct, cast off 3 sts at beg of next 2 rows.

Cast off 2 sts at beg of foll 2 rows.

Dec 1 st at beg of next 2 rows. (114 sts) **

Work 58 rows in patt without further shaping.

Shape shoulders

Next row (RS): Cast off 17 sts at beg of next 2 rows.

Cast off 19 sts at beg of foll 2 rows.

Leave rem 42 sts on a holder.

FRONT

Work as given for back but foll chart for front to **.

Note: Shorter length sweater begins at chart row 17–omit the final row of the first row of badges.

Work 25 rows in patt without further shaping.

Place pocket

Chart row 128 (both lengths): Keeping patt correct, P 18 sts, (K1, P1) 12 times, patt to end.

Chart row 129: Patt 72 sts, (K1, P1) 12 times, patt to end.

Rep last 2 rows once more, then first row again.

Chart row 133: Patt 72 sts, cast off next 24 sts, patt to end.

Chart row 134: Patt 18 sts, break off yarn, and with new yarn cast on 24 sts, turn. Working on these 24 sts only, cont in st st until work measures 10cm from cast on edge ending with a WS row. Patt across rem sts on left hand needle. This completes the pocket.

Work a further 8 rows from chart.

Shape neck

Patt 48 sts, turn, leaving rem sts on a holder.
Work each side of neck separately.

Cast off 4 sts at beg next row and 2 sts at beg of 3 foll alt rows.

Work 3 rows, then dec 1 st at neck edge of next row and the foll 4th row.

Work 2 rows.

Shape shoulder

Cast off 17 sts at beg of next row.

Work 1 row.

Cast off rem 19 sts.

With RS facing, slip centre 18 sts onto a holder, rejoin yarn and patt to end.

Complete to match first side reversing all shaping.

LEFT SLEEVE

Cast on 46 sts using 3¼mm (US 3) needles and yarn A.

Work 10cm in K1, P1 rib.

Change to 4½mm (US 7) needles and foll chart for left sleeve which is worked entirely in st st beg with a K row. AT THE SAME TIME, shape sides by inc 1 st at each end of rows where indicated until there are 98 sts.

Work 14 rows without further shaping for the **ladies** sweater and 24 rows for the **mans** sweater ending with a WS row.

Shape sleeve top

Cast off 5 sts at beg next 2 rows and 3 sts at beg of foll 8 rows. (64sts)

Cast off 4 sts at beg of next 2 rows, 10 sts at beg next 2 rows and then 4 sts at beg next 2 rows.

Cast off rem 28 sts.

RIGHT SLEEVE

Work as for left sleeve **but** reverse the patt so that the badges are worked up the right side of the vertical line.

MAKING UP

Press all pieces (omitting ribbing) on WS using a warm iron over a damp cloth.

Join right shoulder seam using backstitch.

Shirt collar

With RS facing, 3¼mm (US 3) needles and yarn A, pick up and K 32 sts down left front neck, 18 sts from holder at centre front, 32 sts up right front neck and 42 sts from holder at centre back. (124sts)

Work 5 rows in K1, P1 rib.

Next row: Rib 41 sts, turn, leaving rem sts on a holder.

On these 41 sts work a total of 30 rows rib from cast on row.

Cast off evenly in rib.

Return to sts rem on holder.

Work in rib to match first side.

Cast off evenly in rib.

Join left shoulder seam using backstitch.

Join side and sleeve seams.

Press seams.

Crew neck

With RS facing, 3¼mm (US 3) needles and yarn A, pick up and K 28 sts down left front neck, 16 sts from holder at centre front, 28 sts up right front neck and 42 sts from holder at centre back. (114 sts)

Work 16 rows in K1, P1 rib.

Cast off evenly in rib.

Join left shoulder seam using backstitch.

Join neckband seam. Fold neckband in half to WS and slip st into place.

Stitch pocket lining into place on WS.

Set sleeves into armhole using backstitch.

Join side and sleeve seams.

Press seams.

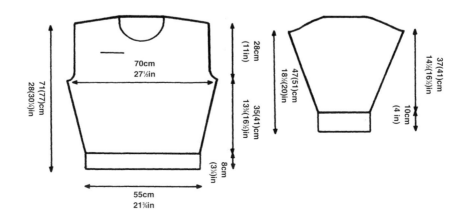

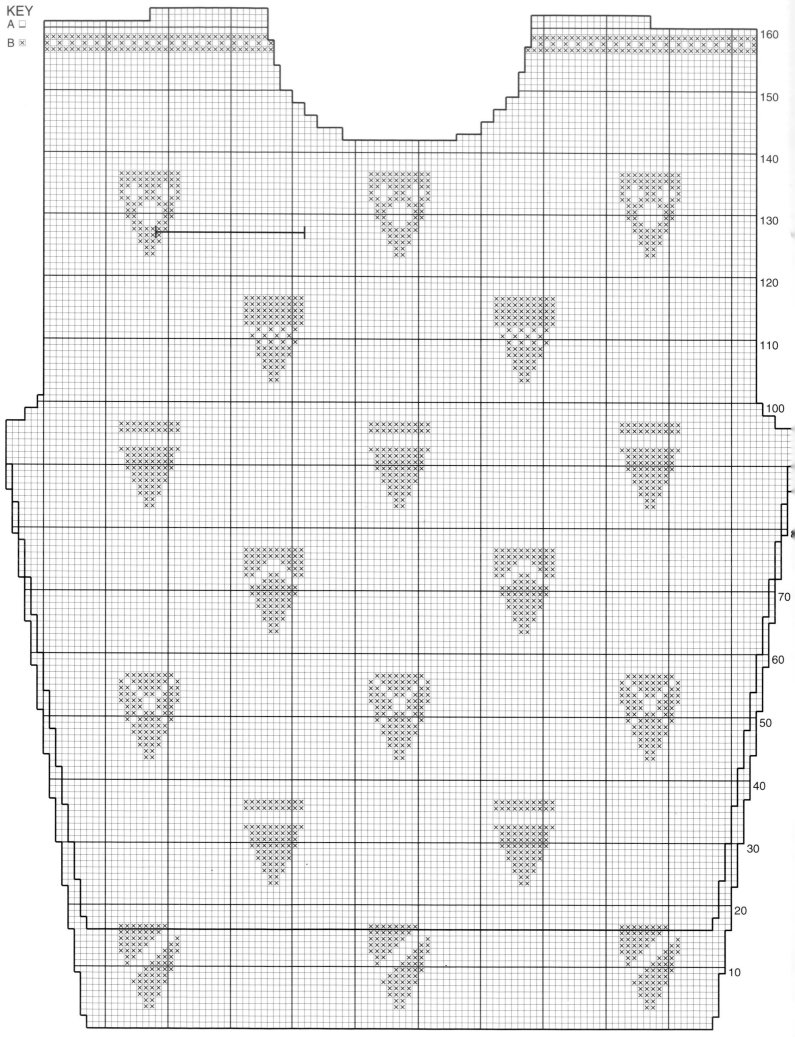

front

28

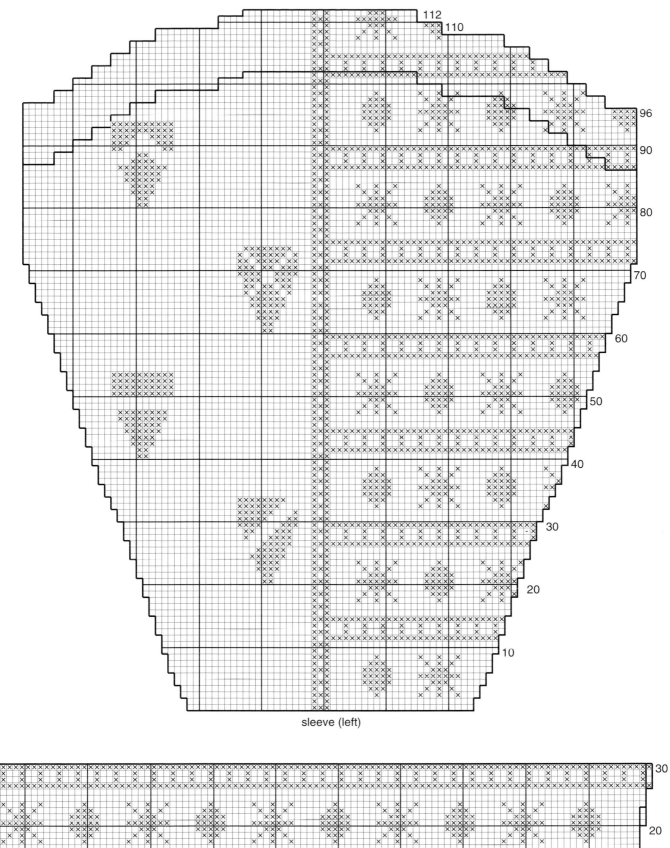

112
110
96
90
80
70
60
50
40
30
20
10

sleeve (left)

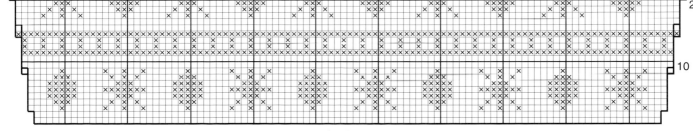

30
20
10

30 row patt rep throughout

back

Aran Sweater with Textured Squares

MARY NORDEN

YARN

Rowan Magpie Aran

S	M	L	
8	8	9	x 100gm

NEEDLES

1 pair 3¾mm (no 9)(US 5)
1 pair 4½mm (no 7) (US 7)

TENSION

21 sts and 30 rows to 10cm measured over pattern using 4½mm (US 7) needles

STITCH NOTE:

Irish moss stitch (worked over a multiple of 2 sts plus 1).

Row 1 (RS): K1, * P1, K1, rep from * to end.
Row 2: P1, * K1, P1, rep from * to end.
Row 3: As 2nd row.
Row 4: As 1st row.
These 4 rows form the patt and are repeated throughout.

BACK

Cast on 94(98:106 sts) using 3¾mm (US 5) needles.
Work in rib as folls:
Row 1 (RS): P2, * K2, P2, rep from * to end.
Row 2: K2, * P2, K2, rep from * to end.
Rep rows 1-2 until rib measures 10cm ending with a RS row.
Next row (inc): Rib 2(5:5), [M1, rib 5(4:4)sts] to last 2(5:5) sts, M1, rib 2(5:5).
(113(121:131)sts)
Change to 4½ mm (US 7) needles and patt, working centre 83 sts from chart and 15(19:24) sts either side in Irish moss stich as outlined in stitch note.
Work as folls:
Row 1: K1(1:0), [(P1, K1) 7(9:12) times], (P2,

K25) 3 times, P2, K1, [P1, K1] 7(9:11) times, P0(0:1).
This row sets position of patt.
Work 136 rows in patt, thus ending chart patt on row 34.
Now work in Irish moss stitch only until back measures 61(63:66)cm from beg ending with a WS row.

Shape back neck

Patt 48(51:54)sts, turn and leave rem sts on a holder.
Work each side of neck separately.
Cast off 5 sts at neck edge on next row and foll alt row.
Work 2 rows.
Cast off rem 38(41:44) sts.
With RS facing, rejoin yarn to rem sts, cast off centre 17(19:23) sts, patt to end.
Complete to match first side reversing all shaping.

FRONT

Work as given for back until front is 6cm shorter than back to shoulder.

Shape front neck

Patt 48(51:54) sts, turn and leave rem sts on a holder.
Work each side of neck separately.
Cast off at neck edge on next row and foll alt rows, 3 sts once, 2 sts twice and 1 st 3 times.
(38(41:44)sts)
Cont without further shaping until front matches back to shoulder.
Cast off.
With RS facing, rejoin yarn to rem sts, cast off centre 17(19:23)sts, patt to end.
Complete to match first side reversing all shaping.

SLEEVES

Cast on 50(54:58) sts using 3¾mm (US 5) needles.
Work 11cm in K2, P2 rib as given for back, ending with a RS row.
Next row (inc): Rib 1(3:5), (M1, rib 12) 4 times, M1, rib 1(3:5). (55(59:63)sts)
Change to 4½mm (US 7) needles and patt, work-

ing centre 29 sts from chart and 13(15:17) sts either side in Irish moss stitch as outlined in stitch note.
Work as folls:
Row 1: K1, (P1, K1) 6(7:8) times, P2, K25, P2, (K1, P1) to last st, K1.
This row sets position of patt.
Cont in patt as set and AT THE SAME TIME, shape sides by inc 1 st at each end of 3rd row and every foll 5th row until there are 109(113:119) sts. Take extra sts into Irish moss stitch side panels as they occur.
Work 3 rows without further shaping. (N.B. 4 complete chart patt repeats for 1st and 2nd sizes, 4 complete chart patt repeats for 3rd size, followed by 5 rows in Irish moss stitch only).
Cast off loosely and evenly.

MAKING UP

Press all pieces as described on the information page.
Join both shoulder seams using backstitch.

Collar

Cast on 26 sts using 3¾mm (US 5) needles.
Work one row in K2, P2 rib as given for back.
Keeping rib patt correct, cast on 10 sts at beg of next 4 rows, 6 sts at beg of next 2 rows, 4 sts at beg of next 16 rows, and 2 sts at beg of next 2(4:6) rows. (146(150:154)sts)
Work one row.
Cast off evenly in rib.
Sew cast on edge of collar to neck edge, overlapping at centre front by 14cm.
Place markers 26(27:28)cm below shoulder seam on back and front.
See information page for finishing instructions, reversing cuff seam 6cm from cast on edge.

KEY

☐ K on RS, P on WS

☒ P on RS, K on WS

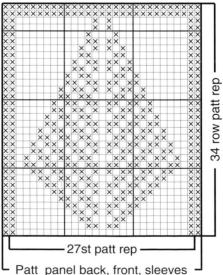

34 row patt rep

27st patt rep

Patt panel back, front, sleeves

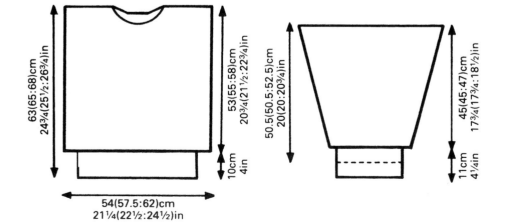

63(65:68)cm
24¾(25½:26¾)in

53(55:58)cm
20¾(21½:22¾)in

10cm
4in

54(57.5:62)cm
21¼(22½:24½)in

50.5(50.5:52.5)cm
20(20:20¾)in

45(45:47)cm
17¾(17¾:18½)in

11cm
4¼in

Moss Stitch and Crossover Chevron

SUE TURTON

YARN

Rowan Magpie Aran
8 x 100gm

NEEDLES

1 pair 3¾mm (no 9) (US 5)
1 pair 4½mm (no 7) (US 7)
Cable needle
3¾mm (no 9) (US 5) circular needle—40cm long
or set of four double-pointed needles for polo collar

TENSION

18 sts and 30 rows to 10cm measured over double moss stitch using 4½mm (US 7) needles

STITCH NOTE

Double moss stitch (worked over odd number of sts)
1st row (RS): * K1, P1, rep from * to last st, K1.
2nd row: * P1, K1, rep from * to last st, P1.
3rd row: As 2nd row.
4th row: As 1st row.
These 4 rows form the double moss st pattern, referred to as MS in the pattern instructions, followed by the number of sts to be worked in this way.

Crossover chevron pattern (worked over 23 sts)
1st row: P2, K1tbl, P6, K2, P1, K2, P6, K1tbl, P2.
2nd row: K2, P1, K6, P2, K1, P2, K6, P1, K2.
3rd row: P2, K1tbl, P6, slip next 3 sts onto a cable needle and hold at back of work, K2, P1, then K2, P1 from cable needle, P5, K1tbl, P2.
4th row: As 2nd row.
5th row: P2, K1tbl, P5, B.Cr, K1, F.Cr, P5, K1tbl, P2.

6th and every foll alt row: K all the K sts and P all the P sts as they face you.
7th row: P2, K1tbl, P4, B.Cr, K1, P1, K1, F.Cr, P4, K1tbl, P2.
9th row: P2, K1tbl, P3, B.Cr, (K1, P1) twice, K1, F.Cr, P3, K1tbl, P2.
11th row: P2, K1tbl, P2, B.Cr, (K1, P1) 3 times, K1, F.Cr, P2, K1tbl, P2.
13th row: P2, K1tbl, P1, B.Cr, (K1, P1) 4 times, K1, F.Cr, P1, K1tbl, P2.
15th row: P2, K1tbl, P1, K2, P3, K2, P1, K2, P3, K2, P1, K1tbl, P2.
Work rows 1-15, then rep rows 2-15 throughout.
This patt will be referred to in the instructions as "Chevron 23"

BACK

Cast on 94 sts using 3¾mm (US 5) needles and work in rib as folls:
1st row: * K2, P2, rep from * to last 2 sts, K2.
2nd row: * P2, K2, rep from * to last 2 sts, P2.
Cont in rib until work measures 8cm ending with a 1st row.
Next row (inc): Rib 2 sts, (M1, rib 9 sts) 10 times, M1, rib 2 sts. (105sts)
Change to 4½mm (US 7) needles and commence patt.
1st row: MS 11sts, work 1st row of Chevron 23, MS 37 sts, work 1st row of Chevron 23, MS 11sts.
This row sets the position of the patt. Rep the 4 row double moss st patt throughout, and at the same time keep continuity of chevron patt panel correct. **
Cont as set until back measures 76cm from beg.
Next row: Cast off 39 sts at beg of next 2 rows.
Leave rem sts on a holder.

FRONT

Work as for back to **.
Cont as set until front measures 68.5cm from beg.

Shape neck

Next row: Patt 47 sts, turn and leave rem sts on a holder.
Work each side of neck separately.
Cast off 2 sts at beg of next row and foll alt row

and 1 st at beg of 4 foll alt rows.
Work straight until front matches back to shoulder.
Cast off rem 39 sts.
With RS facing, return to rem sts and slip centre 11 sts onto a holder for neck ribbing.
Rejoin yarn to sts for right side of neck and complete to match first side, reversing all shaping.

SLEEVES (both alike)

Cast on 46 sts using 3¾mm needles.
Work 8cm in K2, P2 rib as given for back ending with a 1st row.
Next row (inc): Rib 3 sts, (M1, rib 2 sts) 20 times, M1, rib 3 sts. (67sts)
Change to 4½mm (US 7) needles and commence patt.
1st row (RS): MS 3 sts, work 1st row of Chevron 23, MS 15 sts, work 1st row of Chevron 23, MS 3.
This row sets position of patt. Rep 4 row double moss st patt throughout, keeping continuity of chevron patt panel correct and AT THE SAME TIME, shape sides by inc 1 st at each end of every 5th row until there are 109 sts. Take extra sts into double moss st side panels as they occur.
Cont straight until sleeve measures 46cm from beg ending with a WS row.
Cast off loosely and evenly.

MAKING UP

Press all pieces as described on the information page.
Join both shoulder seams using backstitch.

Polo Collar

With RS facing and 3¾mm (US 5) circular needle, pick up and K 25 sts down left front neck, 11 sts from holder at centre front, 25 sts up right front neck and 27 sts from holder at back neck. (88sts)
Work 16cm in K2, P2 rib.
Cast off loosely and evenly.
Place markers 28cm below shoulder seam on back and front.
Stitch sleeves into position between markers.
Join side and sleeve seams.

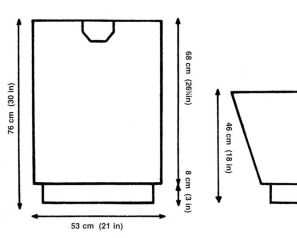

Chenille Jacket

CLAUDINE PERUS

YARN

Rowan Fine Cotton Chenille
8 x 50gm
(photographed in Plum 409)

NOTIONS

3 buttons
One pair shoulder pads

NEEDLES

1 pair 2¾mm (no 12) (US 2) needles

TENSION

23 sts and 36 rows to 10cm measured over moss st pattern using 2¾mm (US 2) needles

BACK

Cast on 116 sts using 2¾mm (US 2) needles.
Work 10 rows in moss st.
Keeping moss st patt correct throughout shape garment as folls:
Next row (RS)(dec): K2tog, patt 27 sts, sl 1, K2tog, psso, patt 52, sl 1, K2tog, psso, patt 27, K2tog. (110sts)
Work 3 rows without shaping.
Next row (RS)(dec): Patt 27, sts, sl 1, K2tog, psso, patt 50 sts, sl 1, K2tog, psso, patt 27. (106sts)
Work 3 rows without shaping.
Next row (RS)(dec): Patt 26 sts, sl 1, K2tog, psso, patt 48 sts, sl 1, K2tog, psso, patt 26. (102sts)
Work 1 row.
Dec 1 st at each end of next row and foll 10th row. (98 sts)
Work 9 rows without shaping.
Next row (RS)(inc): Inc in first st, patt 23 sts, M1, K1, mark this K st with a contrast yarn, M1, patt 48, M1, K1, mark this K st with a contrast yarn, M1, patt 23 sts inc in last st. (104 sts)
Cont to inc at side edges on every foll 6th row (from last inc) to 126 sts and AT THE SAME TIME, M1 either side of the marked sts on the foll two 8th rows (from last inc). (126sts)

Cont without shaping until work measures 28cm from cast on edge ending with a WS row.

Shape armholes

Cast off 10 sts at beg next 2 rows.
Cast off 3 sts at beg next 2 rows and 2 sts beg foll 2 rows.
Work 1 row.
Dec 1 st at each end of next row and foll alt row. (92sts)
Cont without further shaping until work measures 21cm from beg armhole shaping ending with a WS row.

Shape shoulder and back neck

Cast off 8 sts, patt 25 sts, turn and leave rem sts on a holder.
Work each side of neck separately.
Cast off 4 sts, patt to end.
Cast off 8 sts, patt to end.
Cast off 3 sts, patt to end.
Cast off rem 10 sts.
With RS facing rejoin yarn to rem sts and cast off centre 26 sts, patt to end.
Complete to match first side reversing all shaping.

LEFT FRONT

Shape point

Cast on 2 sts using 2¾mm (US 2) needles.
Row 1: K into front and back of 2 sts on needle. (4sts)
Cont in moss stitch inc 1 st at each end of next row and every foll row to 50 sts.
Next row (RS): Cast on 10 sts at beg next row, patt to last st, inc in last st. (61sts)
Point completed.
Work 9 rows in moss st.
Keeping patt correct throughout shape garment as folls:
Next row (RS)(dec): K2tog, patt 27 sts, sl 1, K2tog, psso, patt to end. (58 sts)
Work 3 rows without shaping.
Next row (RS)(dec): Patt 27 sts, sl 1, K2tog, psso, patt to end. (56sts)
Work 3 rows without shaping.
Next row (RS)(dec): Patt 26 sts, sl 1, K2tog, psso, patt to end. (54 sts)
Work 1 row.
Dec 1 st at beg of next row and foll 10th row. (52sts)

Work 9 rows without shaping.
Next row (RS)(inc): Inc in first st, patt 23 sts, M1, K1, mark this K st with a contrast yarn, M1, patt to end. (55sts)
Cont inc at side edge on every foll 6th row (from last inc) to 66 sts and AT THE SAME TIME, M1 either side of the marked st on the foll two 8th rows (from last inc). (66st)
Cont without shaping until work matches back to beg armhole shaping ending with a WS row.

Shape armhole

Cast off 10 sts at beg of next row.
Work 1 row.
Cast off 3 sts at beg next row and 2 sts beg foll alt row.
Work 1 row.
Dec 1 st at beg next row and foll alt row. (49 sts)
Cont without further shaping until work matches back to beg shoulder shaping ending with a WS row.

Shape shoulder

Cast off 8 sts at beg next row and foll alt row.
Work 1 row. Cast off 10 sts and patt to end. (23sts)
Cont on these 23 sts for a further 8.5cm to form collar.
Cast off in moss st.

RIGHT FRONT

Work as for left front reversing all shaping.

SLEEVES (both alike)

Cast on 54 sts using 2¾mm (US 2) needles.
Work 6 rows in moss st.
Keeping moss st patt correct inc 1 st at each end of next row and every foll 6th row to 76 sts and then every foll 4th row to 106 sts.
Cont without further shaping until work measures 40.5cm or length required from cast on edge.

Shape sleevehead

Cast off 2 sts at beg next 2 rows.
Dec 1 st at each end of next row and every foll alt row to 58 sts.
Cast off 2 sts at beg next 14 rows.
Cast off 3 sts at beg next 2 rows. (24sts)
Cast off.

MAKING UP

Press all pieces as described on the information page.
Join both shoulder seams with a fine back stitch seam.
Join cast off edges of collar together at back neck so that the seam is to the underneath when collar turned over.
Slip stitch collar neatly into place around back neck.
See information page for finishing instructions.
Work 3 button loops on right front large enough to take button of your choice. The first to start 6cm from beg lower front edge, the second 12cm from beg lower front edge and third 18cm from beg lower front edge.
Sew buttons into place so that right front overlaps left front by 2.5cm
Slip stitch shoulder pads into place.

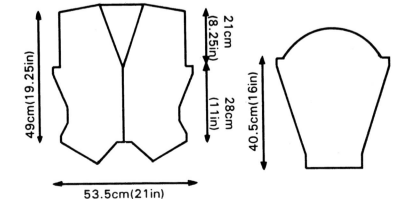

Snowflake Ladies Sweater

ANNABEL FOX

YARN

Rowan Magpie Aran and Magpie Tweed

		M	L		
A	Natural 002	7	8	x	100gm
B	Ember 763	2	2	x	100gm
C	Ivy 765	1	1	x	100gm

NEEDLES

1 pair 4mm (no 8) (US 6)
1 pair 4½mm (no 7) (US 7)
Cable needle

TENSION

18 sts and 25 rows to 10cm measured over stocking stitch using 4½mm (US 7) needles

BACK

Cast on 100(110) sts using 4mm (US 6) needles and yarn A.
Work cable rib as folls:
Row 1 (RS): * K1, P2, K4, P2, K1, rep from * to end.
Row 2: * P1, K2, P4, K2, P1, rep from * to end.
Row 3: As row 1.
Row 4: As row 2.
Row 5: * K1, P2, C4F, P2, K1, rep from * to end.
Row 6: As row 2.
These 6 rows form the patt.
Rep row 1-6 until rib measures 12cm from beg

ending with a RS row.
Next row (inc): Patt 2(1), [M1, patt 8(9)] 12 times, M1, patt 2(1). (113(123) sts)
Change to 4½mm (US 7) needles, and using the INTARSIA technique described on the information page work in patt from chart for back which is worked entirely in st st beg with a K row.
Work 88(92) rows in patt.
Shape armholes
Cast off 4 sts at beg of next 2 rows. (105(115)sts)
Work a further 66 rows in patt (N.B. work only complete snowflakes)
Shape shoulders
Cast off 19(22) sts at beg of next 2 rows and 19(21) sts at beg of foll 2 rows.
Leave rem 29 sts on a holder.

FRONT

Work as given for back until front is 14 rows shorter than back to start of shoulder shaping.
Shape front neck
Patt 47(52) sts, turn and leave rem sts on a holder.
Work each side of neck separately.
Cast off 4 sts at beg of next row, 3 sts at beg of foll alt row and 1 st at beg of foll 2 alt rows. (38(43)sts)
Cont straight for 6 rows ending with a WS row.
Shape shoulder
Cast off 19(22) sts at beg of next row.
Work one row.
Cast off rem 19(21) sts.
With RS facing, slip centre 11 sts onto a holder, rejoin yarn to rem sts and complete to match first side reversing all shaping.

SLEEVES

Cast on 40 sts using 4mm (US 6) needles and

yarn A.
Work 12cm in cable rib as given for back ending with a RS row.
Next row (inc): Patt 2, (M1, patt 2, M1, patt 1, M1, patt 2) 7 times, M1, patt 1, M1, patt 2. (63sts)
Change to 4½mm (US 7) needles and work 78(82) rows in patt, AND AT THE SAME TIME, shape sides by inc 1 st at each end of 3rd row and every foll 4th row to 97 sts.
Shape sleeve top
Cast off 7 sts at beg of next 2 rows, 5 sts at beg of foll 6 rows and 7 sts at beg of next 2 rows.
Cast off rem 39 sts.

MAKING UP

Press all pieces as described on the information page.
Join right shoulder seam using backstitch.
Neckband
With RS facing, using 4mm (US 6) needles and yarn A, pick up and K 18sts down left front neck, 11 sts from holder at centre front, 18 sts up right side front neck and 29 sts from holder at back neck. (76sts)
Work in rib as folls:
Row 1: * K2, P1, rep from * to last st, K1.
Row 2: P across row.
Rep these 2 rows until neckband measures 6cm from beg ending with a WS row.
Change to 4½mm (US 7) needles and work 4cm in st st beg with a K row.
Cast off loosely and evenly.
Join left shoulder seam and neckband.
Sew sleeve top into armhole.
Join side and sleeve seams.
Press seams.

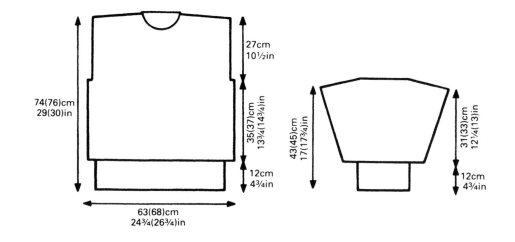

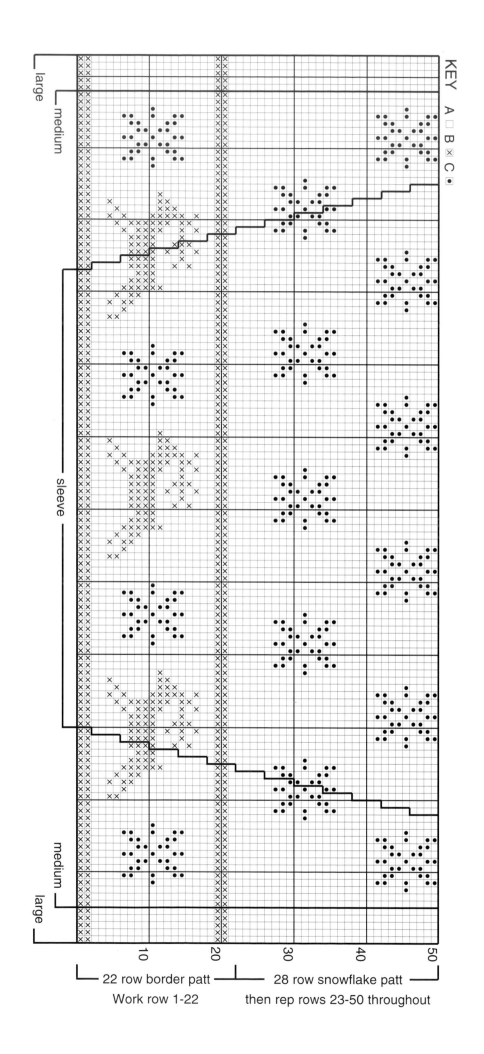

KEY A □ B ☒ C •

large

medium

sleeve

medium

large

10

20

30

40

50

— 22 row border patt — 28 row snowflake patt —

Work row 1-22   then rep rows 23-50 throughout

Cross Patch Waistcoat

KAFFE FASSETT

YARNS

Rowan Lambswool Donegal Tweed

		s	m	l		
A	Dragonfly 488	1	1	1	x	25gm
B	Mulled Wine 461	1	1	1	x	25gm
C	Pepper 473	1	1	1	x	25gm
D	Juniper 482	1	1	1	x	25gm
E	Mist 466	1	1	1	x	25gm
F	Bay 485	1	1	1	x	25gm
G	Dried Rose 462	1	1	1	x	25gm
J	Nutmeg 470	1	1	1	x	25gm
L	Black 491	1	1	1	x	25gm
M	Marram 472	1	1	1	x	25gm
N	Dolphin 478	3	3	4	x	25gm
R	Shale 467	1	2	2	x	25gm
S	Mayfly 463	1	2	2	x	25gm

NEEDLES

1 pair 2¾mm (no 12) (US 2)
1 pair 3¼mm (no 10) (US 3)
Circular needle 2¾mm (no 12) (US 2)–80cm long

BUTTONS

5

TENSION

24st and 36 rows to 10cm measured over patterned st st using 3¼mm (US 3) needles

BACK

Cast on 121(127:133)sts using 2¾mm (US 2) needles and yarn N, work 10 rows in st st beg with a K row.
Next row (RS): Purl to form hemline.
Next row: Purl.
Change to 3¼mm (US 3) needles and work 102(106:110) rows in patt from chart for back using the INTARSIA technique described on the information page and AT THE SAME TIME shape sides by inc 1 st at each end of row 21(25:29) and 5 foll 14th rows to 133(139:145) sts ending with a WS row.

Shape armhole

Cast off 6 sts at beg next 2 rows.
Dec 1 st at each end of next 8(9:10) rows and 3 foll alt rows. (99(103:107)sts)
Cont without further shaping until chart row 196(202:208) completed ending with a WS row.

Shape shoulders and back neck

Cast off 7(9:11)sts at beg next 2 rows.
Cast off 10 sts, patt 14, turn and leave rem sts on a holder.
Work each side of neck separately.
Cast off 4 sts, patt to end.
Cast off rem 10 sts.
With RS facing rejoin yarns to rem sts, cast off centre 37 sts, patt to end.
Complete to match first side reversing shaping.

LEFT FRONT

Cast on 59(62:65) sts using 2¾mm (US 2) needles and yarn N, work 10 rows in st st beg with a K row.
Next row (RS): Purl to form hemline.
Next row: Purl.
Change to 3¼mm (US 3) needles and work 100 rows in patt from chart for left front and AT THE SAME TIME shape side by inc at side edge on row 21(25:29) and 5 foll 14th rows to 65(68:71) sts and ending with a WS row.

Shape front neck

Dec 1 st at neck edge on next row and every foll 4th row to 27(29:31) sts and AT THE SAME TIME when front matches back to armhole shaping, shape armhole as given for back.
Cont without further shaping until front matches back to shape shoulder ending with a WS row.

Shape shoulder

Cast off 7(9:11) sts at beg next row and 10sts at beg foll alt row.
Work 1 row.
Cast off rem 10 sts.

RIGHT FRONT

Work as given for left front following chart for right front and reversing all shaping.

MAKING UP

PRESS all pieces as described on the information page.

Join both shoulder seams using back stitch.

Front bands

With RS facing and using 2¾mm (US 2) circular needle and yarn N, pick up and K 81 sts up right front from hemline to beg front neck shaping, 76(79:82) sts up to shoulder, 43 sts across back neck, 76(79:82) sts down left front to beg front neck shaping and 81 sts to hemline. (357(363:369)sts)
Working in rows and not rounds, work 5 rows in patt from chart B, beg at lefthand side with a P row and working the 6 sts patt 59(60:61) times across row and then first 3 sts once and AT THE SAME TIME make buttonholes on 2nd and 3rd rows as folls:

Ladies waistcoat only

Chart row 2 (RS): K3, (K2tog tbl, (yon) twice, K2tog, patt 13) 4 times, K2tog tbl, (yon) twice, K2tog, patt to end.
Man's waistcoat only
Chart row 2 (RS): Patt to last 75 sts, (K2tog tbl, (yon) twice, K2tog, patt 13) 4 times, k2tog tbl, (yon) twice, K2tog, patt 3.

Both waistcoats

Chart row 3: Patt across row, purling into back of each loop made on previous row.
Cont in yarn N.
Row 6: Knit.
Row 7 (WS): Knit to form foldline.
Work 9 rows in st st beg with a K row and AT THE SAME TIME work buttonholes on 4th and 5th row to correspond with those worked previously.
Cast off very loosely and evenly.
Fold band onto WS along foldline and slip stitch into place.
Armhole edging (both alike)
With RS facing and using 2¾mm (US 2) needles and yarn N, pick up and K 162 sts evenly around armhole edge.
Work 3 rows in patt from chart B, beg at lefthand side with a P row and rep patt 27 times across row.
Cont in yarn N.
Row 4: Knit.
Row 5 (WS): Knit to form foldline.
Work 6 rows in st st beg with a K row.
Cast off very very loosely.
See information page for finishing instructions.
Fold hems onto WS and slip stitch into position.

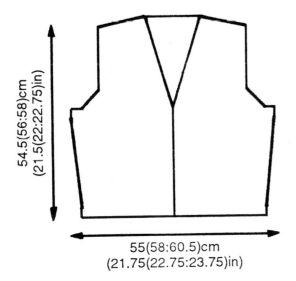

54.5(56:58)cm
(21.5:22.75)in

55(58:60.5)cm
(21.75(22.75:23.75)in)

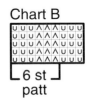

Chart B

└ 6 st ┘
patt

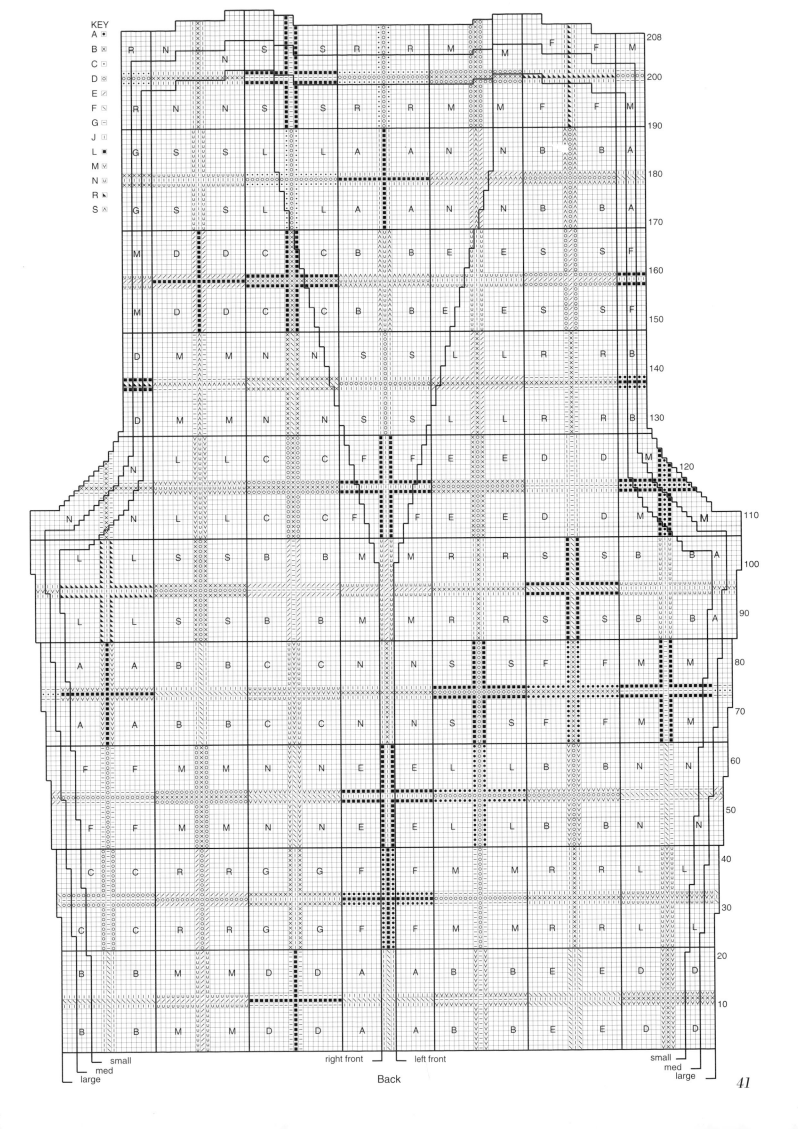

41

Criss Cross
KAFFE FASSETT

Crew neck sweater and Tunic

YARNS

Rowan Donegal Lambswool

			Swt	Tunic	
A	D.L.T.	Oatmeal 469	9	9	x 25gm
B	D.L.T.	Elderberry 490	11	11	x 25gm
C	D.L.T.	Mist 466	2	2	x 25gm
D	D.L.T.	Pepper 473	2	2	x 25gm
E	D.L.T.	Dragonfly 488	1	1	x 25gm
F	D.L.T.	Nutmeg 470	2	2	x 25gm

NEEDLES

1 pair 3mm (no 11) (US 3)
1 pair 3¾mm (no 9) (US 5)

TENSION

26 sts and 30 rows to 10cm measured over patterned stocking stitch using 3¾mm (US 5) needles

TUNIC

BACK

Cast on 150 sts using 3mm (US 3) needles and yarn C.
Work 7 rows in garter st, (ie knit every row)
Next row (WS): Knit 6 sts, leave these 6 sts on a holder, knit to last 6 sts, turn and leave rem 6 sts on a holder. (138sts)
Change to 3¾mm (US 5) needles and using a combination of the FAIR ISLE and INTARSIA techniques described on the information page and cont in patt from chart for tunic back which is worked entirely in st st beg with a K row until chart row 66 completed, ending with a WS row.

Shaping for side vents

Cast on 6 sts at the beg of next 2 rows. (150 sts)
Cont to work from chart until chart row 220 completed, ending with a WS row.

Shape shoulders and back neck

Next row: Cast off 18 sts, patt 39, turn leaving rem sts on a holder.
Work each side of neck separately.
Cast off 2 sts patt to end.
Cast off 17 sts patt to last 2 sts, K2tog.
Cast off 2 st patt to end.
Cast off rem 17 sts.
With RS facing rejoin yarns to rem sts, cast off centre 36 sts, patt to end.
Complete to match first side.

FRONT

Work as for back until chart row 194 completed, ending with a WS row.

Shape front neck

Next row (RS): Patt 67, turn leaving rem sts on a holder.
Work each side of neck separately.
Cast off 4 sts patt to end.
Dec 1 st at neck edge on next 7 rows, 2 foll alt rows and then 2 foll 4th rows. (52 sts)
Cont without further shaping until chart row 220 completed, ending with a WS row.

Shape shoulder

Cast off 18 sts at beg next row and 17 sts foll alt row.

Work 1 row.
Cast off rem 17 sts.
With RS facing rejoin yarn to rem sts, cast off centre 16 sts, patt to end.
Complete to match first side.

Side Vents

Slip 6 sts from first side vent onto a 3mm (US 3) needle and using yarn C cont to work in garter st until band fits up to cast on sts, stretching slightly to give a neat edge.
Cast off.
Slip st neatly into place.
Work other side vents to match.

SLEEVES (both alike)

Cast on 62 sts using 3mm (US 3) needles and yarn C.
Work 8 rows in garter st.
Change to 3¾mm (US 5) needles and work from chart for tunic sleeve until chart row 130 completed and AT THE SAME TIME shape sides by inc 1 st at each end of 3rd row and every foll 3rd row until 116 sts and every foll 4th row to 136 sts.
Cast off loosely and evenly.

Sweater

BACK

Cast on 150 sts using 3mm (US 3) needles and yarn B.
Row 1 (RS): Using yarn B, K2, (P2, K2) to end.
Row 2: Using yarn B, P2, (K2, P2) to end.
Row 3: Using yarn A, work as row 1.
Row 4: Using yarn A, work as row 2.
Rep these 4 rows until 23 rows in all completed.

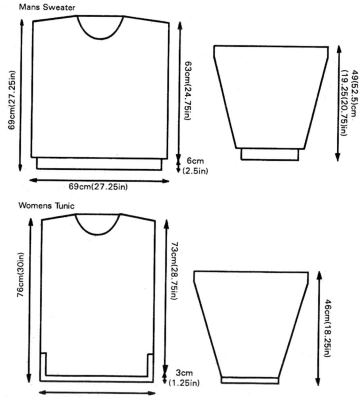

Mans Sweater

69cm(27.25in)
63cm(24.75in)
69cm(27.25in)
6cm (2.5in)
49(52.5)cm (19.25(20.75)in)

Womens Tunic

76cm(30in)
73cm(28.75in)
57.5cm(22.5in)
3cm (1.25in)
46cm(18.25in)

Row 24 (WS)(inc): Using yarn A, rib 3, (M1, rib 5), 29 times, M1, rib 2. (180sts)

Change to 3¾mm (US 5) needles and yarn C, and using a combination of FAIR ISLE and INTARSIA techniques described on the information page, work in patt from chart for sweater back which is worked entirely in st st beg with a K row, until chart row 190 completed, ending with a WS row.

Shape shoulders and back neck

Next row: Cast off 23 sts, patt 49, turn leaving rem sts on a holder.

Work each side of neck separately.

Cast off 2 sts patt to end.

Cast off 22 sts patt to last 2 sts, K2tog.

Cast off 2 st patt to end.

Cast off rem 22 sts.

With RS facing rejoin yarns to rem sts, cast off centre 36 sts, patt to end.

Complete to match first side.

FRONT

Work as for back until chart row 164 completed, ending with a WS row.

Shape front neck

Next row (RS): Patt 82, turn leaving rem sts on a holder.

Work each side of neck separately.

Cast off 4 sts at beg next row.

Dec 1 st at neck edge on next 7 rows, 2 foll alt rows and then 2 foll 4th rows. (67 sts)

Cont without further shaping until chart row 190 completed, ending with a WS row.

Shape shoulder

Cast off 23 sts at beg next row and 22 sts foll alt row.

Work 1 row.

Cast off rem 22 sts.

With RS facing rejoin yarn to rem sts, cast off centre 16 sts, patt to end.

Complete to match first side.

SLEEVES (both alike)

The instructions are given for the shorter sleeve followed by the **longer sleeve in brackets in bold.**

Cast on 50 sts using 3mm (US 3) needles and yarn B, work 23 rows in rib as for back, ending with a WS row.

Row 24 (WS)(inc): Rib 4, (M1, rib 2, M1, rib 3) 9 times, rib 1. (68 sts)

Change to 3¾mm (US 5) needles and yarn C, work from chart for sweater sleeve, shape sides by inc 1 st at each end of 3rd row until 98 sts

and every foll 4th row to 136(**142**) sts.

Cont without further shaping until chart row 130(**140**) completed.

Cast off loosely and evenly.

MAKING UP

Both garments

PRESS all pieces as described on the information page.

Join right shoulder seam using back stitch.

Neckband

With RS facing using 3mm needles and yarn **C for tunic** or yarn **A for sweater**, pick up and K 26 sts down left front neck, 16 sts across centre front, 26 sts up right front and 46 sts across back neck. (114 sts)

Tunic only

Work 8 rows in garter st.

Cast off loosely and evenly.

Sweater only

Work 2 rows in rib using yarn A, setting sts as for sweater back.

Work 2 rows in rib using yarn B.

Rep these 4 rows once more.

Cast off loosely and evenly in rib using yarn B.

See information page for finishing instructions.

KEY
A
B
C
D
E
F

220
210
200
190
180
170
160
150
140
130
120
110
100
90
80
70
60
50
40
30
20
10

Tunic Sleeve
Sweater Sleeve
Tunic
Sweater

45

Patchwork Cardigan

SHARON PEAKE

YARNS

Rowan Cotton Glace

A	Ecru 725	3	x	50gm
B	Pear 780	6	x	50gm
C	Provence 744	2	x	50gm
D	Gentian 743	2	x	50gm
E	Sky 749	2	x	50gm
F	Bloom 784	2	x	50gm
G	Dijon 739	1	x	50gm
H	Crushed rose 793	1	x	50gm
J	Carnival 432	(small amount required)		

NEEDLES

1 pair 2¾mm (no 12) (US 2)
1 pair 3¼mm (no 10) (US 3)

BUTTONS

5

TENSION

23 sts and 32 rows to 10cm measured over patterned stocking stitch using 3¼mm (US 3) needles

BACK

Cast on 116 sts using 2¾mm (US 2) needles and yarn B and work 6 rows in garter st i.e. knit every row.

Change to 3¼mm (US 3) needles and work 24 rows in patt from chart for back using the INTARSIA technique described on the information page and working 2 sts at sides edges in garter st to form side vents.

Cont in patt from chart for back until chart row 152 completed, and AT THE SAME TIME shape sides by inc 1 st at each end of chart rows 55 and 81 ending with a WS row. (120sts)

Shape back neck and shoulders

Cast off 10 sts, patt 30, turn and leave rem sts on a holder.

Work each side of neck separately.

Work 1 row.

Cast off 10 sts at beg next row and foll alt row.

Work 1 row.

Cast off rem 10 sts.

With RS facing rejoin yarns to rem sts, cast off centre 40 sts, patt to end.

Complete to match first side reversing shaping.

LEFT FRONT

Cast on 63 sts using 2¾mm (US 2) needles and yarn B and work 5 rows in garter st.

Next row (WS): K5 and leave these on a holder for front band K to end. (58sts)

Change to 3¼mm (US 3) needles and cont in patt from chart for left front until chart row 24 completed working 2 sts at side edge in garter st to form side vents.

Cont until chart row 133 completed, inc 1 st at side edge on chart rows 55 and 81 as given on chart and ending with a RS row. (60sts)

Shape front neck

Next row (WS): Cast off 20 sts, patt to end. (40sts)

Cont without further shaping until chart row 152 completed ending with a WS row.

Shape shoulder

Cast off 10 sts at beg next row and 2 foll alt rows.

Work 1 row.

Cast off rem 10 sts.

RIGHT FRONT

Cast on 63 sts using 2¾mm (US 2) needles and yarn B and work 5 rows in garter st.

Next row (WS): Knit to last 5 sts, turn and leave rem 5 sts on a holder for front band. (58sts)

Change to 3¼mm (US 3) needles and complete as given for left front foll chart for right front and reversing shaping.

SLEEVES (both alike)

Cast on 58 sts, using 2¾mm (US 2) needles and yarn B and work 4 rows in garter st.

Change to 3¼mm (US 3) needles and work 136 rows in patt from chart working between markers for sleeve and AT THE SAME TIME inc 1 st at each end of 3rd row and every foll 6th row to 100 sts ending with a WS row.

Shape sleevehead

Cast off 9 sts at beg next 10 rows. (10sts)

Cast off rem 10 sts.

MAKING UP

PRESS all pieces as given on the information page.

Join both shoulder seams using back stitch.

Button band

With RS of left front facing slip sts onto a 2¾mm (US 2) needles and cont in garter st until front band fits neatly to beg neck shaping when slightly stretched ending with a WS row.

Slip st into place, leave sts on a holder and break yarn.

Mark position of 5 buttons, the first 4 to come opposite the horizontal bands of reverse st st, the last to come 1 row below neck shaping.

Buttonhole band

Work as given for button band with the addition of 5 buttonholes worked to correspond with markers as folls and ending with a WS row:

Buttonhole row (RS): K1, K2tog, (yon) twice, K2.

Next row: Work across row dropping one of loops made on previous row.

Slip st into place, leave sts on the needle, do not break yarn.

Neckband

With RS of right front facing, using 2¾mm (US 2) needles and yarn B, knit 5 sts from buttonhole band, pick up and knit 20 sts across cast off sts at front neck, place marker, 26 sts up front neck to shoulder, 6 sts down side of back neck, place marker, 40 sts across back neck, place marker, 6 sts up side of back neck, 26 sts down front neck, place marker, and 20 sts across cast off sts of front, knit 5 sts from holder. (154sts) Work 2 rows in garter st ending with a RS row. Cast off knitwise and AT THE SAME TIME reduce sts at each corner by taking 2 sts together either side of each marker to give a neater edge.

See information page for finishing instructions.

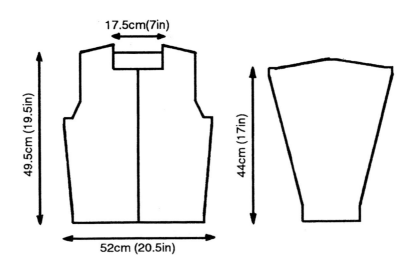

17.5cm(7in)

49.5cm (19.5in)

52cm (20.5in)

44cm (17in)

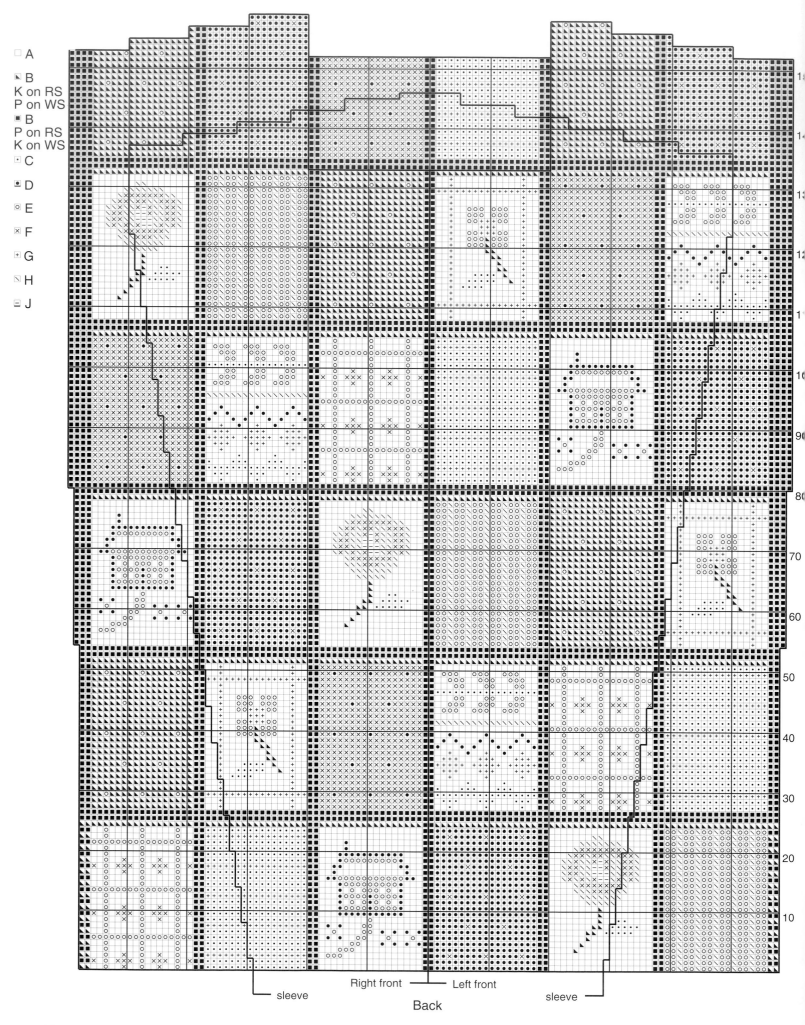

A

B
K on RS
P on WS

B
P on RS
K on WS

C

D

E

F

G

H

J

sleeve

Right front —— Left front

Back

sleeve

Rebbeca

KIM HARGREAVES

YARNS

Rowan True 4-ply Botany

		s	m	l		
A	Jet 546	10	10	11	x	50gm
B	Plum 547	1	1	1	x	50gm
C	Redwood 549	1	1	1	x	50gm
D	Frost 552	1	1	1	x	50gm
E	Avocado 559	1	1	1	x	50gm
F	Pine 553	1	1	1	x	50gm
G	Conker 555	1	1	1	x	50gm
H	Sloe 548	1	1	1	x	50gm
J	Camouflage 562	1	1	1	x	50gm
L	Anjou 554	1	1	1	x	50gm

NEEDLES

1 pair 2¾mm (no 12) (US 2)
1 pair 3¼mm (no 10) (US 3)

BUTTONS

7

TENSION

28sts and 36 rows to 10cm measured over patterned stocking stitch using 3¼mm (US 3) needles

BACK

Cast on 155(163:171)sts using 2¾mm (US 2) needles and yarn A and work in moss st setting sts as folls:
Row 1 (RS): K1, (P1, K1) to end.
Rep this row 9 times more ending with a WS row.
Change to 3¼mm (US 3) needles, cont in patt from chart for back which is worked entirely in st st beg with a K row. Using the INTARSIA and FAIR ISLE technique described on the information page, work until chart row 160(168:176) completed ending with a WS row.

Shape armholes

Cast off 6 sts at beg next 2 rows.
Dec 1 st at each end of next 8 rows.
(127(135:143)sts)
Cont without further shaping until chart row 250(258:266) completed ending with a WS row.

Shape shoulder and back neck

Cast off 8(9:10) sts at beg next 4 rows.
Cast off 8(9:10) sts, patt 22(23:24), turn and leave rem sts on a holder.
Work each side of neck separately.
Cast off 4 st patt to end.
Cast off 8(9:10) sts beg next row, patt to end.
Work 1 row.
Cast off rem 10 sts.
With RS facing rejoin yarn to rem sts, cast off centre 35 sts, patt to end.
Complete to match first side reversing shaping.

LEFT FRONT

Cast on 84(88:92) sts using 2¾mm (US 2) needles and yarn A and work in moss st setting sts as folls:
Row 1 (RS): (K1, P1) to end.
Rep this row 8 times more ending with a RS row.

*Row 10 (WS): Patt 6 and leave these 6 sts on a holder for front band, patt to end. (78(82:86)sts)
Change to 3¼mm (US 3) needles and cont in patt from chart for left front until chart row 160(168:176) completed ending with a WS row.

Shape armhole

Cast off 6st at beg next row.
Work 1 row.
Dec 1 st at armhole edge on next 8 rows.
(64(68:72)sts)
Cont without further shaping until chart row 223(231:239) completed ending with a RS row.

Shape front neck

Cast off 7 sts at beg next row and 4 sts at beg foll alt row.
Dec 1 st at neck edge on next 5 rows, 3 foll alt rows and 3 foll 4th rows. (42(46:50)sts)
Cont without further shaping until chart row 250(258:266) completed ending with a WS row.

Shape shoulder

Cast off 8(9:10) sts at beg next row and 3 foll alt rows.
Work 1 row.
Cast off rem 10 sts.

RIGHT FRONT

Work as given for left front to *.
Row 10 (WS): Patt to last 6 sts, turn and leave rem 6 sts on a holder for front band.
(78(82:86)sts)
Change to 3¼mm (US 3) needles and working from chart for right front complete as given for left front reversing all shaping.

SLEEVES (both alike)

Cast on 63 sts using 2¾mm (US 2) needles and yarn A and work 10 rows in moss st as given for back ending with a WS row.
Change to 3¼mm (US 3) needles and work 162 rows in patt from chart for sleeve and AT THE SAME TIME shape sides by inc 1 st at each end of 3rd row and every foll 4th row to 141 sts and ending with a WS row.

Shape sleevehead

Cast off 6 sts at beg next 2 rows.
Dec 1 st at each end of next 8 rows.
Cast off rem 113sts.

MAKING UP

PRESS all pieces as described on the information page.
Join both shoulder seams using back stitch.

Button band

Slip 6 sts from holder on left front onto a 2¾mm (US 2) needle and using yarn A cont in moss st until band fits neatly when slightly stretched up front to beg neck shaping.
Slip st into place.
Cast off.
Mark position of 7 buttons, the first to come opposite chart row 86, the last to come 1cm down from cast off edge and the rem spaced evenly between.

Buttonhole band

Work as given for button band with the addition of 7 buttonholes worked to correspond with markers as folls:

Buttonhole row (RS): Patt 2, cast off 2, patt to end.
Next row: Patt across row casting on 2 sts over those cast off on previous row.

Collar

Cast on 129 sts using 2¾mm (US 2) needles and yarn A.
Row 1 (RS): K3, moss st to last 3 sts, K3.
Row 2: K3, moss st to last 3 sts, K3.
Row 3 (inc): K3, M1, keeping patt correct work to last 3 sts, M1, K3.
Row 4: K3, patt to last 3 sts, K3.
Keeping st correct as set work 2 rows.
Keeping st correct as set inc as before on next row and every foll 4th row until work measures 6cm from cast on edge ending with a WS row.
* **Next row (RS):** Patt 25, wrap next st (ie. sl 1 st, bring yarn to front of work, put sl st back onto LH needle, turn and work on these 25 sts only), turn, patt to end.
Keeping incs correct as set, shape collar as folls and include inc sts within shaping:
Next row (RS): Patt 18, wrap next st, turn, patt to end.
Next row (RS): Patt 12, wrap next st, turn, patt to end.
Next row (RS): Patt 9, wrap next st, turn, patt to end.
Next row (RS): Patt 6, wrap next st, turn, patt to end.
Next row (RS): Patt 4, wrap next st, turn, patt to end.
Work in patt across all sts working loop and wrapped st together as you go. *
Rep from * to * ending with a WS row.
Patt 1 row.
Cast off in patt.
Slip st cast on edge of collar neatly into place beg and end halfway across front bands and matching centre back of collar with centre back neck.
See information page for finishing instructions.

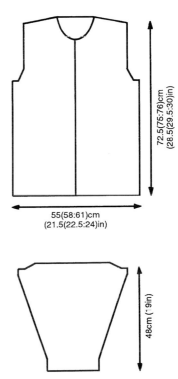

72.5(75:76)cm
(28.5(29.5:30)in)

55(58:61)cm
(21.5(22.5:24)in)

48cm (19in)

KEY

A ☐ K on RS, P on WS
A ⊡ P on RS, K on WS
B ⊙
C ⊠
D ⊡
E ⊟
F ▲
G ▣
H ▨
J ⊡
L ☑

266
260
250
240
230
220
210
200
190
180
170
160
150
140
130
120
110
100
90
80
70
60
50
40
30
20
10

small
medium
large

sleeve
right sleeve   left sleeve

small
medium
large

51

Oriental Leopard

KIM HARGREAVES

YARN

Rowan Magpie, Designer D.K. and Light Weight D.K.

A	Magpie	Raven	62	2	2	2	x	100gm
B	Magpie	Cork	309	1	2	2	x	100gm
C	Magpie	Coffee	310	3	3	3	x	100gm
D	Magpie	Neptune	612	1	1	1	x	100gm
E	DD.K	Wine	663*	2	2	2	x	50gm
F	Lt.Wt.DK	Rose	70*	2	2	2	x	25gm
G	Lt.Wt.DK	Beige	615*	1	1	1	x	25gm
H	Lt.Wt.DK	Airforce	65*	2	2	2	x	25gm
J	Lt.Wt.DK	Gold	9*	3	3	3	x	25gm
L	Lt.Wt.DK	Sand	11*	22	22	23	x	25gm

*USE DOUBLE THROUGHOUT

NEEDLES

1 pair 4mm (no 8) (US 6)
1 pair 5mm (no 6) (US 8)

TENSION

18 sts and 23rows to 10cm measured over patterned stocking stitch using 5mm (US 8) needles

BACK

Cast on 106(110:114) sts using 4mm (US 6) needles and yarn A.
Work in K2, P2 rib for 2.5cm, inc 1 st at end of last row. (107(111:115)sts)
Change to 5mm (US 8) needles and using both the INTARSIA and FAIR ISLE techniques described on the information page, cont in patt from chart for back which is worked entirely in st st beg with a K row, using yarns double where applicable.
Work until chart row 82(88:94) completed, ending with a WS row.

Shape armhole

Cast off 5 sts at beg of next 2 rows. (97(101:105)sts)
Cont without further shaping until chart row 140(146:152) completed.

Shape back neck and shoulders

Patt 32(34:36) sts, turn and leave rem sts on a holder.
Work each side of neck separately.
Cast off 3 sts at beg next row and foll alt row.
Dec 1 st at neck edge on the next 2 rows.
Cast off 7(8:8) sts, patt to last 2 sts, K2tog.

Work 1 row.
Cast off 7(8:9) sts, patt to last 2 sts, K2tog.
Work 1 row.
Cast off rem 8(8:9) sts.
With RS facing, place centre 33 sts on a holder, rejoin yarn to rem sts and patt to end.
Work 1 row.
Complete to match first side reversing all shaping.

FRONT

Work as for back to *.
Cont without further shaping until chart row 116(122:128) completed.

Shape front neck

Patt 38(40:42) sts, turn and leave rem sts on a holder.
Work each side of neck separately.
Cast off 3 sts at beg of next row and foll alt row.
Dec 1 st at neck edge on next 3 rows.
Work 1 row.
Dec 1 st at neck edge on next row and 2 foll alt rows and then on every foll 4th row until there are 22(24:26) sts.
Work 1 row.

Shape shoulder

Cast off 7(8:8) sts at beg next row and 7(8:9) sts at beg foll alt row.
Work 1 row.
Cast off rem 8(8:9) sts.
With RS facing place centre 21 sts on a holder, rejoin yarn to rem sts patt to end.
Work 1 row.
Complete to match first side reversing shaping.

SLEEVES (both alike)

Cast on 52 sts using 4mm (US 6) needles and yarn A.
Work 2.5cm in K2, P2 rib, inc 1 st at end of last row. (53sts)
Change to 5mm (US 8) needles and work 4 rows from chart B, inc 1 st at each end of 3rd row as indicated.
Now cont from main chart, beg at chart row 39 and AT THE SAME TIME, inc 1 st at each end of first row (row39) and every foll alt row to 75 sts and then every foll 4th row to 101 sts.
cont without further shaping until chart row 136 completed.
Cast off loosely and evenly.

MAKING UP

Press all pieces as described on the information page.
Join right shoulder seam using back stitch.

With RS facing, using 5mm (US 8) needles and yarn A, pick up and K 37 sts down left front neck, K across 21 sts from centre holder, pick up and K 37 sts up right front neck to shoulder, 13 sts down right back shaping, K across 33 sts from back neck holder dec 1 st at centre back and pick up and K 13 sts up left back neck shaping. (153 sts)
Work 6 rows in patt from chart C starting row 1 at LH side with a purl row.

Row 7 (dec): (P6, P2tog) 19 times, P1. (134 sts)

Row 8 (dec): (K2tog, K5) 19 times, K1. (115sts)

Row 9 (dec): P2tog, P3, (P2tog, P4) 18 times. (96sts)

Row 10 (dec): K11, (K2tog, K8) 8 times, K2tog, K3. (87sts)

Change to 4mm (US 6) needles and using yarn L, purl 1 row.
Work 2cm in K2, P2 rib.
Cast off loosely and evenly in rib.
See information page for finishing instructions.

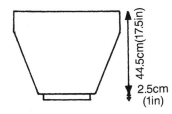

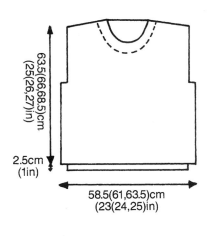

KEY
A ■ B ⊠ C ● D ⊡ E ▽ F ◪ G ⊟ H ◌ J ● L □

CHART B

CHART A

KEY
A ■
B ⊠
C ⊙
D +
E ∨
F ◢
G ⊟
H ⊡
J ⊚
L □

4
1

158
150
140
130
120
110
100
90
80
70
60
50
40
30
20
10

← start
sleeve

small
medium
large

sleeve

back & front

small
medium
large

54

All Blocked Out

MONTSE STANLEY

A piece of knitting fresh off the needles is like a rough diamond waiting to be polished. Blocking out each piece to shape before you sew up a garment will uncurl edges, smooth out wrinkles, and enhance textures.

When you have invested time, money, and creativity into knitting a beautiful designer pattern, it's well worth making just that bit more effort to ensure that the finished result is as perfect as it can be. 'Blocking' is the term used for 'setting' a piece of knitting by pinning it out to shape and treating it with water or steam. Blocking esures that flat fabrics like stocking stitch are perfectly smooth and flat, and that textured knitting like cables, lace, and ribs are as three-dimensional as possible.

Blocking greatly reduces the tendency of fabrics with a stocking-stitch base to curl up, making it easier to join seams and match patterns. Before blocking, the top and bottom of a piece tend to roll out, while the sides roll in. This curling is in the nature of knitted fabric and will never totally vanish, but it can be greatly reduced.

WHAT YOU NEED

A large, flat pinning surface. This can be a bed, a blanket-covered table, a cork-lined board, or even the corner of your living room carpet.

A piece of gingham or other lightweight fabric with bold, bright checks.

A tape measure.

Glass-headed pins, preferably 5 cm (2 in) long.

A water sprayer, steam brush, or steam iron.

Step 1

Sew in all ends before you begin. Cover the pinning surface with the gingham, securing the corners with pins. With a tape measure, mark key positions on the checked fabric following the measurement diagram supplied in your pattern: the cast-on line, the widest and narrowest side points, the start of the armhole, etc. To block a symmetrical piece, start by placing the centre line right in the middle of a check. You can then measure one side and mirror it for the other by counting the checks.

Step 2

With the right side facing upwards, spread the knitting out and pin the key points in place. If there is a ribbed welt, flatten, but don't stretch it. Let the knitting above the rib reach its full width gradually.

Pin along the vertical and horizontal edges, following the lines of the checks. It is best to put one pin at each end, then one at the centre, followed by one in the centre of the two halves and so on. A flat pattern, such as garter or moss stitch, needs few pins. Others, such as stocking stitch, will need more.

The rule is to go on pinning until the line is straight. Use a straight edge such as a ruler to guide you along diagonal lines. When blocking identical or symmetrical pieces such as sleeves or jacket fronts, use the gingham as a guide to get a perfect match; just position the second piece by counting the checks to match the first.

Flatten stocking-stitch-knitted fabrics by patting gently with your hand. To remove the odd bump, push one or more pins down to their heads or place a light weight on top after steaming or spraying.

Bring any distorted stitches into line at this stage, too—an over-large stitch can be made smaller by easing the yarn along the row with the point of a cable needle.

A pattern that draws in, such as a rib, will need stretching slightly. To make it more three-dimensional, run a knitting needle gently along each groove to accentuate the texture.

For cable patterns, run a fine knitting needle gently along the purl lines. Cable crossings can be emphasised by slightly pinching them between your thumb and forefinger. The same can be done to the cables and bobbles of a more complicated pattern.

Some patterns might require different kinds of tricks to help them look their best. Simply decide what the stitch is trying to do and think of ways to accentuate this by closing up, stretching out, or bringing up the texture.

Step 3

Now spray or steam each piece, including

ribs. Both methods are equally effective, although steaming is faster.

To spray, use a fine water sprayer and completely wet the surface of the knitting. You will need to wait several hours for the knitting to dry, which can be a disadvantage if you are in a hurry or can't spare the pinning surface for any length of time.

For steaming, a special steam brush is quick and easy, but can be expensive to buy. If you do a lot of knitting, however, this handy tool is well worth the investment.

An ordinary steam iron will work too, but be sure to keep the iron well above the knitting so that it doesn't touch the fabric and flatten it.

For stocking-stitch knitting only, place a damp cloth over the fabric and press carefully with a dry iron.

Step 4

Now simply leave the pieces to completely dry before removing the pins. Your curled and unformed knitting will have been magically transformed into neatly shaped pieces of fabric, all ready to be joined together into a professional looking, beautifully finished garment.

Eglantine

SASHA KAGAN

YARN

Rowan True 4-ply Botany, Donegal Lambswool Tweed and Fine Cotton Chenille

A	Bot	Snowdrop	545	6	x	50gm
B	D.L.T	Mulberry	459	2	x	50gm
C	F.Chen	Milkshake	405	1	x	50gm
D	F.Chen	Privet	410	1	x	50gm
E	F.Chen	Mousse	418	1	x	50gm

NEEDLES

2¾mm (no 12)(US 2)
1 pair 3¼mm (no 10)(US 3)
Circular needle 2¾mm (no 12)(US 2)–100cm long

Buttons

6

TENSION

28 sts and 36 rows to 10cm measured over patterned stocking stitch using 3¼mm (US 3) needles

BACK

Cast on 139 sts using 2¾mm (US 2) needles and yarn A.
Work in mock cable rib as folls:
Row 1 (WS): K1, (P2, K1) to end.
Row 2: P1, [twist 2 (by knitting into front of second st on left hand needle, than K first st and slip both sts off needle tog), P1], to end.
Rep rows 1 and 2 until rib measures 5cm from beg ending with a WS row, and AT THE SAME TIME, inc 1 st at end of final row. (140 sts)
Change to 3¼mm (US 3) needles and using the

INTARSIA technique described on the information page work in patt from chart which is worked entirely in st st beg with a K row.
Work rows 1-64, then rep rows 22-64 until work measures 30cm from beg ending with a WS row.

Shape armholes

Cast off 7 sts at beg of next 2 rows. (126sts)
Cont without further shaping until work measures 50cm from beg ending with a WS row.

Shape shoulders

Cast off 20 sts at beg of next 4 rows.
Cast off rem 46 sts.

LEFT FRONT

Cast on 67 sts using 2¾mm (US 2) needles and yarn A.
Work 5cm in mock cable rib as given for back ending with a WS row. Do NOT increase on final row.
Change to 3¼mm (US 3) needles and joining in and breaking off colours as required work in patt from chart for left front.
(N.B Do NOT work any motifs along centre front which are less than half complete)
Cont in patt until work measures 23cm from beg ending with a WS row.

Shape front slope and armhole

Dec 1 st at end of next row and at same edge on every foll 5th row until there are 40 sts, and AT THE SAME TIME, when front matches back to armhole shaping, cast off 7 sts at armhole edge.
Cont without further shaping until front measures same as back to shoulder ending with a WS row.

Shape shoulder

Cast off 20 sts at beg of next row, patt to end.
Work one row.
Cast off rem 20 sts.

RIGHT FRONT

Work as given for left front reversing all shaping and foll chart for right front.

SLEEVES (both alike)

Cast on 58 sts using 2¾mm (US 2) needles and yarn A.
Work 5cm in mock cable rib as given for back ending with a RS row.
Next row (WS)(inc): Rib 3, (M1, rib 2, M1, rib 1, M1, rib 2) 10 times, M1, rib 2, M1, rib 3. (90sts)
Change to 3¼mm (US 3) needles and joining in and breaking off colours as required work in patt from chart for sleeves. AT THE SAME TIME, shape sides by inc 1 st at each end of 3rd row and every foll 14th row until there are 112 sts.
Take extra sts into patt as they occur.
Cont without further shaping until work measures 48cm from beg ending with a WS row.
Cast off loosely and evenly.

MAKING UP

Press all pieces as described on the information page.
Join both shoulder seams using back stitch.
Front bands (worked in one piece)
With RS facing, 2¾mm (US 2) circular needle and yarn A, pick up and K 80 sts up right side front edge to start of neck shaping, 100 sts to shoulder seam, 46 sts across back neck, 100 sts down left side front neck to start of neck shaping and 80 sts down left side front edge. (406 sts)
Work 3 rows in mock cable rib.
Next row (buttonholes): Rib 3, cast off 2 sts, (rib 13, cast off 2 sts) 5 times, rib to end.
Next row: Rib, casting on 2 sts in place of those cast off on previous row.
Work 3 more rows in rib.
Cast off loosely and evenly.
Sew sleeve top into armhole using backstitch.
Join side and sleeve seams.
Sew on buttons to correspond with buttonholes.
Press seams.

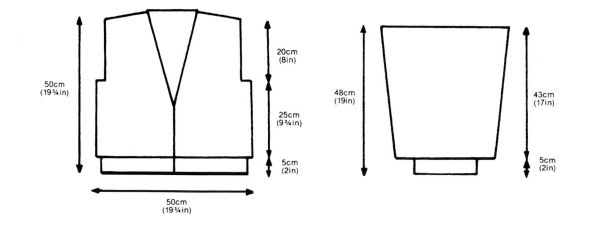

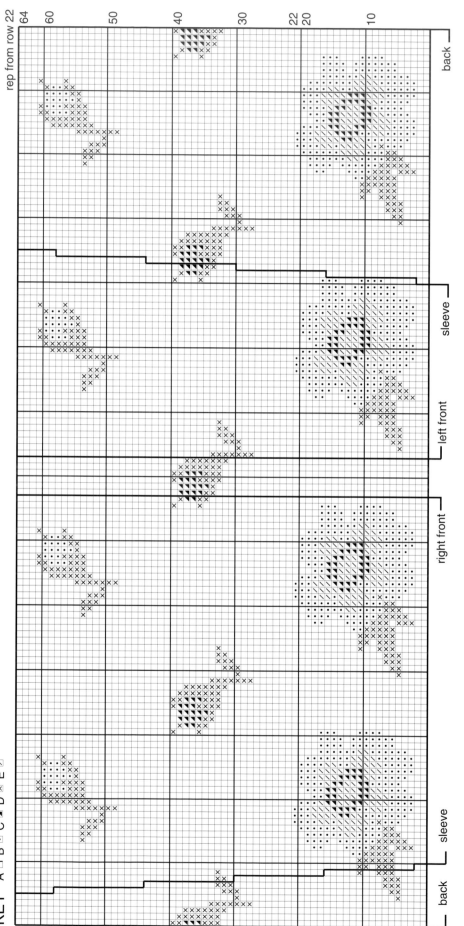

KEY A □ B · C ◀ D × E ◹

Falling Leaves
ANNABEL FOX

YARN
Rowan Magpie Aran & magpie Tweed

			S	M	L		
A	Ivy	765	7	8	9	x	100gm
B	Squirrel	772	2	2	2	x	100gm
C	Ember	763	1	1	1	x	100gm
D	Thunder	764	2	2	2	x	100gm

NEEDLES
1 pair 4mm (no 8)(US 6)
1 pair 4½mm (no 7) (US 7)

TENSION
18 sts and 23 rows to 10cm measured over patterned stocking stitch using 4½mm (US 7) needles

CHART NOTE
Read odd rows (K) from right to left and even rows (P) from left to right.

BACK
Cast on 92(97:102) sts using 4mm (US 6) needles and yarn A.
Work in patterned rib as folls:
Row 1 (RS): * K3, P2, rep from * to last 2 sts, K2.
Row 2: P2, * K2, P3, rep from * to end.
Row 3: * K2, LT, P1, rep from * to last 2 sts, K2.
Row 4: * P2, K1, P1, K1, rep from * to last 2 sts, P2.
Row 5: * K2, P1, LT, rep from * to last 2 sts, K2.
Row 6: * P3, K2, rep from * to last 2 sts, P2.
Row 7: * K2, P1, RT, rep from * to last 2 sts, K2.
Row 8: * P2, K1, P1, K1, rep from * to last 2 sts, P2.
Row 9: * K2, RT, P1, rep from * to last 2 sts, K2.
Row 10: P2, * K2, P3, rep from * to end.
Work row 1-10, then rep rows 3-10 until rib measures 12cm from beg ending with a RS row.
Next row (WS)(inc):
small: P7, (M1, P3) 26 times, M1, P7. (119sts)
medium: P6, (M1, P3, M1, P4) 13 times. (123sts)
large: P3, (M1, P4) 24 times, M1, P3. 127sts)
Change to 4½mm (US 7) needles and using the INTARSIA technique described on the information page work 12 rows in patt from chart A, starting and ending where indicated and rep the 17 patt sts 7 times across row. Now work in patt from chart B. Leaf stems may be swiss darned on completion.
Cont in patt until work measures 42(45:48)cm from beg ending with a WS row.
Shape armhole
Keeping patt correct, cast off 3 sts at beg of next 2 rows.
Cast off 2 sts at beg of next 2 rows.

Dec 1 st at beg of foll 2 rows. (107(111:115)sts) **
Cont straight until work measures 69(72:75)cm from beg ending with a WS row.
Note: Work only complete leaves at shoulder line.
Shape shoulders
Cast off 20(21:22) sts at beg of next 2 rows.
Cast off 19(20:21) sts at beg of foll 2 rows. (29sts)
Leave rem sts on a holder.

FRONT
Work as given for back to **.
Cont straight until work measures 48(51:54) cm from beg ending with a WS row.
Divide for neck
Patt 52(54:56) sts, turn and leave rem sts on a holder.
Work each side of neck separately.
Dec 1 st at neck edge of next row and every foll alt row until 39(41:43) sts rem.
Cont straight until front matches back to shoulder shaping.
Shape shoulder
Cast off 20(21:22) sts at beg of next row.
Work one row.
Cast off rem 19(20:21) sts.
With RS facing, return to rem sts, slip centre 3 sts onto a safety pin, rejoin yarn and work to match first side, reversing all shaping.

SLEEVES (both like)
Cast on 47 sts using 4mm (US 6) needles and yarn A.
Work 10cm in patterned rib as given for back ending with a RS row.
Next row (WS)(inc): P5, (M1, P2) 18 times, M1, P6. (66sts)
Change to 4½mm (US 7) needles and work 12 rows in patt from chart C, rep the 17 patt sts 3 times across row and working first 8 sts and last 7 sts on K rows and first 7 sts and last 8 sts on P rows as indicated. AT THE SAME TIME, shape sides by inc 1st at each end of 5th row and foll 4th row. (70sts)
Now work in patt from chart B, rep patt sts as indicated and cont to shape sides by inc 1 st at each end of 1st row and every foll 4th row until there are 80 sts, then every foll 3rd row until there are 98 sts.
Cont straight until work measures 48cm from beg

ending with a WS row.
Shape top
Cast off 6 sts at beg of next 2 rows, 5 sts at beg of foll 8 rows and then 6 sts at beg of next 2 rows.
Cast off rem 34 sts.

V-NECK INSERT
With RS facing, 4mm (US 6) needles and yarn A, slip 3 sts on safety pin onto left hand needle and work in patterned rib as given for back and shaping as outlined below:
Row 1: Inc in first st, P1, inc in last st. (5sts)
Row 2: P1, K2, P2.
Row 3: Inc in first st, LT, P1 inc in last st.(7sts)
Row 4: P2, K1, P1, K1, P2.
Keeping rib patt correct, cont to inc 1 st at each end of every RS row until there are 31 sts.
Cont straight until work measures 16cm from divide ending with a WS row.
Shape front neck
Patt 11 sts, turn and leave rem sts on a holder.
Work each side of neck separately.
Cast off 4 sts at beg of next row and 2 sts at beg of foll 2 alt rows.
Work one row.
Cast off rem 3 sts.
With RS facing, return to rem sts, slip centre 9 sts onto a holder, rejoin yarn to rem 11 sts and work to match first side reversing all shaping.

MAKING UP
Press all pieces as described on the information page.
Slip stitch side edges of V-neck insert into place.
Join right shoulder seam using back stitch.
Neckband
With RS facing, 4mm (US 6) needles and yarn A, pick up and K 4 sts down left side front neck, 10sts down left side insert, 9 sts from holder at centre front, 10 sts up right side insert, 4 sts up right side front neck and 29 sts from holder at centre back. (66sts)
Work 6cm in K1, P1 rib.
Cast off loosely and evenly in rib.
Join left shoulder seam and neckband.
Fold neckband in half to WS and slip stitch loosely into place.
Sew sleeve top into armhole.
Join side and sleeve seams

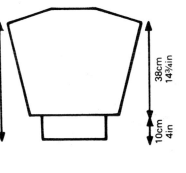

66(68:70)cm
26(26¾:27½)in

69(72:75)cm
27¼(28¼:29½)in

27cm
10¾in

30(33:36)cm
11¾(12¾:14)in

12cm
4¾in

48cm
18¾in

38cm
14¾in

10cm
4in

CHART A

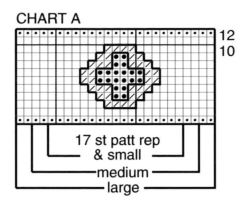

12
10

17 st patt rep
& small
medium
large

CHART B

KEY
A ☐
B ⊡
C ⊙
D ╱

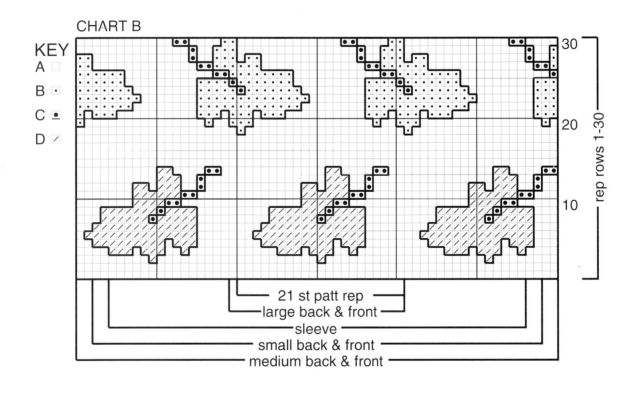

30

20

rep rows 1-30

10

21 st patt rep
large back & front
sleeve
small back & front
medium back & front

CHART C

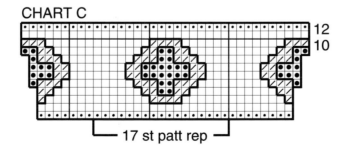

12
10

17 st patt rep

Star

LOUISA HARDING

YARN

Rowan Light Weight D.K. and Donegal
Lambswool Tweed

Ladies' sweater

A	D.L.T.	Bramble 484	15	16	17	x	25gm
B	Lt.Wt.DK.	Old Gold 11	2	3	3	x	25gm
C	D.L.T.	Cinnamon 479	1	1	1	x	25gm
D	D.L.T.	Bay 485	2	2	2	x	25gm
E	Lt.Wt.DK	Forest 73	2	2	2	x	25gm
F	Lt.Wt.DK	Port 602	3	3	3	x	25gm
G	Lt.Wt.DK	Rust 27	1	2	2	x	25gm
H	Lt.Wt.DK	Crimson 46	1	2	2	x	25gm
J	Lt.Wt.DK	Fuschia 94	1	1	1	x	25gm

Man's sweater

A	D.L.T	Dolphin 478	13	13	14	x	25gm
B	Lt.Wt.DK	Blue 52	1	1	2	x	25gm
C	D.L.T.	Black 491	1	1	1	x	25gm
D	Lt.Wt.DK	Petrol 54	1	2	2	x	25gm
E	D.L.T.	Juniper 482	1	1	1	x	25gm
F	D.L.T.	Sapphire 486	1	1	1	x	25gm
G	D.L.T.	Shale 467	1	1	1	x	25gm
H	Lt.Wt.DK	Rose 70	1	1	1	x	25gm
J	Lt.Wt.DK	Fuschia 94	1	1	1	x	25gm

Child's sweater

A	D.L.T.	Ivory 465	6	x	25gm
B	D.L.T.	Black 491	1	x	25gm
C	D.L.T.	Juniper 482	1	x	25gm
D	D.L.T.	Roseberry 480	1	x	25gm

NEEDLES

1 pair 2¾mm (no 12) (US 2)
1 pair 3¼mm (no 10) (US 3)

TENSION

25 sts and 34.5 rows to 10cm measured over patterned stocking stitch using 3¼mm (US 3) needles

Pattern note: The pattern is written for the
child's size, the ladies' and man's sweaters follow
in brackets. Where the mans version differs from
the ladies' this will be shown in **bold**. Where **one**
figure is given this refers to all sizes.

BACK

Cast on 100(152:160:168)(**138:146:154**) sts,
using 2¾mm (US 2) needles and yarn A.

Ladies sweater only

Work 4 rows in garter st, i.e. K every row.

All sizes

Work 2.5(2.5)(**6**) cm in K2, P2 rib ending with a
RS row.

Child's and ladies only

Next row (inc): Inc 1 st, rib to end.
(101(153:161:169)sts)

Man's only

Next row (inc): P6(10:14), (M1, P9) 14 times,
M1, P6(10:14). (153(161:169)sts)

All sizes

Change to 3¼mm (US 3) needles and using the
INTARSIA technique described on the information page and starting at row 1 for ladies and row
51 for child's and man's, cont in patt from chart
for back, which is worked entirely in st st beg with
a K row, until chart row 178(144)(**170**) completed.

Ladies' and man's only

Shape armhole

Cast off 4 sts at beg next 2 rows. (145(153:161)sts)
Cont without further shaping until chart row
228(**254**) completed.

All sizes

Shape shoulders and back neck

Cast off 11(11:15:19) sts at beg of next 2 rows.
Cast off 11(19) sts at beg of next row, patt 15(24)
sts, turn and leave rem sts on a holder.
Work each side of neck separately.
Cast off 4 sts patt to end.
Cast off rem 11(20) sts.
With RS facing rejoin yarn to rem sts, cast off
centre 27(37) sts, patt to end.
Complete to match first side reversing all shaping.

FRONT

Work as for back until chart row 160(196)(**222**)
completed.

Shape front neck

Patt 43(64:68) sts, turn and leave rem sts on a
holder.
Work each side of neck separately.
Cast off 3(4) sts at beg next row.
Dec 1 st at neck edge on next 5(4) rows.
Work a row.
Dec 1 st at beg of next row and foll 1(5) alt rows.
(33(50:54:58)sts)
Cont without further shaping until front matches
back to shoulder ending with a WS row.

Shape shoulder

Cast off 11(11:15:19) sts at beg next row and
11(19) beg foll alt row.
Work 1 row.
Cast off rem 11(20) sts.
With RS facing, rejoin yarn to rem sts.
Cast off centre 15(17)sts, patt to end.
Complete to match first side reversing all shaping.

SLEEVES (both alike)

Cast on 44(64) sts using 2¾mm (US 2) needles
and yarn A.
Work in K2, P2 rib for 2.5(12)cm, inc 1 st at end
of last row. (45(65)sts)
Change to 3 mm (US 3) needles, starting at chart
row 51, cont in patt from sleeve chart.
Work until chart row 134(200) completed and AT
THE SAME TIME, inc 1 st at each end of 3rd row
and every foll 3rd(4th) row to 89(133) sts.
Cast off loosely and evenly.

MAKING UP

Press all pieces as described on the information
page.
Join right shoulder seam using back stitch.

Neckband

With RS facing using 2¾mm (US 2) needles and
yarn A, pick up and K 19(26) sts down left front
neck, 15(17) sts across centre front, 19(26) sts up
right front neck and 35(45) sts from back neck.
(88(114)sts)
Work 2.5(7.5)(6) cm in K2, P2 rib.

Ladies' sweater only

Work 4 rows in garter st.

All sizes

Cast off evenly in rib.
See information page for finishing instructions.

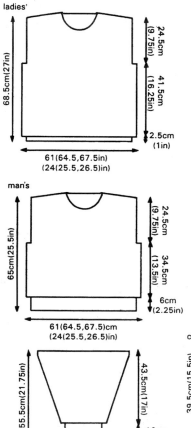

ladies'
24.5cm (9.75in)
68.5cm(27in)
41.5cm (16.25in)
2.5cm (1in)
61(64.5,67.5in)
(24(25.5,26.5)in)

man's
24.5cm (9.75in)
65cm(25.5in)
34.5cm (13.5in)
6cm (2.25in)
61(64.5,67.5)cm (24(25.5,26.5)in)

55.5cm(21.75in)
43.5cm (17in)
12cm (4.75in)

child's
37cm (14.5in)
39.5cm(15.5in)
2.5cm (1in)
40.5cm (16in)

27cm(10.75in)
24.5cm (9.75in)
2.5cm (1in)

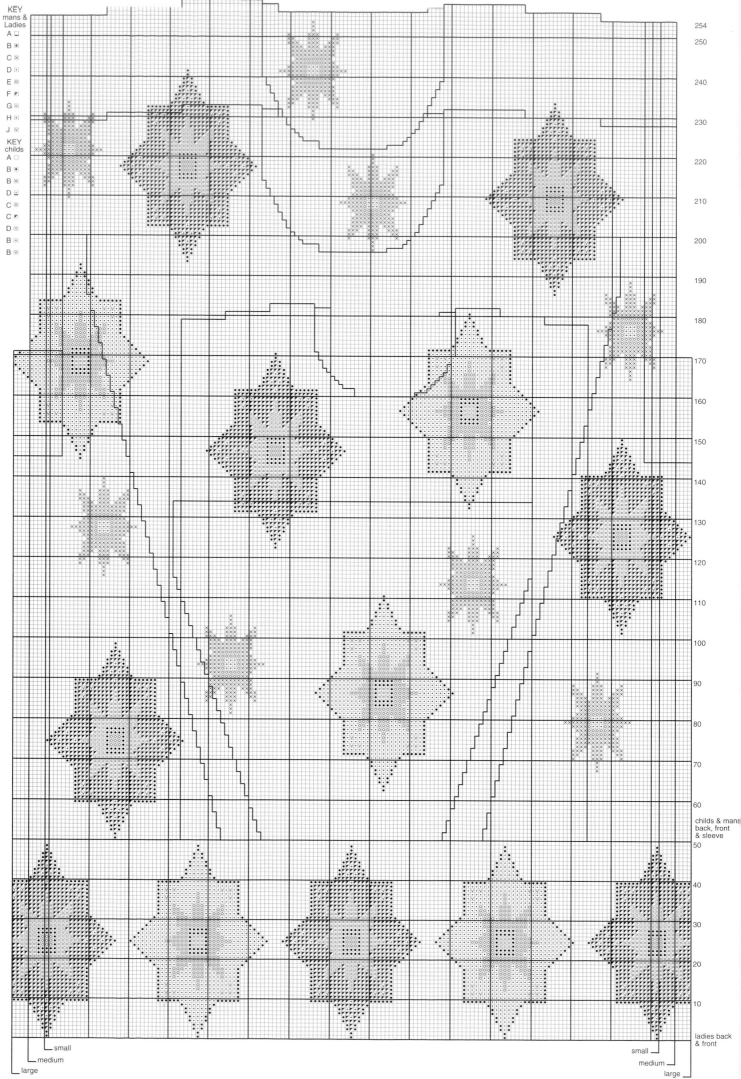

KEY
mans &
Ladies
A □
B ⊙
C ✕
D ⊡
E ⊠
F ☑
G ⊟
H ⊡
J ☑

KEY
childs
A □
B ☑
B ⊠
D ⊡
C ⊙
C ☑
D ⊟
B ⊙
B ☑

254
250
240
230
220
210
200
190
180
170
160
150
140
130
120
110
100
90
80
70
60

childs & mans
back, front
& sleeve

50
40
30
20
10

ladies back
& front

└ small
└ medium
└ large

small ┘
medium ┘
large ┘

64

Patch

AMANDA GRIFFITHS

Crew neck sweater

YARNS

Rowan Donegal Lambswool Tweed

		s	m	l		
A	Don L.T.	12	12	13	x	25gm
B	Don L.T.	12	12	13	x	25gm

One strand of each colour are used together throughout.
(Photographed in 471 Sedge and 469 Oatmeal)

NEEDLES

1 pair 5mm (no 6) (US 8)
1 pair 5½mm (no 5) (US 9)
One 5mm (no 6) (US 8) circular

TENSION

17 sts and 24 rows to 10cm measured over patterned stocking stitch using 5½mm (US 9) needles

Use 1 strand A and 1 strand B together throughout.

BACK

Cast on 104(108:112) sts using 5mm (US 8) needles.
Work 4 rows in patt from chart for back.
Change to 5½mm (US 9) needles and cont until chart row 90 completed ending with a WS row.

Shape armholes

Cast off 3 sts at beg next 2 rows and 2 sts beg foll 2 rows.
Dec 1 st at each end of next row. (92(96:100)sts)
Cont until chart row 146 completed, ending with a WS row.

Shape shoulders and back neck

Next row: Cast off 10(10:10)sts, patt 20(22:24), turn leaving rem sts on a holder.
Work each side of neck separately.
Next row: K2tog, patt to end.

Cast off 10(10:10) sts patt to end.
Work 1 row.
Cast off rem 9(11:13) sts.
With RS facing rejoin yarns to rem sts, cast off centre 32 sts, patt to end.
Complete to match first side reversing shaping.

Pattern note: The front is a mirror image of the back. This image is achieved by reversing the symbols (see chart key). Note that the odd rows (which are worked from right to left of chart) are now WS rows.

FRONT

Work as for back until chart row 134 completed ending with a WS row and reversing symbols (see Key and patt note).

Shape front neck

Next row (RS): Patt 39(41:43) sts, turn leaving rem sts on a holder.
Work each side of neck separately.
Dec 1 st at neck edge on next 10 rows. (29(31:33)sts)
Cont without further shaping until chart row 146 completed ending with a WS row.

Shape shoulder

Cast off 10(10:10) sts at beg next row and foll alt row.
Work 1 row.
Cast off rem 9(11:13) sts.
With RS facing rejoin yarn to rem sts, cast off centre 14 sts, patt to end.

Complete to match first side reversing shaping.

SLEEVES (both alike)

Cast on 52 sts using 5mm (US 8) needles.
Work 4 rows in patt from chart for sleeve.
Change to 5½mm (US 9) needles and cont from chart until chart row 20 completed and AT THE SAME TIME inc 1 st at each end of next row and every foll 5th row. (60sts)
Cont in st st beg with a K row, inc 1 st at each end of every 5th row as before until 90 sts on needle.
Cont without further shaping until sleeve measures 52cm, or length required, from cast on edge, ending with a WS row.
Cast off loosely and evenly.

MAKING UP

PRESS all pieces as described on the information page.
Join both shoulder seams using back stitch.

Neckband

With RS facing using 5mm (US 8) circular needle and starting at left shoulder seam, pick up and K 14 sts down left front neck, 14 sts across centre front, 14 sts up right front and 36 sts across back neck. (78 sts)
Round 1 to 12: P15, K12, P27, K12, P12.
Round 13 to 16: K15, P12, K27, P12, K12.
Cast off loosely and evenly in rib patt as set.
See information page for finishing instructions.

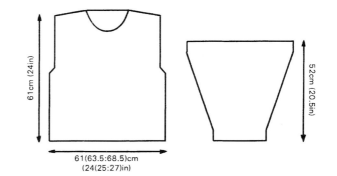

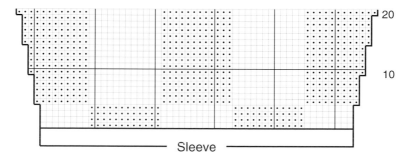

Sleeve

Key

On back   ☐ = K on RS, P on WS   ⊡ = P on RS, K on WS
and sleeves

On front   ☐ = P on RS, K on WS   ⊡ = K on RS, P on WS

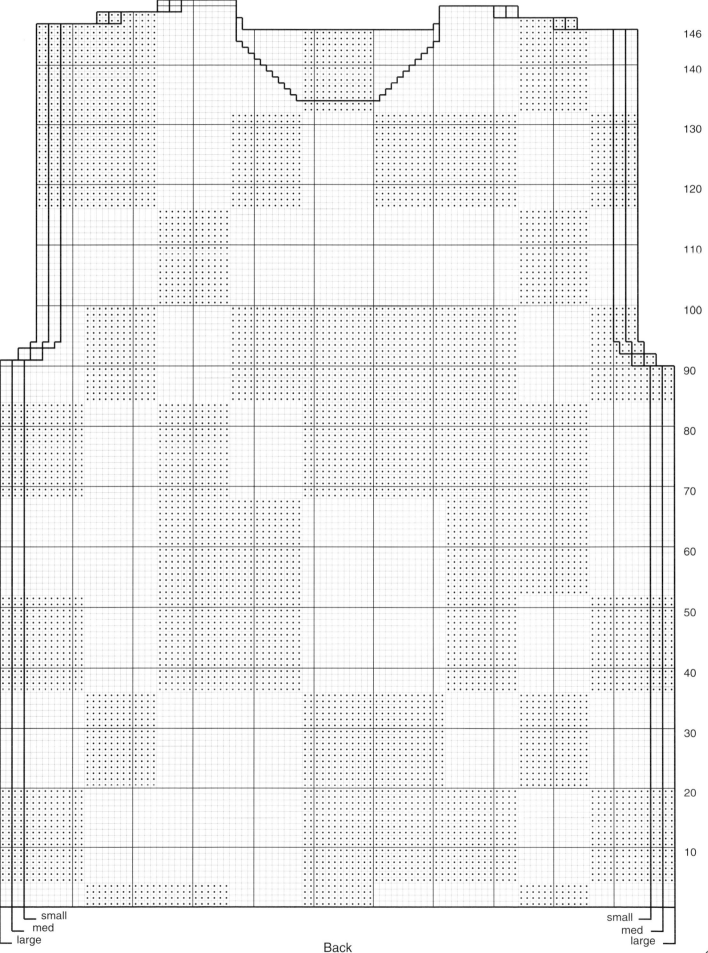

146
140
130
120
110
100
90
80
70
60
50
40
30
20
10

small
med
large

small
med
large

Back

67

Monotone Waistcoat

JEAN MOSS

YARN

Rowan True 4-ply Botany

med	large		
4	4	x	50gm

NEEDLES

1 pair 2¼mm (no 13) (US 1)
1 pair 3¼mm (no 10) (US 3)
Cable needle

Buttons

5

TENSION

30 sts and 40 rows to 10cm measured over pattern using 3¼mm (US 3) needles

BACK

Cast on 110(118) sts using 2¼mm (US 1) needles and work 2cm in K1, P1 rib.
Change to 3¼mm (US 3) needles and work in patt from chart beg at row 1. AT THE SAME TIME, shape sides by inc 1 st at each end of 7th row and every foll 6th row until there are 136(144) sts. Take extra sts into patt as they occur.
Work a further 5(11) rows in patt, ending with a WS row.

Shape armholes

Keeping patt correct, cast off 5(6) sts at beg of next 2 rows, 4 sts at beg of foll 2 rows, 3(4) sts at beg of foll 2 rows and 2 sts at beg of next 4 rows.
Dec 1 st at each end of next row and every foll alt row until 98(102) sts rem.
Work a further 73(77) rows in patt ending with a WS row.

Shape shoulders

Cast off 8(9) sts at beg of next 2 rows and 9 sts at beg of foll 2 rows.
Cast off rem 64(66) sts.

LEFT FRONT

Cast on 2 sts using 3¼mm (US 3) needles and work in patt from chart for left front beg as indicated on chart.
Row 1 (RS): Knit.
Cont as chart and AT THE SAME TIME, * cast on 4 sts at end of next row and 2 sts at end of foll row; rep from * 4 more times. (32sts)
Work one row.
Next row: Cast on 21(25) sts at beg of row, patt across next 32 sts, cast on 2 sts at end of row. (55(59) sts)
Now cont in patt from chart for left front and AT THE SAME TIME, shape side edge by inc 1 st at beg of chart row 7 and every foll 6th row until there are 68(72) sts.
Work 5(11) rows in patt without further shaping.

Shape armhole and neck

Cast off 5(6) sts at beg of next row, patt to last 2 sts, k2tog.
Cont to shape armhole as for back and AT THE

SAME TIME, dec 1 st at neck edge on every foll 3rd row until there are 35(39) sts, then every foll 4th row until there are 26(28) sts.
Cont without further shaping until front matches back to shoulder ending with a WS row.

Shape shoulder

Cast off 8(9) sts at beg of next row and 9 sts at beg of foll alt row.
Work one row.
Cast off rem 9(10) sts.

RIGHT FRONT

Cast on 2 sts using 3¼mm (US 3) needles and work in patt from chart for right front beg as indicated on chart.
Row 1 (RS): Knit.
Cont in patt and AT THE SAME TIME, * cast on 2 sts at end of next row and 4 sts at end of foll row; rep from * 4 more times. (32sts)
Next row: Patt 32 sts, cast on 2 sts at end of row.
Next row: Patt 34 sts, cast on 21(25) sts at end of row. (55(59)sts)
Now complete to match left front, reversing all shaping and foll chart for right front.

MAKING UP

Press all pieces as described on the information page.
Join both shoulder seams using backstitch.

Armbands (both alike)

With RS facing and 2¼mm (US 1) needles, pick up and K 166(178) sts evenly around armhole edges.
Work 2cm in K1, P1 rib.
Cast off evenly in rib.

Front bands and neckband

(one piece)
Cast on 10 sts using 2 mm (US 1) needles and work in K1, P1 rib until band (when slightly stretched) first along bottom of left front to point, ending with a WS row.
Now form mitre in foll way:
Cast off 3 sts at beg of next row and foll 2 alt rows. (1 st remains)
With WS facing, cast on 3 sts at end of next row and foll 2 alt rows. (10sts)
Cont straight until band reaches centre front, ending with a WS row. Sew band in place as worked.
Form a second mitre in same way as before.
Cont around front edges, sewing band in place as worked and making a further 2 mitres on right front to correspond to left front shaped edge(take care to ensure that mitre is formed on side to be attached to front). AT THE SAME TIME, mark position of 5 buttons on left front band with pins to ensure even spacing, the first to come 1.5cm up from mitred corner, the last level with start of neck shaping and the remaining 3 spaced evenly between. Work buttonholes on right front to correspond with marked positions as folls:
Next row (buttonhole): Rib 4 sts, cast off 2 sts, rib 4 sts.
Next row: Work across row, casting on 2 sts in place of those cast off on previous row.
Cast off evenly in rib.
Stitch remainder of band into place.
Sew mitred edges together very neatly.
Join side seams using backstitch.
Sew on buttons to correspond with buttonholes.
Press seams.

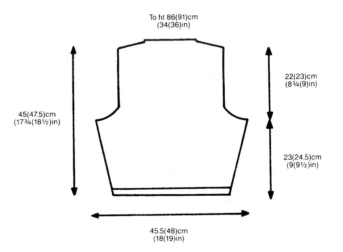

To fit 86(91)cm
(34(36)in)

22(23)cm
(8¾(9)in)

45(47.5)cm
(17¾(18½)in)

23(24.5)cm
(9(9½)in)

45.5(48)cm
(18(19)in)

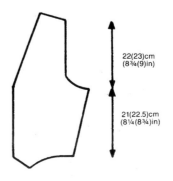

22(23)cm
(8¾(9)in)

21(22.5)cm
(8¼(8¾)in)

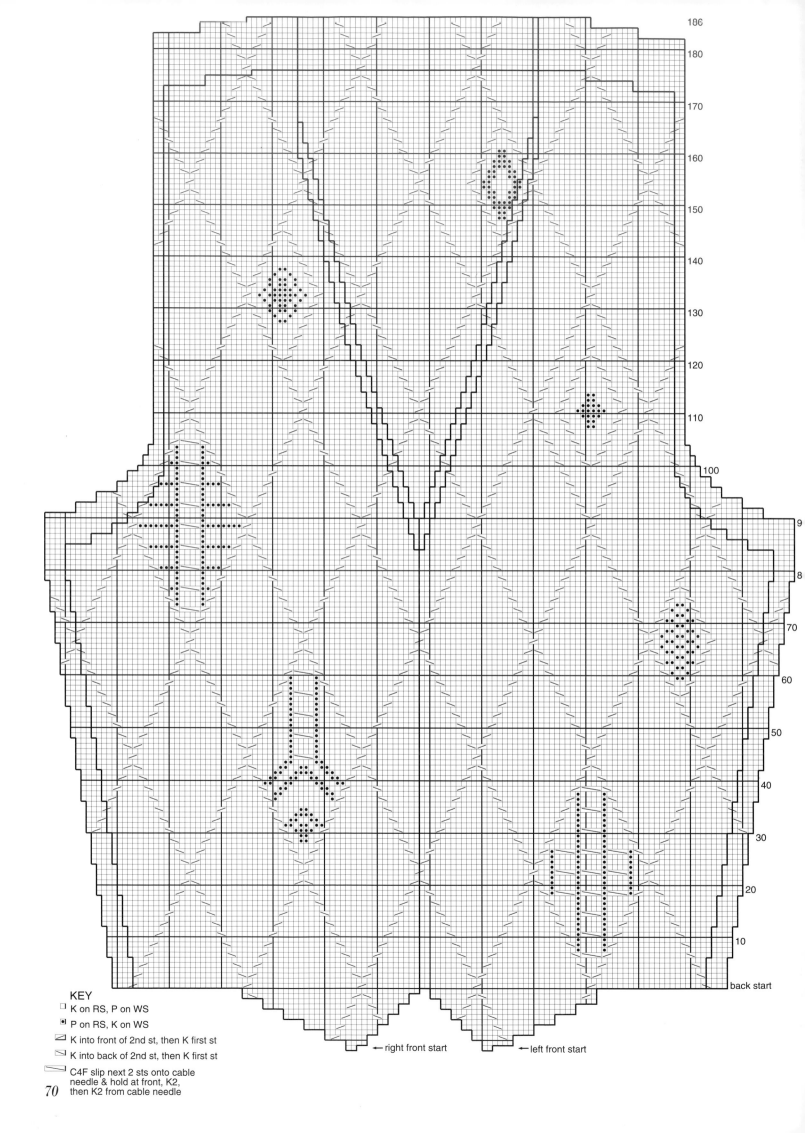

186
180
170
160
150
140
130
120
110
100
9
8
70
60
50
40
30
20
10
back start

← right front start ← left front start

KEY

☐ K on RS, P on WS

▣ P on RS, K on WS

⧄ K into front of 2nd st, then K first st

⧅ K into back of 2nd st, then K first st

▱ C4F slip next 2 sts onto cable
needle & hold at front, K2,
then K2 from cable needle

70

October Leaves

SASHA KAGAN

YARNS

Rowan Magpie, Fine Chenille, Chunky Chenille, Designer D.K. and Kid Silk

A	Magpie	Raven 62	9 x 100gm
B	F.Chen	Ruby 407*	2 x 50gm
C	D.D.K.	Pine 685*	1 x 50gm
D	D.D.K	Donkey 698*	3 x 50gm
E	Kid Silk	Holly 990*	2 x 25gm
F	Ch.Chen	Aubergine 356	1 x 100gm
G	Ch.Chen	B/currant 381	1 x 100gm
H	Kid Silk	Smoke 998*	3 x 25gm
J	F.Chen	Privet 410*	1 x 50gm

* Yarns used double throughout

NEEDLES

1 Pair 4mm (no 8) (US 6)
1 Pair 5mm (no 6) (US 8)

BUTTONS

7

TENSION

18 sts and 24 rows to 10 cm measured over stocking stitch pattern on size 5mm (US 8) needles.

BACK

Cast on 113 sts using 4 mm (US 6) needles and yarn A.
Row 1 (RS): K1, (P1, K1) to end.
Row 2: Work as row 1.
These 2 rows form Moss st.
Rep these 2 rows until work measures 2.5cm from cast on edge ending with a WS row and inc 1 st at end of last row. (114sts)
Change to 5mm (US 8) needles and using the INTARSIA technique described on the information page cont in patt from chart for back which is worked entirely in st st beg with a K row.
Work until chart row 122 completed ending with a WS row.

Shape armholes

Cast off 7 sts at beg next 2 rows. (100sts)
Cont without further shaping until chart row 188 completed ending with a WS row.

Shape shoulders and back neck

Cast off 9 sts at beg next 2 rows.
Cast off 9 sts, patt 21 sts, turn leaving rem sts on a holder.
Work each side of neck separately.
Next row: P2tog, patt to end.
Next row: Cast off 9 sts, patt to last 2 sts, K2tog.
Work 1 row.
Cast off rem 10 sts.
With RS facing rejoin yarn to rem sts, cast off centre 22 sts, patt to end.
Complete to match first side reversing shaping.

POCKET LINING (make 2)

Cast on 25 sts using 5mm (US 8) needles and yarn A.

Work 44 rows in st st beg with a K row.
Leave sts on a holder.

LEFT FRONT

Cast on 55 sts using 4 mm (US 6) needles and yarn A.
Work 2.5cm in moss st as given for back, inc 1 st at end of last row. (56sts)
Change to 5mm (US 8) needles and cont in patt from chart for left front until chart row 58 completed.
Place pocket
Row 59 (RS): Patt 16 sts, slip next 25 sts onto a holder and in place of these patt across sts of first pocket lining, patt to end.
Cont from chart until chart row 122 completed ending with a WS row.

Shape armhole

Cast off 7 sts at beg next row. (49sts)
Cont without further shaping until chart row 169 completed ending with a RS row.
Shape front neck
Next row (WS): Cast off 5 sts, patt to end.
Dec 1 st at neck edge on next 3 rows and 4 foll alt rows. (37sts)
Cont without further shaping until front matches back to shoulder shaping ending with a WS row.

Shape shoulder

Cast off 9 sts at beg next row and 2 foll alt rows.
Work 1 row.
Cast rem 10 sts.

RIGHT FRONT

Work as given for left front foll chart for right front and reversing all shaping and position of pocket.

SLEEVES (both alike)

Cast on 49 sts using 4mm (US 6) needles and yarn A.
Work 2.5cm in moss st as given for back and inc 1 st at end of last row. (50sts)
Change to 5mm (US 8) needles and cont in patt from chart for sleeve until chart row 110 completed and AT THE SAME TIME shape sides by inc 1 st at each end of 3rd row and every foll 4th row to 100 sts ending with a WS row and working all extra stitches in background colour.
Cast off loosely and evenly.

MAKING UP

PRESS all pieces as described on the information page.

Buttonhole band

With RS facing using 4mm (US 6) needles and yarn A, pick up and K148 sts evenly along right front edge.
Work 3 rows in moss st.
Next row (RS): Patt 36, cast off 2 sts, (patt 16, cast off 2 sts) 6 times, patt 2.
Next row: Keeping moss st correct, cast on 2 sts over those cast off on previous row.
Work 2 rows moss st.
Cast off evenly in patt.

Button band

Work as given for buttonhole band omitting buttonholes.

Collar

Cast on 89 sts using 4mm (US 6) needles and yarn A.
Row 1 (RS): K2, * P1, K1, rep from * to last st, K1.
Row 2 : Work as row 1.
Next row (inc): K2, M1, * P1, K1, rep from * to last 2 sts, M1, K2.
Work 10cm in moss st inc 1 st (as before) at each end of every 4th row.
Cast off evenly in patt.

Pocket Tops (both alike)

With RS facing using 4mm (US 6) needles and yarn A knit across sts on holder.
Work 5 rows in moss st.
Cast off evenly in patt.
Join shoulder seams using back stitch.
Slip stitch cast on edge of collar into place starting and ending halfway across front bands and matching centre of collar to centre back neck.
See information page for finishing instructions.

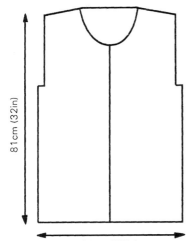

81cm (32in)

64cm (25in)

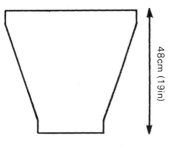

48cm (19in)

Key
A
B
C
D
E
F
G
H
J

188
180
170
160
150
140
130
120
110
100
90
80
70
60
50
40
30
20
10

Right front

Left Front

Sleeve

73

Colour Works

JULIA COWPER

Knitting with more than one colour can be confusing if you're not sure of the techniques involved. Why do some charts only show a small square of pattern, while others display a shaped piece, complete with motifs? How are you supposed to make yarns stretch across the back of the knitting without pulling it completely out of shape? And how on earth do you knit a motif in the middle of a cardigan front?

Simply put, colour knitting can be divided into two main categories: patterns where only two or three colours are used in every row and where all the yarns are carried across the back of the work—this is called 'Fair Isle' knitting, and patterns where a different length of yarn is used for each separate area of colour—this is called 'intarsia' knitting.

Working from charts

Most multicoloured designs, whether Fair Isle or intarsia, use charts to simplify the written knitting instructions. Charts are set out on graph paper, with one square representing one stitch, and each horizontal line of squares representing one row. Blank squares usually denote the background colour, and the different symbols in the squares relate to the different colours to be knitted.

For example;

= main colour
X = 1st contrast colour
* = 2nd contrast colour
- = 3rd contrast colour
0 = 4th contrast colour

If there are large areas of colour to be worked in an intarsia design, they will sometimes be outlined and a coded number or letter will be given for that area, rather than a symbol for each square.

If working from symbols is hard on your eyes, try using coloured pencils or felt-tip pens to fill in each square with the appropriate colour first. This will make your knitting and the chart look the same.

Most colour charts are worked in stocking stitch—one row knit, one row purl—unless the pattern states otherwise. The first and every odd-numbered row are knit rows, and are knitted following the chart from right to left. The second and every even-numbered row are purl rows, and are purled following the chart from left to right. Charts usually have numbers running up one or both sides to help you keep track of where you are. Keep your place on the chart with sticky Post It labels, and move them up row by row as you work your way up.

Fair Isle

In most Fair Isle charts only a section of the pattern will be shown, usually one full repeat with stitches either side to make sure the pattern matches up neatly on the side seams. To knit the first pattern row, knit the few stitches on the right of the chart as indicated for the size you are knitting, repeat the pattern stitches as many times as instructed, then knit the stitches on the left. On the second pattern row, a purl row, the reverse should be done—purl the required stitches on the left, repeat the pattern stitches across the row, then purl the stitches on the right. Continue to work all the pattern rows the same way.

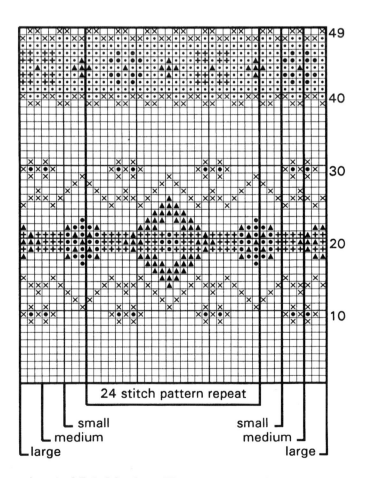

A typical Fair Isle chart. The centre 24 stitches are repeated across the row, with stitches worked either side

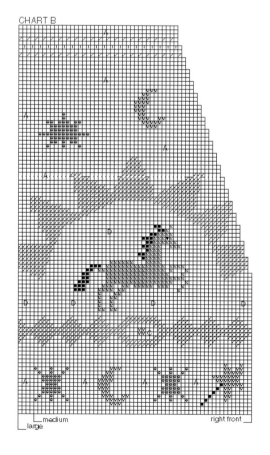

Intarsia charts usually show the motifs in position-nand all shaping too

Stranding yarns

The colours in Fair Isle knitting are carried across every row, with only one of the colours being worked at a time. The yarn or yarns not in use are stranded across the back of the work. It is important that the stranded colours are not pulled tightly, or the knitted fabric will pucker out of shape. One way to avoid this is to make sure that the stitches on the right-hand needle are spread out and that the strand, or float, is long enough to comfortably span these stitches before making the next stitch. Another key point when changing colours is to be consistent about keeping the main yarn above, and the contrast yarns below. This way, the floats will lie flat on the fabric and the balls of yarn will not need untangling at the end of each row. Another way to avoid tangling the yarns is to turn the point of the right-hand needle (with the knitting on it) away from you at the end of every knit row, and towards you at the end of every purl row.

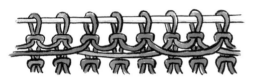

Stranding yarns. The main yarn should lie on top, the contrast yarn below to keep the floats flat against the fabric

Weaving yarns

Carrying a yarn across more than four or five stitches will produce long floats on the back of the work which can catch. To avoid this, weave in unused yarns by taking them first above, then below the yarn that is being knitted.

Take the tail of the second yarn up and. . .

. . . over the top to the yarn that is being worked

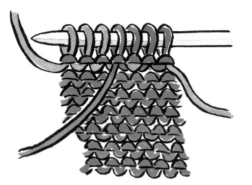

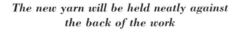

The new yarn will be held neatly against the back of the work

Intarsia

Intarsia knitting is very different from Fair Isle knitting, both in appearance and in the way it is worked. Charts usually show the knitted piece in its entirety, with all shapings clearly marked. This ensures that all colour areas and motifs are properly placed on the chart. Each area of colour is knitted with separate lengths (not balls) of yarn, which are twisted together at the joins and left in position until required on the following row. They are not carried across the back of the work, so the resulting fabric is more flexible and not as thick as a piece of Fair Isle knitting. The single most useful tip for intarsia knitting is to use 'manageable' lengths of yarn, about one to one-and-a-half metres long. If there are a lot of colours being used in a small area they inevitably get tangled, and if these were all balls of yarn, you would spend more time untangling them than you would knitting! But if the yarns are used as short lengths, when a particular colour is needed it can easily be pulled free of the others.

Twisting yarns at colour joins

Twisting yarns when changing from one colour to another is vital when working intarsia. Work to the colour change point, then take the colour you

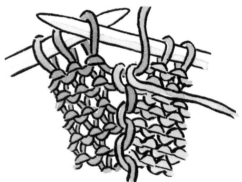

Twisting yarns together on a knit row

Twisting yarns together on a purl row

have just been using over the top of the yarn you are about to use. Pick up the new yarn and, pulling firmly, work the next stitch. This will prevent gaps being made in the work where two colours meet and will make a neat join on the wrong side.

Joining yarn

So what do you do in the middle of a piece of intarsia when the lengths of yarn run out? Just cut off a new length of the right colour and start working with it, weaving in the new end as you go along as shown in the illustrations at left and above. Leave a 15cm 'tail' on the new colour and, starting approximately 10 stitches before it is needed, take the tail above the working yarn on every other stitch. The tail will be caught into the work at least five times and will be secure enough to cut off.

Once you learn and practise a few basic techniques, and get to know some of the tricks designed to make knitting simpler, working with more than one colour can become as easy as knitting plain or textured designs, and will open up a whole new world of pattern and design.

Duffy

LUCY GUY

YARN

Rowan True 4-ply Botany

			s	m		
A	Blond	564	6	7	x	50gm
B	Jet	546	2	2	X	50gm

NEEDLES

1 pair 3mm (no 11) (US 3)
Circular needle 40cm long 2¾mm (no 12) (US 2)

TENSION

28 sts and 36 rows to 10cm measured over patterned stocking stitch using 3 mm (US 3) needles

STITCH NOTE

Border

Cast on 7 sts.

Row 1 (RS): Knit.
Row 2: K5, K into front and back of next st, K1.
Row 3: K 1, K into front and back of next st, K6.
Row 4: K7, K into front and back of next st, K1.
Row 5: K1, K into front and back of next st, K8.
Row 6: K9, K into front and back of next st, K1.
Row 7: K1, K into front and back of next st, K10.
Row 8: K11, K into front and back of next st, K1.
Row 9: K1, K into front and back of next st, K12.
Row 10: K12, K2tog, K1.
Row 11: K1, K2tog, K11.
Row 12: K10, K2tog, K1.
Row 13: K1, K2tog, K9.
Row 14: K8, K2tog, K1.
Row 15: K1, K2tog, K7.
Row 16: K6, K2tog, K1.
Row 17: K1, K2tog, K5.
Rep rows 2-17.

BACK

Cast on 7 sts using 3mm (US 3) needles and yarn A.
Work 14(15) repeats of brder patt outlined in STITCH NOTE.
Cast off.
Then with RS facing, 3mm (US 3) needles and yarn A, pick up and K 116(124) sts evenly along straight edge of border.
Then, joining in and breaking off yarn B as required work 4 rows in patt from chart D which is worked entirely in st st beg with a P row. Rep 9 st patt 12(13) times across row and work first 5(0) sts and last 3(7) sts on RS rows and first 3(7) sts and last 5(0) sts on WS rows as indicat-
ed.
Work 5(9) rows in st st using yarn A only and AT THE SAME TIME, begin shaping sides by inc 1

st at each end of 2nd(4th) row and for medium size only foll 5th row. (118(128)sts)
Work 70(62) rows in patt from chart and AT THE SAME TIME, shape sides by inc 1 st at each end of 1st(5th) row and every foll 6th(5th) row until there are 140(148) sts. **

Shape raglan

Dec 1 st at each end of next row and every foll alt row until ther are 60 sts. N.B. From row 121 onwards work in patt from chart B for back neck.
Work one row. (Row 150 chart B)

Shape back neck

K2tog, patt 14 sts, turn and leave rem sts on a holder.
Work each side of neck separately.
Cast off 9 sts at beg of next row, patt to end.
Next row: K2tog at beg of row, patt to end.
Work one row.
Cast off rem 5 sts.
With RS facing, return to rem sts, leave centre 28 sts on a holder, rejoin yarn to rem sts, patt to end.
Complete second side to match first side revers-
ing all shaping.

FRONT

Work as given for back to **.

Shape raglan

Dec 1 st at each end of next row and every foll alt row until ther are 72 sts.
Work one row. (Row 138 chart A)

Shape front neck

K2tog, patt 20 sts, turn and leave rem sts on a holder.
Work each side of neck separately.
Cast off at beg of next row and foll alt rows, 4 sts once, 3 sts once, 2 sts twice and 1 st once and AT THE SAME TIME, cont to dec 1 st at arm-
hole edge on every alt row as before until 2 sts rem.
Work one row.
Cast off.
With RS facing, return to rem sts, leave centre 28 sts on a holder, rejoin yarn to rem sts, patt to end.
Complete second side to match first side revers-
ing all shaping.

SLEEVES (both alike)

Cast on 7 sts using 3mm (US 3) needles and yarn A.

Work 9 repeats of border patt outlined in STITCH NOTE.
Cast off.
With RS facing, 3mm (US 3) needles and yarn A, pick up and K 74 sts evenly along straight edge of border.
Then, joining in and breaking off yarn B as required work 4 rows in patt from chart D which is worked entirely in st st beg with a P row. Rep 9 patt sts 7 times across row and work first 6 sts and last 5 sts on RS rows and first 5 sts and last 6 sts on WS rows as indicated. AT THE SAME TIME, begin shaping sides by inc 1 st at each end of 2nd row. (76sts)
Work 5(9) rows in st st using yarn A only and cont to shape sides on medium size only by inc 1 st at each end of 4th row. (76(78) sts)
Then, joining in and breaking off yarn B as required work 94(90) rows in patt from chart C and AT THE SAME TIME, cont in shape sides by inc 1 st at each end of 2nd(1st) row and every foll 9th(6th) row until there 96(108) sts.

Shape raglan

Dec 1 st at each end of next row and every foll alt row until there are 12(16)sts.
Work one row.
Cast off.

MAKING UP

Press all pieces as described on information page.
Join all raglan seams usisng backstitch.

Collar

With RS facing, 2¾mm (US 2) circular needle and yarn A, pick up and K 18 sts down left side front neck, 28 sts from holder at centre front, 18 sts up right side front neck, 10(14) sts across sleeve top, 12 sts down right side back neck, 28 sts from holder at centre back, 12 sts up left side back neck and 10(14) sts across rem sleeve top. (136(144) sts.
Mark centre front point with coloured thread.
work 1.5cm in K1, P1 rib, ending at coloured thread.

Divide for collar

Then, working backwards and forwards and not in rounds, cont in rib as set until collar measures 10cm from pick up row.
Cast off loosely and evenly in rib.
Join side and sleeve seams.
Press seams.

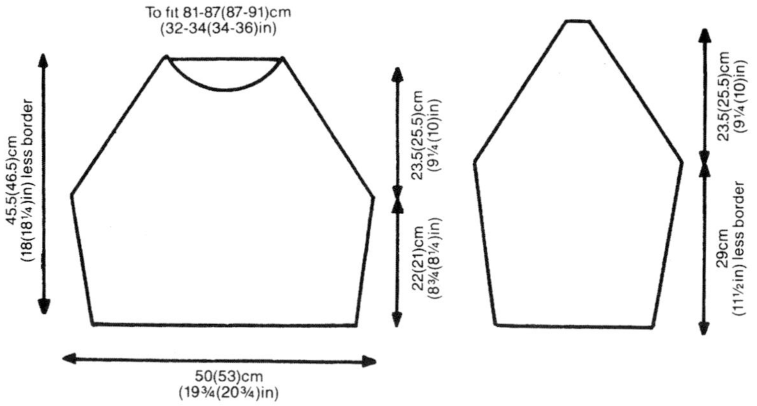

To fit 81-87(87-91)cm
(32-34(34-36))in

45.5(46.5)cm
(18(18¼)in) less border

23.5(25.5)cm
(9¼(10)in)

22(21)cm
(8¾(8¼)in)

50(53)cm
(19¾(20¾)in)

23.5(25.5)cm
(9¼(10)in)

29cm
(11½in) less border

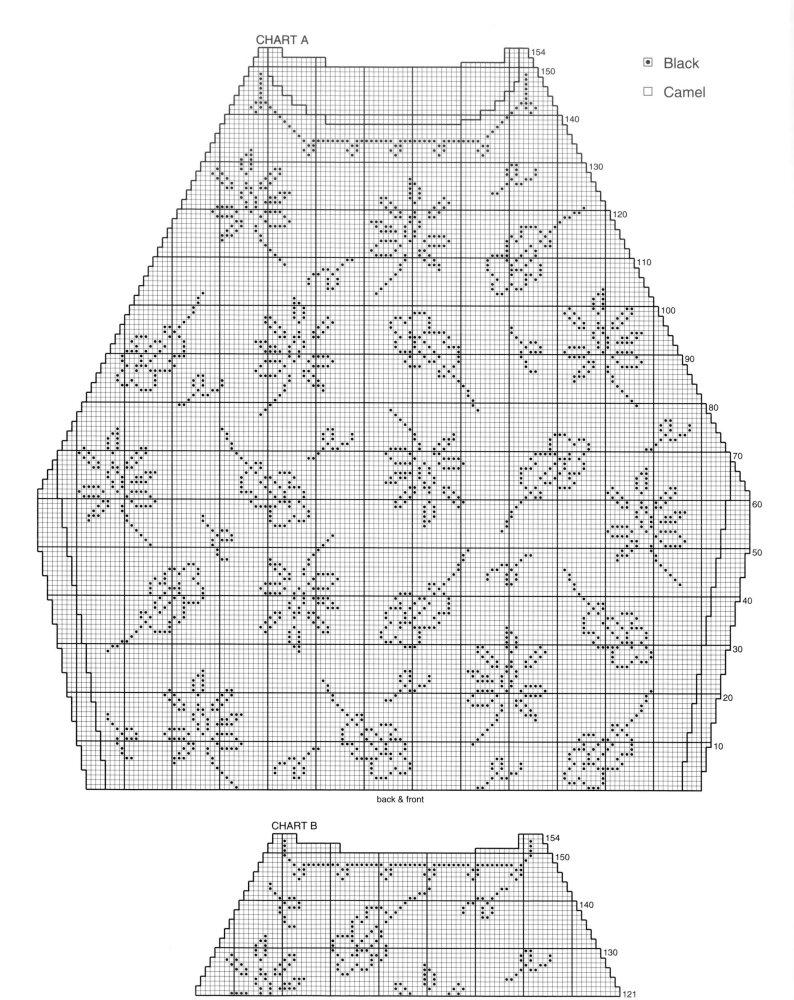

CHART A

154
150
140
130
120
110
100
90
80
70
60
50
40
30
20
10

■ Black
□ Camel

back & front

CHART B

154
150
140
130
121

back neck (rows 121 onwards)

CHART C

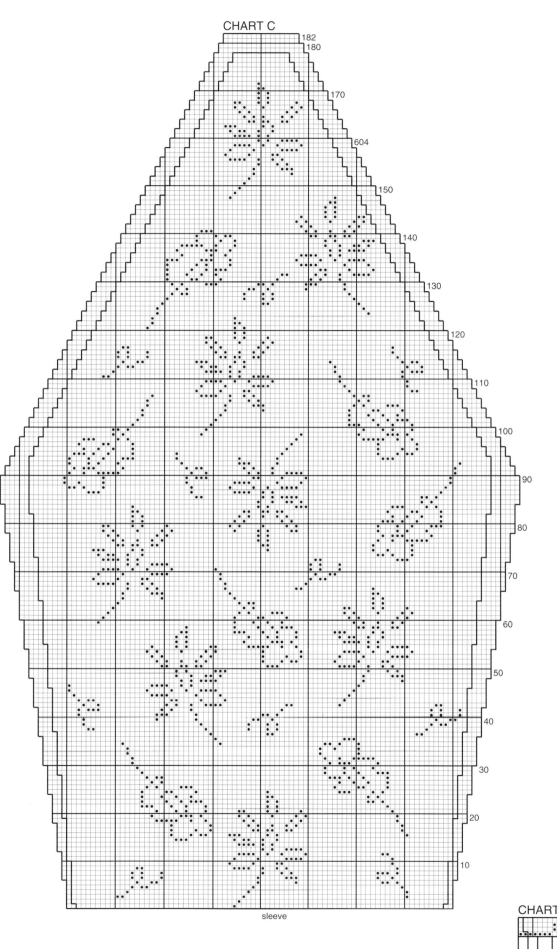

sleeve

CHART D

9 sts patt rep

medium - back

small - back

both sizes - sleeve

Peacock Jacket and Sweater

KIM HARGREAVES

YARN

Rowan Magpie, Magpie Tweed and Light Weight DK

Jacket and Sweater

A	Magpie	Dapple	450	7	x 100gm
B	Mag Twd	Squirrel	772	3	x 100gm
C	Lt.Wt.DK	Beige	615*	2	x 25gm
D	Lt.Wt.DK	Musk	148*	2	x 25gm
E	Lt.Wt.DK	Sage	418*	4	x 25gm
F	Lt.Wt.DK	Duckegg	665*	2	x 25gm
G	Lt.Wt.DK	Mink*	145	2	x 25gm

* USE DOUBLE THROUGHOUT

NEEDLES

1 pair 4mm (no 8) (US 6)
1 pair 5mm (no 6) (US 8)

Buttons

10 (jacket only)

TENSION

18 sts and 23 rows to 10cm measured over patterned stocking stitch using 5 mm (US 8) needles

Jacket

BACK

Cast on 120 sts using 4mm (US 6) needles and yarn B.

Join in yarn A and work 2-colour rib as folls:

Row 1 (RS): P1A, (K2B, P2A) to last 3 sts, K2B, P1A.

Row 2: K1A, (P2B, K2A) to last 3 sts, P2B, K1A.

Rep these 2 rows twice more, inc 1 st at end of last row. (121sts)

Change to 5mm (US 8) needles and using both FAIR ISLE and INTARSIA techniques as described on the information page, cont in patt from chart for back which is worked entirely in st st beg with a K row, i.e. work first 21 rows of border patt in Fair Isle , then work rest of chart in a mixture of Fair Isle and Intarsia. **
Work 148 rows in patt.

Shape shoulders

Cast off 40 sts at beg of next 2 rows.
Cast off rem 41 sts.

LEFT FRONT

Cast on 60 sts using 4mm (US 6) needles and yarn B.

Join in yarn A and work 6 rows in 2-colour rib as given for back BUT do not inc at end of last row.

Change to 5mm (US 8) needles and joining in and breaking off colours as required work 131 rows in patt from chart for left front.

Shape front neck

With WS facing, cast off 5 sts at beg of next row and 3 sts at beg of foll 2 alt rows.
Dec 1 st at neck edge on next 8 rows.

Work one row.
Dec 1 st at neck edge on next row, patt to end. (40sts)
Work a further 2 rows.
Cast off.

RIGHT FRONT

Work as given for left front reversing all shaping and foll chart for right front.

SLEEVES (both alike)

Cast on 44 sts using 4mm (US 6) needles and yarn B.

Join in yarn A and work 6 rows in 2-colour rib as given for back, inc 1 st at end of last row. (45sts)

Change to 5mm (US 8) needles and work 100 rows in patt from chart for sleeve, and AT THE SAME TIME, shape sides by inc 1 st at each end of 3rd row and every foll 4th row until there are 91 sts.

Cast off loosely and evenly.

MAKING UP

Press all pieces as described on the information page.

Join both shoulder seams using backstitch.

Neckband

With RS facing, 4mm (US 6) needles and yarn A, pick up and K 24 sts up right side front neck, 40 sts across back neck and 24 sts down left side front neck. (88sts)

Join in yarn B and work 2-colour rib as folls:

Row 1 (WS): K1A, (P2B, K2A) to last 3 sts, P2B, K1A.

Row 2: P1A, (K2B, P2A) to last 3 sts, K2B, P1A.

Rep these 2 rows twice more.
Cast off evenly in rib using yarn B.

Button band

With RS facing, 4mm (US 6) needles and yarn A, pick up and K 108 sts evenly down left front.

Join in yarn B and work 6 rows in 2-colour rib as given for neckband.
Cast off evenly in rib using yarn B.

Buttonhole band

With RS facing, 4mm (US 6) needles and yarn A, pick up and K 108 sts evenly up right front.

Join in yarn B and work 2 rows in 2-colour rib as given for neckband.

Next row (buttonhole): Keeping 2-colour rib correct, rib 3, (cast off 3, rib 8) 9 times, cast off 3, rib 3.

Next row: Work across row in rib casting on 3 sts in place of those cast off on previous row.
Work a further 2 rows in 2-colour rib.
Cast off evenly in rib using yarn B.
Place markers 25.5cm below shoulder seam on back and front.
Set in sleeves between markers using backstitch.
Join side and sleeve seams.
Press seams.
Sew on buttons to correspond with buttonholes.

Sweater

BACK

Work as given for jacket back.

FRONT

Work as given for jacket back to **.
Work 132 rows in patt.

Shape front neck

Patt 55 sts, turn and leave rem sts on a holder.
Work each side of neck separately.
Cast off 3 sts at beg of next row and foll alt row.
Dec 1 st at neck edge on next 8 rows.
Work one row, then dec 1 st at neck edge on next row.
Work 2 rows.
Cast off rem 40 sts.
With RS facing, rejoin yarn to rem sts, cast off centre 11 sts, patt to end.

To fit up to 102cm (40in)

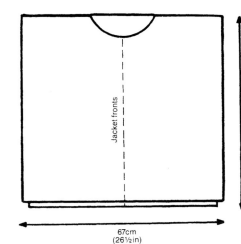

67cm (26½in)

67cm (26½in)

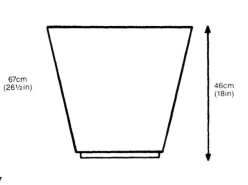

46cm (18in)

Work one row, then complete second side to match first side reversing all shaping.

SLEEVES (both alike)
Work as given for jacket sleeves.

MAKING UP
Press all pieces as described on the information page.

Join right shoulder seam using backstitch.
Neckband
With RS facing, 4mm (US 6) needles and yarn A, pick up and K 18 sts down left side front neck, 11 sts across centre front, 18 sts up right side front neck and 41 sts across back neck. (88sts)
Join in yarn B and work 6 rows in 2-colour rib as given for jacket neckband.

Cast off evenly in rib using yarn B.
Join left shoulder seam and neckband.
Place markers 25.5cm below shoulder seam on back and front.
Set in sleeves between markers using backstitch.
Join side and sleeve seams.
Press seams.

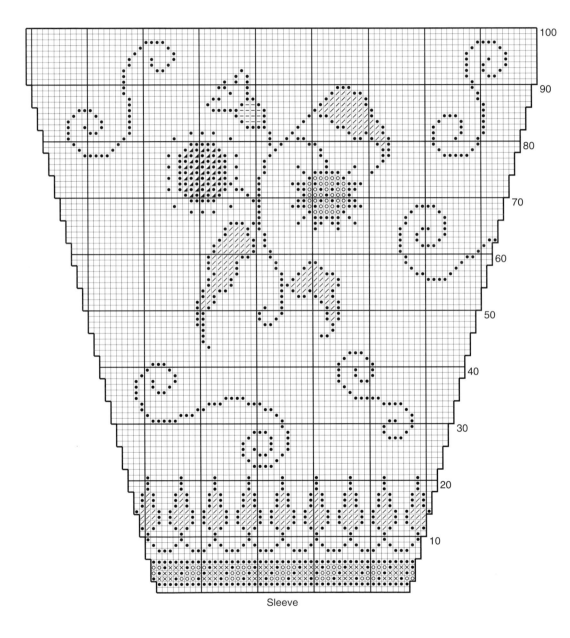

Sleeve

KEY
A □
B •
C ☒
D ⊙
E ⊘
F ⊟
G ◿

Right front ⌐ ⌐ Left front

Back

Baclava

KAFFE FASSETT

YARN

Rowan Donegal Lambswool Tweed and Kid Silk

Jacket

				s	m	l		
A	D.L.Twd	Roseberry	480	6	6	7	x	25gm
B	D.L.Twd	Dolphin	478	4	5	5	x	25gm
C	D.L.Twd	Sedge	471	2	3	3	x	25gm
D	D.L.Twd	Leaf	481	1	1	1	x	25gm
E	D.L.Twd	Tarragon	477	2	3	3	x	25gm
F	D.L.Twd	Pickle	483	1	1	2	x	25gm
G	D.L.Twd	Cinnamon	479	2	3	3	x	25gm
H	D.L.Twd	Pepper	473	1	1	1	x	25gm
J	KidSilk	Old Gold	989	2	3	3	x	25gm
L	D.L.Twd	Rainforest	489	1	2	2	x	25gm
M	D.L.Twd	Elderberry	490	1	1	2	x	25gm
N	D.L.Twd	Mist	466	2	2	3	x	25gm
R	D.L.Twd	Storm	468	2	2	3	x	25gm
S	D.L.Twd	Marram	472	2	2	2	x	25gm
T	D.L.Twd	Rye	474	2	2	2	x	25gm
U	D.L.Twd	Bramble	484	1	1	2	x	25gm
V	D.L.Twd	Bay	485	1	1	1	x	25gm
W	Kid Silk	Holly	990	3	4	4	x	25gm
2	Kid Silk	Steel	991	2	2	3	x	25gm
3	Kid Silk	Pot pourri	996	2	2	3	x	25gm
4	Kid Silk	Smoke	998	1	1	2	x	25gm

Sweater

				s	m	l		
A	D.L.Twd	Roseberry	480	5	5	6	x	25gm
B	D.L.Twd	Dolphin	478	3	3	4	x	25gm
C	D.L.Twd	Sedge	471	2	2	3	x	25gm
D	D.L.Twd	Leaf	481	1	1	1	x	25gm

E	D.L.Twd	Tarragon	477	2	3	3	x	25gm
F	D.L.Twd	Pickle	483	1	1	2	x	25gm
G	D.L.Twd	Cinnamon	479	2	3	3	x	25gm
H	D.L.Twd	Pepper	473	1	1	1	x	25gm
J	KidSilk	Old Gold	989	2	3	3	x	25gm
L	D.L.Twd	Rainforest	489	2	2	2	x	25gm
M	D.L.Twd	Elderberry	490	1	1	2	x	25gm
N	D.L.Twd	Mist	466	2	3	3	x	25gm
R	D.L.Twd	Storm	468	2	3	3	x	25gm
S	D.L.Twd	Marram	472	2	2	3	x	25gm
T	D.L.Twd	Rye	474	2	2	3	x	25gm
U	D.L.Twd	Bramble	484	2	2	2	x	25gm
V	D.L.Twd	Bay	485	1	1	1	x	25gm
W	Kid Silk	Holly	990	4	4	5	x	25gm
2	Kid Silk	Steel	991	2	2	3	x	25gm
3	Kid Silk	Pot pourri	996	2	2	3	x	25gm
4	Kid Silk	Smoke	998	1	1	2	x	25gm

** ALL YARNS TO BE KNITTED DOUBLE

NEEDLES

1 pair 4mm (no 8) (US 6)
1 pair 5mm (no 6) (US 8) needles

BUTTONS

7

TENSION

17 sts and 24 rows to 10cm measured over patterned stocking stitch using 5mm (US 8) needles

BACK

Cast on 86(90:96) sts using 4mm (US 60 needles and yarn A.
Work 19 rows in K1, P1 rib in the foll colour sequence:
1 row A, 2 rows B, 1 row C, 1 row D, 1 row E, 2 rows F, 1 row G, 1 row C, 2 rows B, 1 row J, 1 row A, 1 row C, 2 rows E, 1 row L and 1 row M.
Next row (inc): Using yarn M, rib 1(3:6), (M1, rib 3) 28 times, M1, rib 1(3:6). (115(119:125)sts)
Change to 5mm (US 8) needles and using the INTARSIA technique described on the information page, work from chart for back which is worked entirely in st st beg with a K row. *
Cont from chart until row 144 completed marking each end of rows 7 and 40 for pocket openings and each end of row 70 for position of sleeve.

Shape back neck

Patt 44(46:49) sts, turn and leave rem sts on a holder.
Work each side of neck separately.
Cast off 4 sts patt to end.
Cast off rem 40(42:45) sts.
With RS facing rejoin yarns to rem sts, cast off centre 27 sts, patt to end.
Work one row.
Complete to match first side reversing all shaping.

LEFT FRONT

Cast on 44(46:49) sts using 4mm (US 6) needles and yarn A.
Work 19 rows in K1, P1 rib as given for back.
Next row (inc): Using yarn M, rib 1(2:3), (M1, rib 3) 14 times, M1, rib 1(2:4). (59(61:64)sts)
Change to 5mm (US 8) needles and cont from chart for left front until chart row 79 completed, ending with a RS row, marking position of pocket openings and sleeve, on side edge as for back.

Shape front neck

Cast off 3 sts at beg of next row.
Work 2 rows.
Dec 1 st at neck edge on next row and every foll

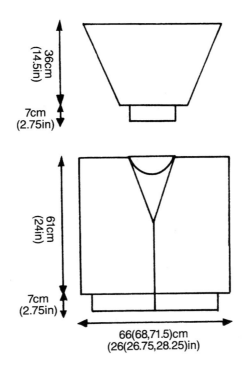

36cm (14.5in)

7cm (2.75in)

61cm (24in)

7cm (2.75in)

66(68,71.5)cm (26(26.75,28.25)in)

3rd row until there are 40(42:45) sts.

Cont without further shaping until front matches back to shoulder.

Cast off evenly.

RIGHT FRONT

Work as given for left front and foll chart for right front, reversing all shaping.

SLEEVES (both alike)

Cast on 42 sts using 4mm (US 6) needles and yarn A.

Work 19 rows in K1, P1 rib as for back.

Next row (inc): Using yarn M, (rib 3, M1) 13 times, rib 3. (55sts)

Change to 5mm (US 8) needles and cont in patt from chart for sleeve and AT THE SAME TIME, inc 1 st at each end of the 3rd row and every foll alt row 11 times, then every foll 3rd row to 111 sts.

Cont without further shaping until chart row 86 completed.

Cast off loosely and evenly.

COLLAR

Cast on 150 sts using 4mm (US 6) needles and yarn A.

Cont in K1, P1 rib in colour sequence outlined below and AT THE SAME TIME, shape collar by casting off 3 sts at beg of row 11 and every foll row until 42 sts rem.

Colour sequence: 1 row A, 2 rows B, 1 row C, 2 rows D, 2 rows E, 3 rows F, 1 row G, 1 row C, 2 rows B, 2 rows J, 2 rows A, 1 row C, 3 rows E, 2 rows L, 2 rows M, 1 row A, 2 rows B, 1 row C, 2 rows D, 2 rows E, 3 rows F, 1 row G, 1 row C, 2 rows B, 2 rows J, 2 rows A.

Cast off loosely and evenly in rib using yarn A.

MAKING UP

Press all pieces as described on the information page.

Pocket edgings (both alike)

With RS facing, 4mm (US 6) needles and yarn B, pick up and K 34 sts evenly between markers on side edge of front.

Knit 1 row to form hemline.

Work a further 4 rows in st st beg with a knit row.

Cast off evenly.

Left pocket lining

With RS facing, 5mm (US 8) needles and yarn B, pick up and K 34 sts evenly between markers on left side edge of back and cont in st st beg with a purl row and AT THE SAME TIME, cast on 8 sts at beg of first row and dec 1 st at end of 5th row and every foll alt row until 22 sts remain.

Cast off evenly.

Right pocket lining

Work as given for left pocket lining reversing all shaping.

Button band

With RS facing, 4mm (US 6) needles and yarn B, pick up and K 67 sts evenly along right front edge for womans jacket, or left front edge for a mans.

Next row (buttonhole): P2, (cast off 2 sts, P8) 6 times, cast off 2 sts, P3.

Next row: K across row casting on 2 sts to replace those cast off on previous row.

Next row: Purl.

Change to yarn A and knit 2 rows (to form foldline).

Work a further 8 rows in st st beg with a K row and work buttonholes on rows 2 and 3 to correspond with those made previously.

Cast off loosely and evenly.

Buttonband

Work as given for buttonhole band omitting buttonholes.

Join shoulder seams using back stitch.

Fold front bands to WS along foldline and slip st loosely into place.

Attach shaped edge of collar neatly to neckline, having centre back of cast off row to centre back neck and cast on edge of collar and foldlines in one continuous line.

Set in sleeves between markers.

See information page for finishing instructions.

SWEATER

BACK

Work as given for back of jacket.

SLEEVES

Work as given for sleeves of jacket.

FRONT

Work as for back of jacket to *.

Work until chart row 120 completed, marking each end of row 70 for sleeve position.

Shape front neck

Patt 52(54:57) sts, turn and leave rem sts on a holder.

Work each side of neck separately.

Cast off 3 sts patt to end.

Dec 1 st at neck edge on next 6 rows and foll 3 alt rows. (40(42:45)sts)

Cont without further shaping until front matches back to shoulder.

Cast off evenly.

With RS facing rejoin yarn to rem sts, cast off centre 11 sts, patt to end.

Work one row.

Complete to match first side reversing all shaping.

MAKING UP

Press all pieces as described on the information page.

Join right shoulder seam using back stitch.

Neckband

With RS facing using 4mm (US 6) needles and yarn G, pick up and K 29 sts down left front neck, 11 sts across centre front, 29 sts up right front neck and 35 sts across back neck. (104sts)

Work 7 rows in K1, p1 rib in the foll colour sequence:

1 row F, 1 row E, 1 row D, 1 row C, 2 rows B, 1 row A.

Cast off loosely and evenly in rib using yarn A.

Set in sleeves between markers.

See information page for finishing instructions.

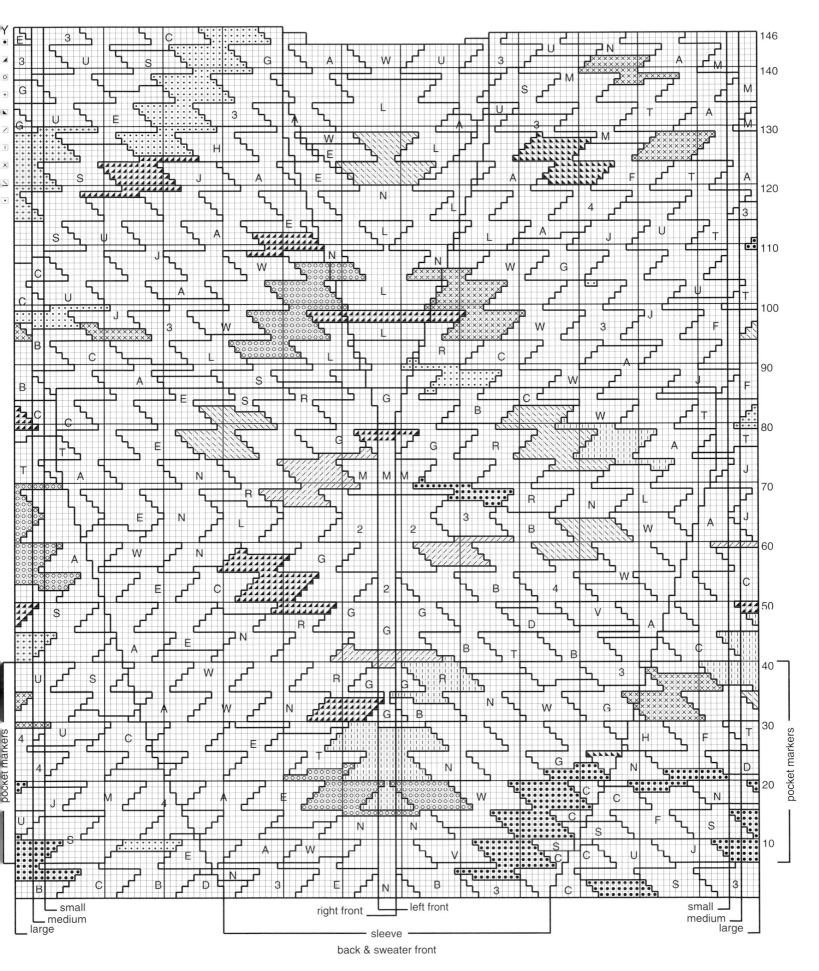

pocket markers

┌ small
└ medium
large

right front ─── left front

small
medium
large

pocket markers

─ sleeve ─

back & sweater front

Petal

SUSAN DUCKWORTH

YARN

Rowan Cotton Glace

A	Oyster 730	10	x	50g
B	Lilac Wine 440	1	x	50g
C	Fiesta 437	1	x	50g
D	Mint 748	1	x	50g
E	Provence 744	1	x	50g
F	Parade 430	1	x	50g
G	Dijon 739	1	x	50g
H	Dusk 439	1	x	50g
J	Carnival 432	1	x	50g
L	Delft 782	1	x	50g
N	Petunia 789	1	x	50g
M	Black—2 metres for flower centres			

NEEDLES

1 pair 2¾mm (no 12) (US 2)
1 pair 3¼mm (no 10) (US 3)

BUTTONS

5

TENSION

23 sts and 32 rows to 10cm measured over stocking stitch using 3¼mm (US 3) needles

Note: K1b = knit into back of stitch.

BACK

Cast on 115 sts using the two-needle method, 2¾mm (US 2) needles and yarn A.
Row 1 (WS): P1, (K1b, P1) to end.
Row 2: K1b, (P1, K1b) to end.
Rep these 2 rows once more and then 1st row again ending with a WS row.
Change to 3¼mm (US 3) needles and joining in and breaking off colours as required and using the INTARSIA technique described on the information page, cont in patt from chart for back which is worked entirely in st st beg with a K row. Work until chart row 56 completed and AT THE SAME TIME shape sides by inc 1 st at each end of 11th row and every foll 10th row to 125 sts, ending with a WS row.

Shape armhole

Cast off 5 sts at beg next 2 rows. (115sts)
Cont without further shaping until chart row 128 completed ending with a WS row.

Shape shoulders and back neck

Cast off 13 sts at beg next 2 rows.
Cast off 13 sts, patt 19 sts, turn leaving rem sts on a holder.
Work each side of neck separately.
Cast off 4 sts patt to end.
Cast off rem 15 sts.
With RS facing rejoin yarns to rem sts, cast off centre 25 sts, patt to end.
Complete to match first side reversing shaping.

LEFT FRONT

Cast on 3 sts using two needle method, 2¾mm (US 2) needles and yarn A.

Row 1 (RS): P1, K1b, P1.
Row 2: K1b, P1, K1b, turn and cast on 5 sts. (8 sts)
Row 3: (K1b, P1) to end.
Row 4: (K1b, P1) to end, turn and cast on 5 sts. (13sts)
Row 5: P1, (K1b, P1) to end.
Row 6: K1b, (P1, K1) to end, turn and cast on 5 sts. (18sts)
Row 7: (K1b, P1) to end.
Row 8: (K1b, P1) to end, turn and cast on 5 sts. (23sts)
Cont increasing thus in patt until there are 58 sts on needle ending with a WS row.
Work 4 rows in twisted rib without further shaping ending with a WS row.
Change to 3¼mm (US 3) needles and cont in patt from chart for left front until chart row 56 completed and AT THE SAME TIME shape side as indicated on chart ending with a WS row. (63sts)

Shape armhole

Cast off 5 sts at beg next row. (58sts)
Cont without shaping until chart row 64 completed.

Shape front neck

Dec 1 st at neck edge on next row and every foll 4th row to 42 sts ending with a RS row.
Work 3 rows.

Shape shoulder

Cast off 13 sts at beg next row, patt to last 2 sts, K2tog.
Work 1 row.
Cast off 13 sts at beg next row, patt to end.
Work 1 row.
Cast off rem 15 sts.

RIGHT FRONT

Cast on 3 sts using two needle method, 2¾mm (US 2) needles and yarn A.
Row 1 (RS): K1b, P1, K1b, turn and cast on 5 sts. (8 sts)
Row 2: (K1b, P1) to end.
Row 3: (K1b, P1) to end, turn and cast on 5 sts. (13sts)
Row 4: P1, (K1b, P1) to end.
Row 5: K1b, (P1, K1) to end, turn and cast on 5 sts. (18sts)
Row 6: (K1b, P1) to end.
Row 7: (K1b, P1) to end, turn and cast on 5 sts. (23sts)
Cont increasing thus in patt until there are 58 sts on needle and ending with a RS row.
Work 5 rows in twisted rib without further shaping ending with a WS row.
Change to 3¼mm (US 3) needles and complete as for left front following chart for right front and reversing all shaping.

LEFT SLEEVE

Cast on 53 sts using two needle method, 2¾mm (US 2) needles and yarn A.
Work 10cm in rib as given for back ending with a WS row.
Change to 3¼mm (US 3) needles, starting at chart row 13 and working between markers for left sleeve, cont until 114 patt rows completed and AT THE SAME TIME shape sides by inc 1

st at each end of 3rd row and every foll 4th row to 105 sts working all extra sts in yarn A and ending with chart row 126.
Cast off loosely and evenly.

RIGHT SLEEVE

Work as for left sleeve following chart for right sleeve.

MAKING UP

PRESS all pieces as described on the information page.
Join shoulder seams using back stitch.
Front band (worked in one piece)
Cast on 7 sts using 2¾mm (US 2) needles and yarn A.
Row 1 (RS): K1b, (K1b, P1) twice, K2b.
Row 2: K1b, (P1, K1b) 3 times.
Rep these 2 rows until band fits, when slightly stretched, up left front around back neck and down right front to neck shaping stretching slightly to give a neat edge.
Slip st into place.
Mark position of 5 buttons, the first to come 1.5 cm from cast on edge, the last to come 1.5cm from beg front neck shaping and others spaced evenly between.
Complete band to match first side working buttonholes to correspond with markers as folls:
Buttonhole row: Rib 3 sts, yon, K2tog, rib to end.
Cast off.
Slip st into place.
See information page for finishing instructions.

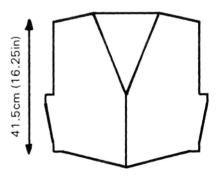

54.5cm (21.5in)
41.5cm (16.25in)

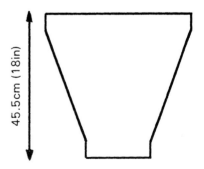

45.5cm (18in)

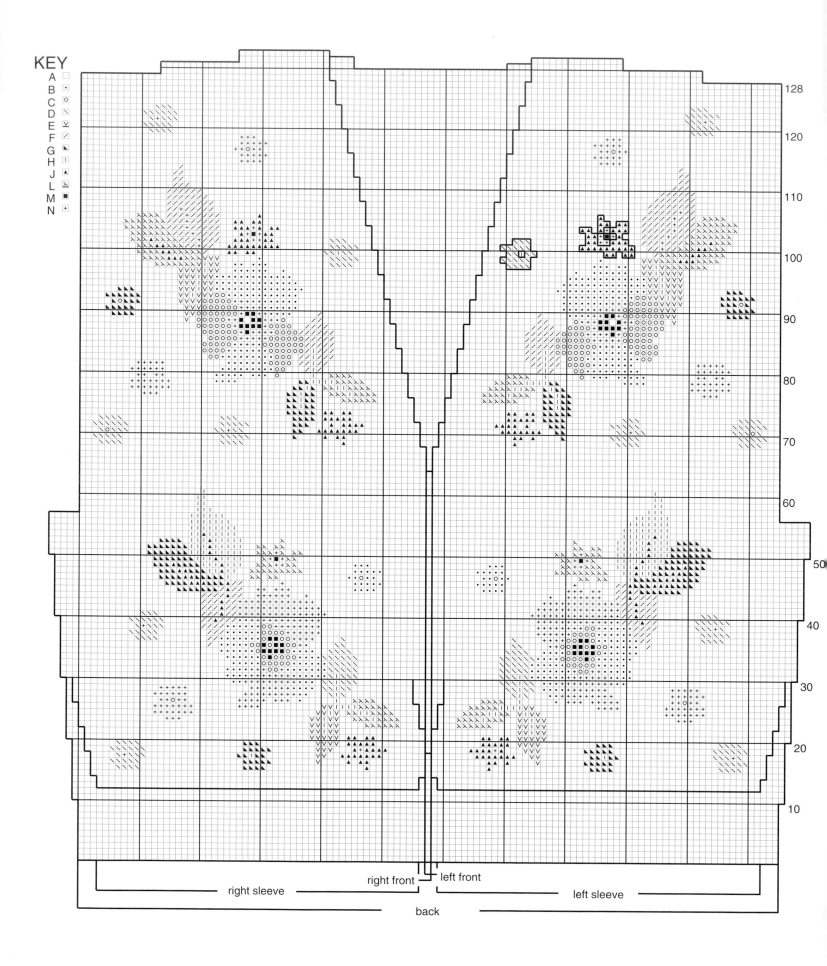

KEY
A □
B ·
C ○
D ⊠
E ✓
F ◣
G ▯
H ▲
J ◿
L ■
M +
N ⊞

128

120

110

100

90

80

70

60

50

40

30

20

10

right sleeve
right front ⌐ left front
left sleeve
back

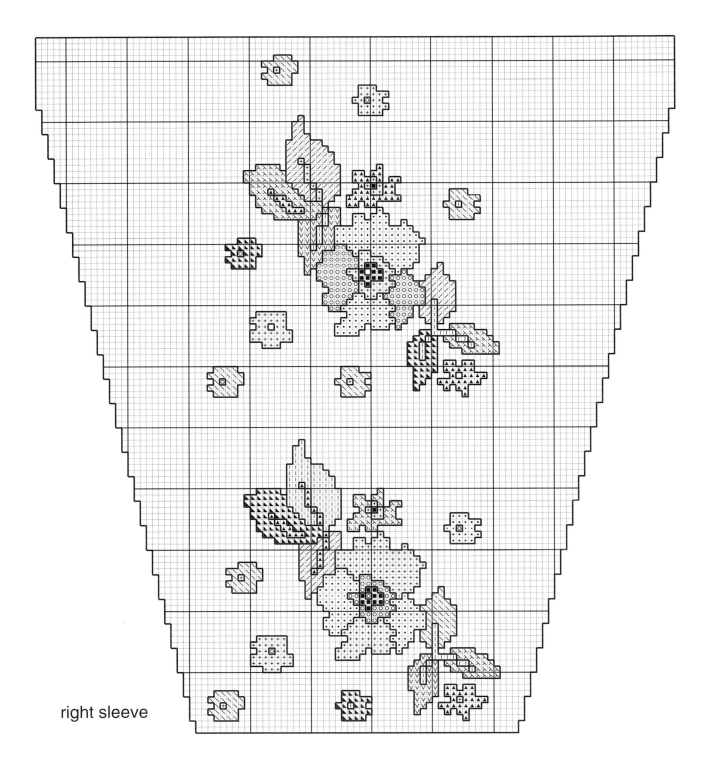

right sleeve

Blue Diamonds

KAFFE FASSETT

YARN

Rowan Light Wt D.K. and Donegal Lambswool Tweed

Jacket

Shade		Amount	No	s	m	l	
A	D.L.T.	Bramble	484*	4	4	5	x 25gm
B	Lt. Wt. DK	Burgundy	602*	2	2	2	x 25gm
C	D.L.T.	Bay	485*	5	5	5	x 25gm
D	D.L.T.	Juniper	482*	4	5	5	x 25gm
E	Lt. Wt. DK	Navy	97*	5	5	5	x 25gm
F	Lt. Wt. DK	Petrol	54*	5	5	5	x 25gm
J	Lt. Wt. DK	Purple	99*	5	6	6	x 25gm
K	Lt. Wt. DK	Jade	91*	4	5	5	x 25gm
M	Lt. Wt. DK	Royal	57*	1	2	2	x 25gm
N	D.L.T.	Sapphire	486*	7	7	7	x 25gm
P	Lt. Wt. DK	Black	62*	1	1	1	x 25gm
R	D.L.T.	Roseberry	480*	1	1	1	x 25gm

* ALL YARNS IN JACKET USED DOUBLE THROUGHOUT

Sweater

both sizes

A	D.L.T.	Bramble	484	4	x 25gm
B	Lt. Wt. DK	Burgundy	602	1	x 25gm
C	D.L.T.	Bay	485	3	x 25gm
D	D.L.T.	Juniper	482	4	x 25gm
E	Lt. Wt. DK	Navy	97	4	x 25gm
F	Lt. Wt. DK	Petrol	54	4	x 25gm
J	Lt. Wt. DK	Purple	99	4	x 25gm
K	Lt. Wt. DK	Jade	91	3	x 25gm
M	Lt. Wt. DK	Royal	57	1	x 25gm
N	D.L.T.	Sapphire	486	3	x 25gm
P	Lt. Wt. DK	Black	62	1	x 25gm
R	D.L.T.	Roseberry	480	1	x 25gm

NEEDLES
Jacket
1 pair 4mm (no 8) (US 6)
1 pair 5mm (no 6) (US 8)
Sweater
1 pair 2¾(no 12) (US 2)
1 pair 3 (no 10) (US 3)
Circular needle 2¾mm (no 12) (US 2) short
Circular needle 3¼mm (no 10) (US 3) short

BUTTONS (jacket only)
7

TENSION
Jacket
17½ sts and 24 rows to 10cm measured over patterned stocking stitch using 5mm (US 8) needles
Sweater
25 sts and 36 rows to 10cm measured over patterned stocking stitch using 3¼mm (no 10) (US 3) needles

Jacket
BACK AND FRONTS (yarns used double throughout jacket)

Beg at lower back edge, cast on 86(90:96) sts using 4mm (US 6) needles and yarn K.
Work 19 rows in K1, P1 rib in the foll colour sequence:
2 rows F, 2 rows C, 3 rows N, 2 rows R, 2 rows B, 2 rows J, 1 row M, 1 row J, 3 rows E and 1 row N.
Next row (inc): Using yarn N, rib 1(3:6), (M1, rib 3) 28 times, M1, rib 1(3:6).
(115(119:125) sts)
Change to 5mm (US 8) needles and using the INTARSIA technique described on the information page, work from chart for back which is worked entirely in st st beg with a K row.*
Cont from chart until row 148 completed marking each end of row 7 and 40 for pocket openings and each end of row 74 for position of sleeve.

Divide for neck
Next row (RS): Patt 44(46:49) sts turn and leave rem sts on a holder.
Work each side of neck separately.
Cast off 4 sts patt to end.
Row 150: Work across row in patt.
This marks the shoulder line, from this point onwards work back down the rows to row 1 beg at row 149.
Cont working down chart until chart row 1 completed and AT THE SAME TIME shape from neck by inc 1 st at neck edge on chart row 127 and every foll 3rd row until 56 (58:61) sts and casting on 3 sts at neck edge on chart row 80.
(59(61:64) sts)
Mark position of pocket openings and sleeve on side edge as for back.
Change to 4mm (US 6) needles and work in K1, P1 rib as folls:
Next row (dec): Using yarn N, rib 0(1:3), (K2tog, K2) 14 times, K2tog, rib 1(2:3).
(44(46:49) sts)
Cont to work in K1, P1 rib reversing colour sequence as given for back.
Work 1 row in rib using yarn K.
Cast off in rib using yarn K.
With RS facing rejoin yarns to sts on holder.
Cast off centre 27 sts patt to end.
Work 1 row.
Complete to match first side.

SLEEVES (both alike)
Cast on 42 sts using 4mm (US 6) needles and yarn K.
Work 19 rows in K1, P1 rib as for back
Next row (inc): Using yarn N, (rib 3, M1) 13 times rib 3. (55sts)
Change to 5mm (US 8) needles, cont in patt from chart for sleeve and AT THE SAME TIME, inc 1 st at each end of the 3rd and every foll alt row 11 times, then every foll 3rd row to 111 sts.
Cont without further shaping until chart row 86 completed.
Cast off loosely and evenly.

COLLAR
Cast on 150 sts using 4mm (US 6) needles and yarn K.
Cont in K1, P1 rib in colour sequence outlined below and AT THE SAME TIME, shape collar by casting off 3 sts at beg of row 11 and every foll row until 42 sts rem.
Colour sequence:
2 rows F, 2 rows C, 3 rows N, 2 rows R, 2 rows B, 2 rows J, 1 row M, 1 row J, 3 rows E, 2 rows N, 2 rows C, 2 rows D, 1 row N, 2 rows F, 2 rows C, 3 rows N, 2 rows R, 2 rows B, 2 rows J, 1 row M, 1 row J, 3 rows E, 2 rows N and 1 row C.
Cast off loosely using yarn C.

MAKING UP
PRESS all pieces as described on the information page
Pocket edgings (both alike)
With RS facing, 4mm (US 6) needles and yarn N pick up and knit 34 sts evenly between markers on side edge of front.
Knit 1 row to form hemline.
Work a further 4 rows in st st beg with a knit row.
Cast off evenly.
Left pocking lining
With RS facing, 5mm (US 8) needles and yarn N pick up and knit 34 sts evenly between markers on left side edge of back and cont in st st beg with a purl row and AT THE SAME TIME, cast on 8 sts at beg of first row and dec 1 st at end of 5th row and every foll alt row until 22 sts rem.
Cast off evenly.
Right pocket lining
Work as given for left pocket lining reversing all shaping.
Buttonhole band
With RS facing, 4mm (US 6) needles and yarn N, pick up and knit 67 sts evenly along right front edge for womans jacket, left front edge for a mans.
Next row (buttonhole): P2 (cast off 2 sts, P8) 6 times, cast off 2 sts, P3.
Next row: K across row casting on 2 sts to replace those cast off on previous row.
Next row: Purl.
Change to yarn K and knit 2 rows (to form foldline).
Work a further 8 rows in st st beg with a K row and work buttonholes on rows 2 and 3 to correspond with those made previously.
Cast off loosely and evenly.
Buttonband
Work as given for buttonhole band omitting buttonholes.
Join shoulder seams using back stitch.
Fold frontbands to WS along foldline and slip st loosely into place.
Attach shaped edge of collar neatly to neckline, having centre back of cast off row to centre back neck and cast on edge of collar and foldlines in one continuous line.
Set in sleeves between markers.
See information page for finishing instructions.

Sweater
BACK AND FRONT (worked in one piece)
Beg at lower back edge, cast on 134(146) sts using 2¾mm (US 2) needles and yarn K.
Work 25 rows in K1, P1, rib in the foll colour sequence:

2 rows F, 2 rows C, 3 rows N, 2 rows R, 2 rows B, 2 rows J, 1 row M, 1 row J, 3 rows E, 2 rows N, 2 rows C, 2 rows D, 1 row N.

Next row (WS)(inc): Using yarn N, rib 7(13) (M1, rib 5) 24 times, M1, rib (7)13. (159(171 sts)

Change to 3¼mm (US 3) and using INTARSIA technique described on the information page cont from chart for back until chart row 214 completed.

Divide row (RS): Patt 63(69) sts turn and leave rem sts on a holder.

Work each side separately.

Cast off 4 sts at beg of next row and foll alt row.

Work 1 row.

Cast off 2 sts patt to end. (53(59)sts)

Work 1 row.

Chart row 222: Work across row in patt. This marks the shoulder line, from this point onwards work back down the rows to row 1 beg at row 221.

Work 7 rows in patt beg at row 221.

Shape front neck

Inc 1 st at neck edge on next row and 5 foll alt rows.

Inc 1 st at neck edge on next 10 rows. (69(75)sts)

Leave sts on a spare needle for right side front neck.

With RS facing, return to rem sts, slip centre 33 sts onto a holder, rejoin yarn to rem sts, patt to end.

Work 1 row.

Complete to match first side.

Leave sts on a spare needle for left side front neck.

With RS facing rejoin yarns to sts for right side front neck, patt to end, turn and cast on 21sts, work in patt across 69(75)sts for left side front neck. (159(171 sts)

Cont working down chart until chart row 1 completed.

Change to 2¾mm (US 2) needles and work at folls:

Next row (dec): Using yarn N, rib 17(23), (rib 2 tog, rib 3) 25 times, rib 17(23). 134(146sts)

Cont to work in K1, P1 rib reversing colour sequence as given for back.

Work 1 row in rib using yarn K

Cast off evenly in rib using yarn K.

SLEEVES (both alike)

Cast on 62 sts using 2¾mm (US 2) needles and yarn K.

Work 25 rows in K1, P1 rib as given for back

Using yarn N work in rib across row inc 1 st at end. (63 sts)

Change to 3 mm (US 3) needles and work 148 rows in patt from chart for sleeve and AT THE SAME TIME shape sides by inc 1 at each end of 3rd and every foll 4th row until 127 sts.

Cast off loosely and evenly.

MAKING UP

PRESS all pieces as described on information page.

Neck border (knitted flat)

With RS facing 3¼mm (US 3) double pointed needles and yarn B, beg at left shoulder pick up and K 40 sts to centre front, 39 sts to right shoulder seam and 54 sts across back neck. (133 sts)

Beg at row 2 of chart, work 8 rows (ie work backwards and fowards and NOT in rounds) in patt from chart, working between markers for neck border. Note that yarn X is replaced by yarn O on first traingle in order that patt will match.

Neckband (knitted in rounds)

Change to 2¾mm (US 2) double pointed needles and work 9 rounds in K1, P1 in foll colour sequence:

2 round C, 1 round N, 2 rounds E, 1 round J, 1 round M, 1 round J, 1 round F.

Cast off evenly in rib using yarn K.

Sew seam in neck border.

See information page for finishing instructions.

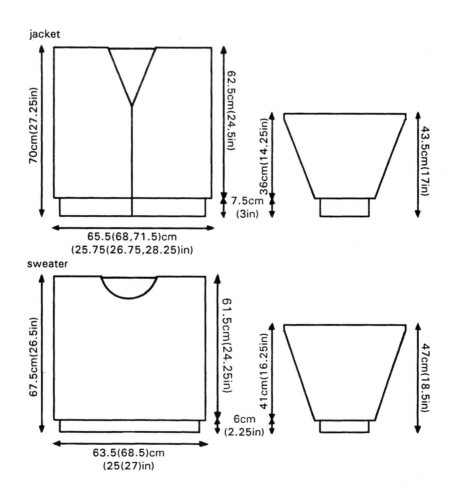

Petunia

KAFFE FASSETT

YARN

Rowan Donegal Lambswool Tweed and Kid Silk

				s	m	l		
A	D.L.T.	Pickle	483	3	3	3	x	25gm
B	D.L.T.	Rainforest	489	2	2	2	x	25gm
C	D.L.T.	Shale	467	1	1	1	x	25gm
D	D.L.T.	Sedge	471	1	1	1	x	25gm
E	D.L.T.	Pepper	473	1	1	2	x	25gm
F	D.L.T	Rye	474	1	2	2	x	25gm
G	D.L.T.	Tarragon	477	1	1	1	x	25gm
H	D.L.T.	Dolphin	478	1	1	1	x	25gm
J	D.L.T.	Cinnamon	479	1	2	2	x	25gm
L	D.L.T.	Roseberry	480	1	1	2	x	25gm
M	D.L.T.	Leaf	481	1	1	2	x	25gm
N	D.L.T.	Bay	485	1	1	1	x	25gm
R	D.L.T.	Elderberry	490	1	1	1	x	25gm
S	D.L.T.	Black	491	1	1	1	x	25gm
T	K.Silk	Steel	991	1	1	1	x	25gm
U	K.Silk	Pot Pourri	996	1	1	1	x	25gm
W	K.Silk	Smoke	998	1	1	1	x	25gm

NEEDLES

1 pair 2¾mm (no 12) (US 1)
1 pair 3mm (no 11) (US 2)
1 pair 3¼mm (no 10) (US 3)
Circular needle 2¾mm (no 12) (US 2)–80cm long

BUTTONS

5

TENSION

25 sts and 36 rows to 10cm measured over pat-terned stocking stitch using 3¼mm (US 3) needles

BACK

Cast on 117(125:131) sts using 2¾mm (US 1) needles and yarn A.
Work 11 rows in st st beg with a K row.
Next row (foldline): Knit.
Change to 3mm (US 2) needles and using the FAIRISLE technique as described on the information page, work 9 rows from chart for back which is worked entirely in st st beg with a K row. *
Next row (inc): P1(3:3), [M1, P23(24:25)] 5 times, M1, P1(2:3). (123(131:137)sts)
Change to 3¼mm (US 3) needles and using the INTARSIA technique as described on the infor-mation page cont in patt from chart until chart row 132(138:142) completed, AT THE SAME TIME, shape sides by inc 1 st at each end of the 3rd row and every foll 6th row until there are 139(147:153) sts ending with a WS row.
Shape armhole
Cast off 5 sts at beg next 2 rows.
Dec 1 st at each end of the next 11 rows and 3 foll alt rows. (101(109:115)sts)
Cont without further shaping until chart row 226(232:236) completed ending with a WS row.
Shape shoulder
Cast off 9(11:12) sts at beg next 2 rows.

Cast off 9(10:11) sts at beg next row, patt 13(14:15) sts, turn and leave rem sts on a holder.
Work each side of neck separately.
Cast off 4 sts at beg next row, patt to end.
Cast off rem 9(10:11) sts.
With RS facing rejoin yarn to rem sts, cast off centre 39 sts, patt to end.
Complete to match first side reversing all shap-ing.

POCKET LINING (make two)

Cast on 34 sts using 3¼mm (US 3) needles and yarn B.
Work 32 rows in st st beg with a K row.
Leave sts on a holder.

LEFT FRONT

Cast on 57(61:64) sts using 2¾mm (US 1) nee-dles and yarn A.
Work as given for back to *.
Next row (inc): P15(16:16), [M1, P14(15:16)] 3 times. (60(64:67)sts)
Change to 3¼mm (US 3) needles and foll chart for left front, shaping side edge as given for back, AT THE SAME TIME, when chart row 42 completed place pocket as folls:
Row 43: Patt 12(16:19) sts, place next 34 sts on a holder and in place of these patt across sts of pocket lining, patt to end.
Cont in patt from chart until row 104(110:114) completed.
Shape front neck
Dec 1 st at neck edge on the next row and on every foll 4th row until 27(31:34) sts rem, AT THE SAME TIME, when chart row 132(138:142) completed work armhole as given for back.
Cont without further shaping until front matches back to shoulder ending with a WS row.
Shape shoulder
Cast off 9(11:12) sts at beg next row and 9(10:11) sts on foll alt row.
Work 1 row.
Cast off rem 9(10:11) sts.

RIGHT FRONT

Work as given for left front foll chart for right front and reversing all shaping and pocket posi-tion.

MAKING UP

Press all pieces as described on the information page.
Join both shoulder seams using back stitch.
Armhole edgings (both alike)
With RS facing using 2¾mm (US 1) needles and yarn B, pick up and K 130 sts evenly around armhole edge.
Work 2 rows in st st beg with a P row.
Change to yarn A and purl 1 row.
Next row (RS): Purl to form foldline.
Work 4 rows in st st beg with a P row.
Cast off evenly.
Pocket tops (both alike)
With RS facing using 2¾mm (US 1) needles place sts from holder onto LH needle and cont in patt from chart for 5 rows more.
Change to yarn A and purl 1 row.

Next row (RS): Purl to form foldline.
Work 6 rows in st st beg with a P row.
Cast off evenly.
Frontband (worked in one piece)
With RS facing using 2¾mm (US 2) circular nee-dle and yarn H, pick up and K 72(76:80) sts up right front from foldline to beg neck shaping, 85 sts up right front neck shaping to shoulder, 46(45:45) sts across back neck, 85 sts down left front to beg of shaping and 72(76:80) sts down left front edge to foldline. (360(367:375)sts)
Joining in and breaking off colours as required, working in rows not rounds, work 9 rows in patt from chart for frontband beg at left hand side with a P row and starting and finishing at appro-priate markers and working 90 st rep 4 times in between and AT THE SAME TIME, make but-tonholes on row 5 and 6 as folls:
Row 5: P4, [cast off 3 sts, P11(12:13)] 4 times, cast off 3 sts, patt to end.
Row 6: Patt across row casting on 3 sts across those sts cast off on previous row.
Cont in patt from chart until row 9 completed.
Row 10: Change to yarn A and knit 1 row.
Row 11: Knit to form foldline.
Work 12 rows in st st beg with a K row making buttonholes on row 7 and 8 to correspond with those already worked.
Cast off evenly.
See information page for finishing instructions.
Turn bottom hem and armhole edgings onto WS along foldline and slip st into place.
Turn frontbands onto WS along foldline and slip stitch into place.

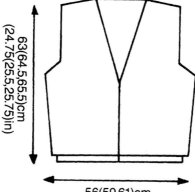

63(64.5,65.5)cm
(24.75(25.5,25.75)in)

56(59,61)cm
(22(23.25,24)in)

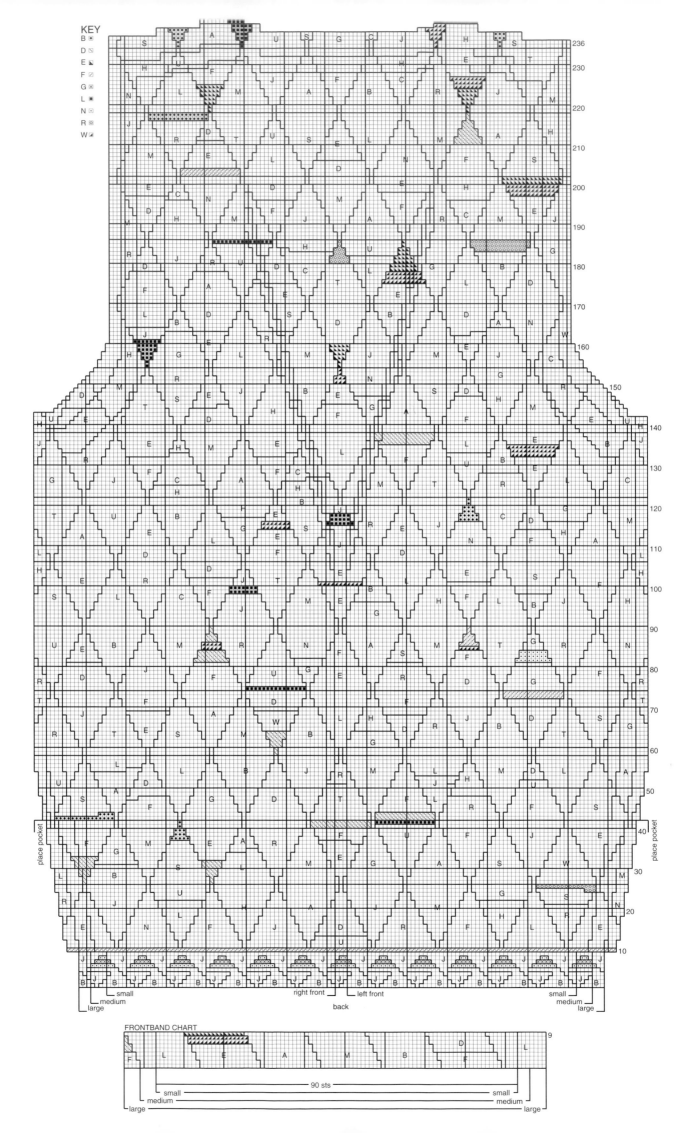

98

Jester

BRANDON MABLY

YARN

Rowan Donegal Lambswool Tweed, Light Weight
D.K. and Kid Silk

A	Lt.Wt.DK Corn 8	2	x	25gm
B	Lt.Wt.DK Apricot 86	2	x	25gm
C	Lt.Wt.DK Rust 77	4	x	25gm
D	Lt.Wt.DK Straw 5	3	x	25gm
E	Lt.Wt.DK Cobolt 53	3	x	25gm
F	Lt.Wt.DK Sand 11	3	x	25gm
G	D.L.T. Juniper 482	1	x	25gm
H	D.L.T. Leaf 481	2	x	25gm
J	D.L.T. Cinnamon 479	8	x	25gm
L	D.L.T. Sapphire 486	2	x	25gm
M	D.L.T. Roseberry 480	2	x	25gm
N	D.L.T. Pickle 483	1	x	25gm
P	K.Silk Holly 990	3	x	25gm

NEEDLES

1 pair 3mm (no 11) (US 3) needles
1 pair 3¾mm (no 9) (US 5) needles
Circular needle 3mm (no 11) (US 3)–60cm long

TENSION

26 sts and 30 rows to 10cm measured over
fairisle pattern using 3¾mm (US 5) needles

Special note:

The pattern comprises of a series of interlocking
diamond motifs, use separate length of yarn for
each diamond, link the colours together as
described on the information page, but carry the
outline colour, yarn J, loosely across back of
work weaving in every 3 or 4 sts.

BACK AND FRONT (knitted in one piece)

Commencing at lower back edge cast on 131 sts
using 3mm (US 3) needles and yarn P.
Work 25 rows in K1, P1 rib in the foll colour
sequence: 2 rows P, 3 rows A, 3 rows C, 3 rows
B, 3 rows M, 3 rows D, 3 rows E, 3 rows A and 2
rows J.

Next row (WS)(inc): P5, (M1, P6) 20 times,
M1, P6. (152sts)
Change to 3¾mm (US 5) needles and using
INTARSIA and FAIR ISLE techniques described
in special note, cont in patt from chart for back
which is worked entirely in st st beg with a K
row, noting that all the outlines are worked in
yarn J. (See special note)
Work until chart row 164 completed.

Shape back and front neck

Row 165 (RS): Patt 64 sts, turn and leave rem
sts on a holder.
work each side separately.
Next row: Cast off 6 sts, patt to end.
Dec 1 st at neck edge on next 4 rows. (54sts)
Cont without shaping until chart row 184 com-
pleted.
Inc 1 st at neck edge on next 5 rows.
Next row (WS): Cast on 3 sts at beg next row
and foll 2 alt rows. (68sts)
Work one row.

Leave sts on a holder.
With RS facing cont on sts for left shoulder.
Cast off 24 sts, patt to end.
Work one row.
Complete as for first side reversing all shaping
and until chart row 195 completed. (68sts)
Row 196 (WS): Patt across row, turn and cast
on 16 sts, patt across 68 sts of first side. (152sts)
Work without further shaping until chart row 200
completed.
Now cont in patt from chart for back beginning at
row 140 with a K row, working backwards
through the rows ending at row 1 with a P row.
Next row (dec): RS facing and using yarn J,
K5, (K2tog, K5) 20 times, K2tog, K5. (131sts)
Change to 3mm (US 3) needles and work 25 rows
in K1, P1 rib, reversing colour sequence given
for back.
Work one row in yarn P.
Cast off evenly in rib using yarn P.

SLEEVES (both alike)

Cast on 71 sts, using 3mm (US 3) needles and
yarn P.
Work 25 rows in K1, P1 rib in colour sequence
as for back.

Next row (WS)(inc): P4, (M1, rib 8) 8 times,
M1, P3, (80sts)
Change to 3¾mm (US 5) needles and foll sleeve
markings, work 130 rows from chart and AT
THE SAME TIME, inc 1 st at each end of 5th
row and every foll 4th row to 140 sts.
Cast off loosely and evenly.

MAKING UP

Press all pieces as described on the information
page.

Neckband

With RS facing, using 3mm (US 3) circular needle and yarn J, pick up and knit 27 sts evenly
down left front neck beg at left shoulder line, 16
sts across centre front, 27 sts up right front to
shoulder line, 10 sts down back neck shaping 24
sts across back neck and 10 sts up back neck
shaping. (114sts)
Work 13 rounds in K1, P1 rib in the foll colour
sequence: 2 rounds J, 3 rounds B, 3 rounds C, 3
rounds A and 2 rounds P.
Cast off loosely in rib using yarn P.
See information page for finishing instructions.

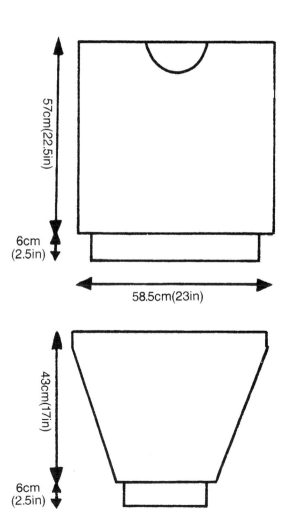

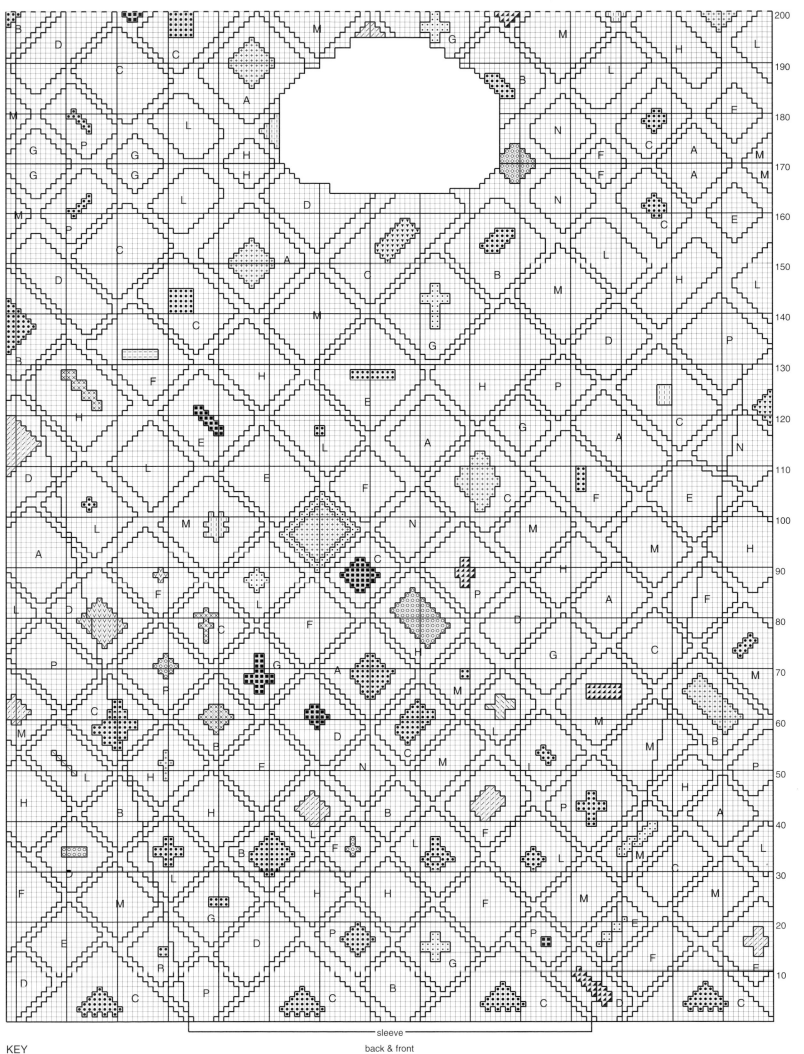

KEY

A ◩ B ⊡ C ◪ D ⊡ E ⊙ F ▾ G ▾ H ◿ J ● L ▽ M ⨯ N − P ⊞

sleeve

back & front

101

Knitting Workshop

KATE BULLER

THE IMPORTANCE OF TENSION

Many knitters don't realise the importance of getting the correct tension before starting their garment. But because the tension determines the finished size of the garment, it is crucial to spend a little time getting it right. Your pattern always tells you how many stitches and rows you need to produce a piece of knitting that will measure 10cm (4 in). All knitters vary enormously in the way they work, so you may well find that you need to use a needle size larger or smaller than the one suggested.

MAKING A TENSION SWATCH

Cast on the number of stitches given in the tension guide plus ten more. If the stitches are to be measured over a pattern, cast on the correct multiple of stitches to knit the pattern. Work in the required pattern until the swatch measures approximately 12cm (5 in). Then break the yarn, slip it through the stitches and slip the stitches off the needle. Don't cast off—this could distort the swatch.

COUNTING THE STITCHES

Lay the swatch down on a flat surface and, in the centre of the swatch, place a ruler horizontally on the square, lining it up along the bottom of a row of stitches. Place a pin at zero and another at the 10cm (4 in) mark. Count the stitches between the pins, including half stitches, if any. Make sure you are absolutely accurate, as even half a stitch out will make the finished garment the wrong size.

ADJUSTING YOUR TENSION

If you have less stitches than that given in the tension measurement, your knitting is too loose and the garment will be too big. Knit up another swatch using smaller needles. If you have more stitches than given, your knitting is too tight and the garment will be too small. Knit up another swatch with larger needles. As long as you get the right tension, it doesn't matter what size needles you use. Remember that if you have to make any adjustment to the size of needles for the main garment, adjust needles for ribs and necklines accordingly.

COUNTING THE ROWS

Lay the swatch down and place a ruler vertically on the square, lining it up along one side of a column of stitches. Place a pin on the zero mark and another at the 10cm (4 in) mark. Count the rows between the pins, including half rows, if any. If you have the right tension stitchwise, the rows are likely to be correct. Row tension is less important than stitch tension since patterns usually give lengths as measurements, not number of rows.

TIPS
- When you are measuring garter stitch, don't forget that each ridge represents two rows.
- When measuring rib, remember to count purl stitches which may have disappeared between knit stitches.

- If you are knitting with mohair, hold the swatch up to the light to count the stitches.

SEWING UP

After you have spent time knitting a Rowan garment, it is well worth knowing how to put the final touches to it for a professional finish. It's just a matter of giving that little extra and knowing the right methods.

MATTRESS STITCH

Use this stitch wherever you want an invisible seam. If you have never tried it, you will be amazed at how much better your seams look.

With the right sides facing, lay the two pieces of knitting to be joined together side by side. Thread a blunt ended needle with yarn and secure the yarn on the back of the work. Bring the needle through to the front and insert it between the edge stitch and the second stitch on the first row. Pass the needle under two rows, then bring it back to the front. On the opposite piece of knitting, take the needle under the two opposing rows and repeat this zigzag action back and forth. After a few centimetres, pull the yarn to join the seam, pulling it a little tighter than necessary at first, then stretch the seam back into shape.

Take the needle under two rows on the left hand piece of knitting.

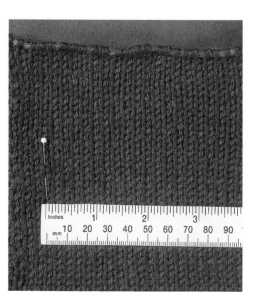

Take it across and under two rows on the right hand piece.

JOINING RIBS

When joining two ribbed sections, take only half a stitch from either side each time, so that when the seam is joined, the two half stitches make one complete stitch.

JOINING A CAST-OFF EDGE TO A SIDE EDGE

Use this method for joining the top of a drop shouldered sleeve to a side edge. Lay the two pieces in position, then pin them together with safety pins at both ends. Pin halfway between the two pins, then place pins at each halfway point until there are pins approximately every 3cm. Zigzag across the seam as for mattress stitch, but work under one or two rows or stitches as necessary to keep the seam flat. Remove pins as you go.

TIPS

• Always use a new length of yarn, rather than an end used for casing on or off, for sewing up.

• Always use matching yarn where possible when you are joining seams. (We have used contrasting yarn for our photographs for clearness only.)

• It is easier to sew up a garment with the pieces laid flat on a table rather than on your lap.

DARNING IN ENDS

When you have knitted a garment in lots of colours, you will have many ends of yarn left at the edges after you have finished. It is important

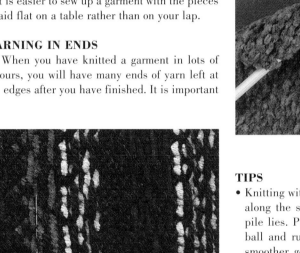

to darn them in securely before sewing up. Thread a darning needle with each end and weave it in horizontally at the back of the work. Snip off, leaving an end approximately 0.5cm long.

KNITTING WITH CHENILLE

As cotton chenille has no natural elasticity, the stitches need to be pushed closely together as you knit to avoid bars appearing between the stitches.

TIPS

• Knitting with chenille will be easier if you feel along the strand to determine which way the pile lies. Pull a strand from the centre of the ball and run your fingers down it. If it feels smoother going toward the ball, cast on with this end. If it feels rough, cast on with the end from the outside of the ball.

• Do not use chenille to sew up a garment—it has no natural stretch and will break. Use a DK yarn in a matching colour instead.

• Always use bamboo needles for knitting with chenille. You will find that the stitches run more smoothly than knitting with metal needles.

Patchwork Sweater
KIM HARGREAVES

YARN

Rowan Design D.K. and Rowan Fine Cotton Chenille

A	D.D.K	Cream	649	16	x	50gm
B	D.D.K	Rust	691	1	x	50gm
C	F.Chen	Mousse	418	1	x	50gm
D	F.Chen	Privet	410	1	x	50gm
E	F.Chen	Cornflower	412	1	x	50gm
F	D.D.K	Purple	636	1	x	50gm
G	D.D.K	Plum	637	1	x	50gm
H	D.D.K	Rose	630	1	x	50gm

NEEDLES

1 pair 3¼mm (no 10)(US 3)
1 pair 4mm (no 8)(US 6)
3mm crochet hook

BUTTONS

4

TENSION

23 sts and 30 rows to 10cm measured over patterned stotcking stitch using 4mm (US 6) needles

BACK

Cast on 118 sts using 3¼mm (US 3) needles and yarn A.
Work 10cm in K2, P2 rib ending with a RS row.
Next row (WS)(inc): Rib 4, (M1, rib 4, M1, rib 3, M1, rib 4) 10 times, M1, rib 4. (149sts)
Change to 4mm (US 6) needles and using the INTARSIA technique described on the information page work in patt from chart for back which is worked in a mixture of st st and reversed st st as indicated. **
Work 150 rows in patt from chart.

Divide for centre back opening

Patt 74 sts, turn and leave rem sts on a holder.
Work each side of neck separately.
Work a further 45 rows in patt.

Shape shoulder

Cast off 51 sts at beg of next row, patt to end.
Work 1 row.
Cast off rem 23 sts.
With RS facing, rejoin yarn to rem sts, K2tog, patt to end.
Complete second side to match first side reversing all shaping.

POCKET LININGS (make 2)

Cast on 36 sts using 4mm (US 6) needles and yarn A.
Work 34 rows in st st beg with a K row.
Leave sts on a holder.

FRONT

Work as given for back to **.
Work 34 rows in patt from chart.

Place pocket linings

Patt 15 sts, slip next 36 sts onto a holder and in place of these, patt across sts of first pocket lining, patt next 47 sts, slip next 36 sts onto a holder and in place of these, patt across sts of second pocket lining, patt to end.
Work a further 139 rows in patt.

Shape front neck

Patt 66 sts, turn and leave rem sts on a holder.
Work each side of neck separately.
Cast off 3 sts at beg of next row, patt to end.
Dec 1 st at neck edge on next 7 rows.
Work one row, then dec 1 st at neck edge on next row and 4 foll alt rows.
Work 3 rows.
Cast off rem 51 sts.
With RS facing rejoin yarn to rem sts, cast off centre 17 sts, patt to end.
Complete second side to match first side, reversing all shaping.

SLEEVES (both alike)

Cast on 65 sts using 3 mm (US 3) needles and yarn A.
Work 20 rows in patt from chart for sleeve cuff.
Change to 4mm (US 6) needles and foll chart for sleeve, working between sleeve markers and omitting any incomplete motifs at side and top of sleeve. Work 106 rows in patt and AT THE SAME TIME, shape sides by inc 1 st at each end of 3rd row and every foll 4th row until there are 117 sts.
Note: If a shorter sleeve length is preferred, work 96 rows in patt and AT THE SAME TIME, shape sides by inc 1 st as given for longer length sleeve until there are 113 sts).
Cast off loosely and evenly.

MAKING UP

Press all pieces as described on the information page.

Pocket tops

With RS facing, 3¼mm (US 3) needles and yarn A, slip sts from holder onto left hand needle and work 3cm in K2, P2 rib.

Cast off evenly in rib.
Sew pocket linings into position on WS and pocket tops on RS.
Join both shoulder seams using backstitch.

Collar

With RS facing, 3¼mm (US 3) needles and yarn A, pick up and K 22 sts across left side back neck, 32 sts to centre front, mark centre with a pin, 32 sts front centre front to right shoulder seam and 22 sts across right side back neck. (108sts)
Next row: K1, (P2, K2) to last 3 sts, P2, K1.
Work a further 7 rows in rib as set.

Divide collar

Next row: Rib 54 sts, turn and leave rem sts on a holder.
Work each side of collar separately.
Cont in rib as set until collar measures 11cm from beg.
Cast off evenly in rib.
Return to rem sts, rejoin yarn and complete to match first side.

Centre back opening

Place markers 1cm up from pick up row of collar on both sides of centre back opening.
With RS facing and 3mm crochet hook, beg at marker on right side of collar, work evenly in dc down right side neck opening and up left side neck opening, ending at marker on left side of collar.
Place 4 markers, evenly spaced along right edge of back opening, to show position of buttonholes.
Buttonhole row: 1ch, work 1 dc into each dc to end and AT THE SAME TIME, (work 2ch, miss 2 sts) to correspond with each marker for buttonhole.
Fasten off.
Place markers 25cm below shoulder seam on back and front.
Set in sleeves between markers using backstitch.
Join side and sleeve seams.
Sew on buttons to correspond with buttonholes.

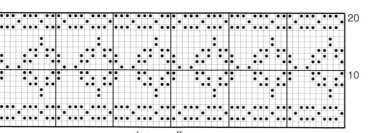

sleeve cuff

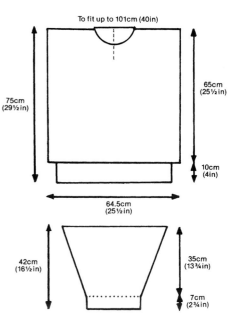

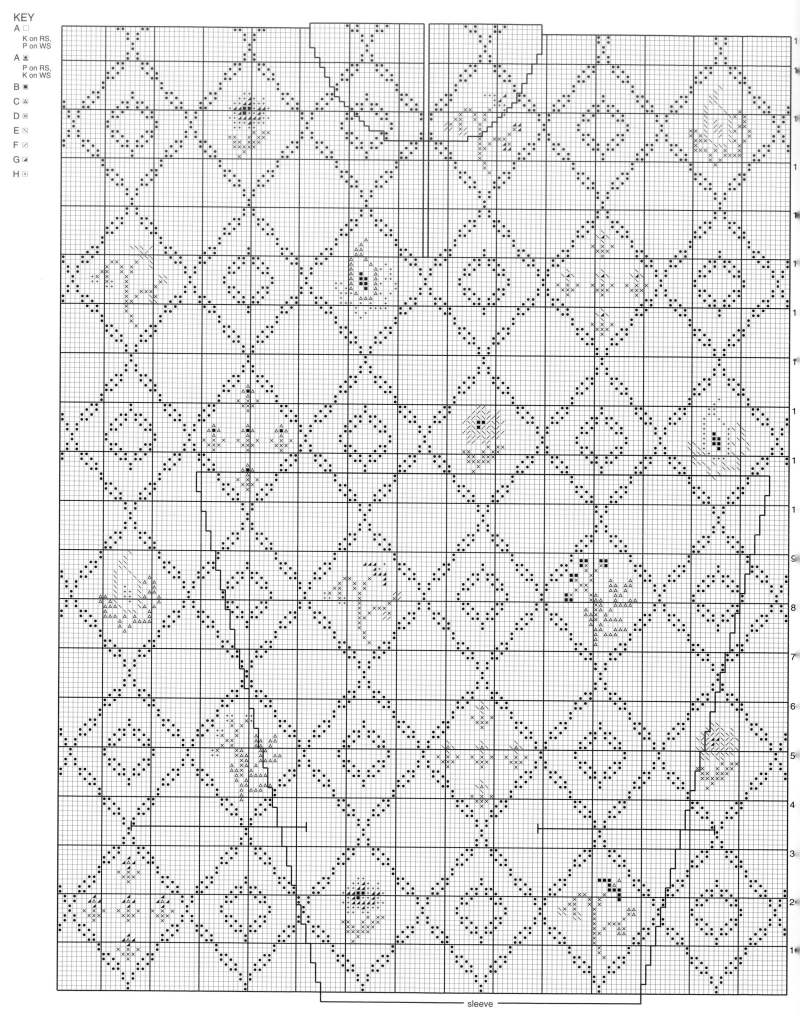

KEY

A ☐ K on RS,
P on WS

A ▣ P on RS,
K on WS

B ■

C △

D ⊠

E ◳

F ◲

G ◢

H ⊡

sleeve

back & front

Carpet Rose
KIM HARGREAVES

YARN

Rowan Cotton Glace and Handknit D.K. Cotton

			s	m	l		
A	Glace	Oyster	730	13	14	14	x 50gm
B	Glace	Matador	742	1	1	1	x 50gm
C	Glace	Provence	744	1	1	2	x 50gm
D	Glace	Corn	791	1	1	1	x 50gm
E	Glace	Terracotta	786	3	3	3	x 50gm
F	Glace	Carnival	432	1	1	1	x 50gm
G	Glace	Blood Orange	445	1	1	1	x 50gm
H	Glace	Dusk	439	1	1	1	x 50gm
J	Glace	Airforce	442	2	2	2	x 50gm
L	Glace	Parade	430	1	1	1	x 50gm
M	Glace	Mint	748	1	1	1	x 50gm
N	H.DK	Pecan	213	3	3	3	x 50gm

NEEDLES

1 pair 2¾mm (no 12) (US 2) needles
1 pair 3¼mm (no 10) (US 3) needles

TENSION

28 sts and 31 rows to 10cm measured over patterned stocking stitch using 3¼mm (US 3) needles

BACK

Cast on 178(184:190) sts using 2¾ mm (US 2) needles and yarn N.
Join in yarn E and work two colour rib as folls:
Row 1 (RS): P2(0:2) E, (K2N, P2E) rep to end.
Row 2: (K2E, P2N) to last 2(0:2) sts, K2E.
Rep these 2 rows until work measures 2.5cm, inc 1 st at end of last row. (179(185:191) sts)

Change to 3¼mm (US 3) needles and using the INTARSIA and FAIR ISLE techniques described on the information page, cont in patt from chart for back which is worked entirely in st st beg with a K row.
Work until chart row 110(118:126) completed ending ending with a WS row.

Shape armhole

Cast off 8 sts at beg next 2 rows. **
Cont without further shaping until chart row 196(204:212) completed ending with a WS row.

Shape shoulders and back neck

Cast off 18(19:20) sts at beg next 2 rows.
cast off 18(19:20) sts, patt 23(24:25) sts, turn and leave rem sts on a holder.
Work each side of neck separately.
Cast off 4 st at beg of next row.
Cast off rem 19(20:21) sts.
With RS facing rejoin yarn to rem sts, cast off centre 45 sts, patt to end.
Complete to match first side reversing all shaping.

FRONT

Work as given for back to **.
Cont without further shaping until chart row 172(180:188) completed ending with a WS row.

Shape front neck

Patt 73(76:79) sts, turn and leave rem sts on a holder.
Work each side of neck separately.
Cast off 3 sts at beg of next row and foll alt row.
Dec 1 st at neck edge on next 7 rows.
Work one row.
Dec 1 st at neck edge on next row and foll 4 alt rows. (55(58:61)sts)
Cont without further shaping until front matches back to shoulder.

Shape shoulder

Cast off 18(19:20) sts at beg of next row and foll

alt row.
Work 1 row.
Cast off rem 19(20:21) sts.
With RS facing rejoin yarn to rem sts, cast off centre 17 sts, patt to end.
Complete to match other side reversing all shaping.

SLEEVES (both alike)

Cast on 70 sts using 2¾mm (US 2) needles and yarn N.
Join in yarn E and work 2 colour rib as folls:
Row 1 (RS): P2E, * K2N, P2E, rep from * to end.
Row 2: K2E, * P2N, K2E, rep from * to end.
Rep these 2 rows until work measures 2.5cm, inc 1 st at end of last row. (71sts)
Change to 3¼mm (US 3) needles and work 126 rows from chart for sleeve, and AT THE SAME TIME shape sides by inc 1 st at each end of 3rd row and every foll alt row until there are 137 sts and then every foll 4th row until there are 157 sts.
Cast off evenly.

MAKING UP

Press all pieces as described on the information page.
Join right shoulder seam using back stitch.

Neckband

With RS facing, using 2¾mm (US 2) needles and yarn A, pick up and K 31 sts down left front neck, 17 sts across centre front, 31 sts up right front neck and 53 sts across back neck. (132sts)
Work 2cm in K2, P2 rib.
Cast off in rib.
Join left shoulder seam and neckband.
See information page for finishing instructions.

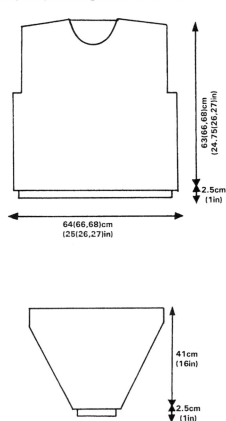

63(66,68)cm
(24.75(26,27)in)

2.5cm
(1in)

64(66,68)cm
(25(26,27)in)

41cm
(16in)

2.5cm
(1in)

KEY

A ☐
B ◉
C ◪
D ◹
E ⊡
F ▲
G ■
H ●
J ⊙
L ⊞
M ⊡
N ⊠

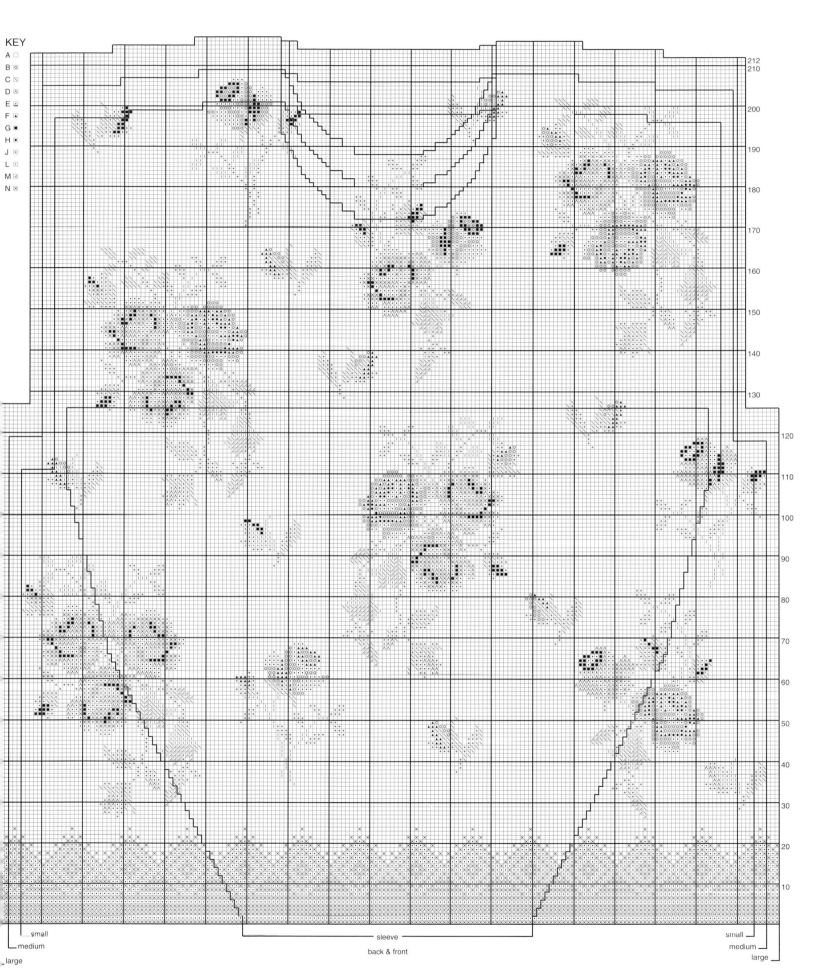

212
210
200
190
180
170
160
150
140
130
120
110
100
90
80
70
60
50
40
30
20
10

small
medium
large

sleeve
back & front

small
medium
large

Dales Aran
MARTIN STOREY

YARNS

Rowan Magpie Tweed

13   14   x   100gm hanks

(photographed in Dolphin 770)

NEEDLES

1 pair 3¾mm (no 9) (US 5)

1 pair 4½mm (no 7) (US 7)

Cable needle

TENSION

17 sts and 25 rows to 10 cm measured over stocking stitch using 4½mm (US 7) needles.

Special Abbreviations

RT = right twist: K2tog, leaving sts on left hand needle, then insert right hand needle from the front between the sts just knitted together and knit the first st again, slip both sts from needle together.

LT = left twist: With right hand needle behind left hand needle, skip one stitch and knit the second st in back loop, then insert right hand needle into the backs of both stitches (the skipped st and the second st) and K2tog through back loop.

BACK

Cast on 148(156) sts using 3¾mm (US 5) needles, work in rib patt as folls:

Row 1: (RS): K4(K3), (P1, RT, K1, P1, K4) to end.

Row 2: (P4, K1, P3, K1) to last 4(3) sts, P4(3).

Row 3: K4(3), (P1, K1, LT, P1, K4) to end.

Row 4: Work as row 2.

Rep these 4 rows until 23 rows completed.

Row 24 (WS)(inc): Patt 18(22), (M1, patt 16) 7 times, M1, patt 18(22). (156(164)sts)

Change to 4½mm (US 7) needles.

Chart row 1 (RS): (K1, P1) 8(10) times, K9, P2, * P6, C5R, P1, C5L, P6, * P2, K8, P2, K4, P8, C8F, P8, K4, P2, K8, P2; rep from * to *, P2, K8, (K1, P1) 8(10) times, K1.

Chart row 2: (P1, K1) 8(10) times, P9, K2, * K6, P5, K1, P5, K6 * K2, P8, K2, P4, K8, P8, K8, P4, K2, P8, K2; rep from * to *, K2, P8, (P1, K1) 8(10) times, P1.

Chart row 3: (P1, K1) 8(10) times, P1, C8F, P2, * P5, C5R, P1, K1, P1, C5L, P5, * P2, C8B, P2, K4, P8, K8, P8, K4, P2, C8F, P2; rep from * to *, P2, C8B, (P1, K1) 8(10) times, P1.

Chart row 4: (K1, P1) 8(10) times, K1, P8, K2, * K5, P5, K1, P1, K1, P5, K5, * K2, P8, K2, P4, K8, P8, K8, P4, K2, P8, K2; rep from * to * K2, P8, (K1, P1) 8(10) times, K1.

This sets the sts, cont in patt from chart until chart row 32 completed.

Rep the 32 row patt until work measures 71cm from cast on edge, ending with a WS row.

Shape back neck and shoulders

Keeping patt correct shape back neck as folls:

Next row (RS): Patt 59(63) sts, turn leaving rem sts on a holder.

Work each side of neck separately.

Dec 1 st at neck edge on next 5 rows. (54(58)sts)

Cast off rem sts.

With RS facing slip centre 38 sts onto a holder, rejoin yarn to rem sts, patt to end.

Complete to match first side reversing all shaping.

FRONT

Work as for back until work measures 64.5cm from cast on edge, ending with a WS row.

Shape front neck

Keeping patt correct shape front neck as folls:

Next row (RS): Patt 68(72) sts, turn leaving rem sts on a holder.

Work each side of neck separately.

Next row: Cast off 5 sts, patt to end.

Work 1 row.

Dec 1 st at neck edge to 54(58) sts.

Cont without further shaping until front matches back to shoulder, ending with a WS row.

Cast off rem sts.

With RS facing slip centre 20 sts onto a holder, rejoin yarn and patt to end.

Complete to match first side reversing all shaping.

SLEEVES (both alike)

Cast on 40 sts using 3¾mm (US 5) needles.

Work 23 sts in rib patt as given for smaller size back.

Row 24 (WS)(inc): Patt 1, (M1, patt 3) 6 times, (M1, patt 1) twice, (M1, patt 3) 6 times, M1, patt 1. (55sts)

Change to 4½mm (US 7) needles.

Chart row 1 (RS): (K1, P1) 3 times, work 43 sts in patt from chart, working between markers for sleeve as folls: K8, P8, C5R, P1, C5L, P8, K8, 6 sts rem, (P1, K1) 3 times.

Chart row 2: (P1, K1) 3 times, work 43 sts from chart as folls: P8, K8, P5, K1, P5, K8, P8, 6 sts rem, (K1, P1) 3 times.

Chart row 3: (P1, K1) 3 times, work 43 sts from chart as folls: C8F P7, C5R, P1, K1, P1, C5L, P7, C8B, 6 sts rem, (K1, P1) 3 times.

Chart row 4: (K1, P1) 3 times, P8, K7, P5, K1, P1, K1, P5, K7, P8, 6 sts rem, (P1, K1) 3 times.

Keeping 32 row patt correct, inc 1 st at each end of next row and every foll alt row to 101 sts and then every 4th row to 119 sts, taking the extra stitches into the double moss st pattern.

Cont without further shaping until sleeves measures 48cm from cast on edge or length required, ending with a WS row.

Cast off loosely in patt.

MAKING UP

PRESS all pieces as described on the information page.

Join right shoulder seam using back stitch.

Neckband

With RS facing and using 3¾mm (US 5) needles, pick up and knit 26 sts down left front neck, work across sts from front neck holder as folls: (K1, K2tog) 3 times, K2, (K2tog, K1) 3 times: pick up and knit 25 sts up right front neck and 6 sts down left back neck, work across sts from back neck holder as folls: (K1, K2tog) 6 times, K2, (K2tog, K1) 6 times: pick up and knit 6 sts up right back neck. (103 sts)

Beg with row 2, work 9cm in rib patt as given for smaller back, rep the 4 row patt throughout and ending with a WS row.

Cast off evenly in patt.

Join left shoulder and neckband seam.

See information page for finishing instructions.

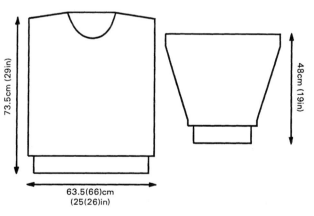

73.5cm (29in)

63.5(66)cm (25(26)in)

48cm (19in)

Back

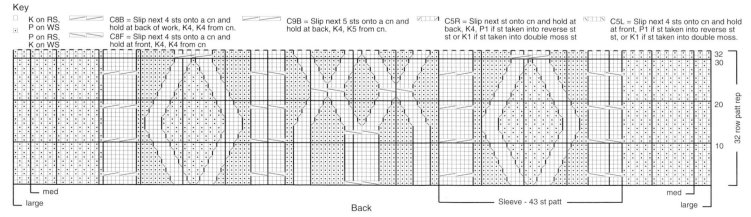

Key

☐ K on RS, P on WS

P on RS, K on WS

C8B = Slip next 4 sts onto a cn and hold at back of work, K4, K4 from cn.

C8F = Slip next 4 sts onto a cn and hold at front, K4, K4 from cn

C9B = Slip next 5 sts onto a cn and hold at back, K4, K5 from cn.

C5R = Slip next st onto cn and hold at back, K4, P1 if st taken into reverse st st or K1 if st taken into double moss st

C5L = Slip next 4 sts onto cn and hold at front, P1 if st taken into reverse st st, or K1 if st taken into double moss.

med

large

Sleeve - 43 st patt

med

large

32 row patt rep

Short Raglan Sweater

AMANDA GRIFFITHS

Rowan Magpie Aran
7   x   100gm
(photographed in Cloud Blue 507)

NEEDLES
1 pair 5mm (no 6) (US 8)
1 pair 5½mm (no 5) (US 9)
Circular needle 40cm long 5mm (no 6) (US 8)
Cable needle

TENSION
15½ sts and 22 rows to 10cm measured over
stocking stitch using 5½mm (US 9) needles

SPECIAL ABBREVIATIONS
C4B slip next 2 sts onto cable needle and hold
at back, K2, then K2 from cable needle.
C4F slip next 2 sts onto cable needle and hold
at front, K2, then K2 from cable needle.

BACK
Knotted edging
Cast on 8 sts using 5½mm (US 9) needles.
Work 26 rows in st st beg with a K row.
Break yarn and leave sts on a holder.
Make 11 more strips in the same way.
Slip all 12 strips onto left-hand 5½mm (US 9)
needle with right sides facing.
Working on first 2 strips only and keeping right
sides facing at all times, cross first strip in front
of second strip then bring cast on edge of second
strip up in front of first strip and tuck it between
the 2 strips and behind the first. Beginning at
row 1 of chart for back work first 8 sts of patt
across sts of first strip and AT THE SAME
TIME, catch in every alt cast on st of second
strip. Next tuck rem cast on edge of first strip
behind sts of second strip and work the next 8
sts of patt across these sts, catching in every alt
cast on st of first strip, thus completing the knot.
Work 5 more knots in the same manner, continu-
ing across row 1 of pattern. (96 sts)
Work a further 31 rows in patt from chart ending
with a WS row.
Shape armholes
Next row (RS)(dec): Cast off 4 sts, P2, K4,
P1, sl 1, K1, psso, K to end.
Next row: Cast off 4 sts, K2, P4, K1, P to last
7 sts, K1, P4, K2.
Next row: P2, C4B, P1, sl 1, K1, psso, K to
last 9 sts, K1, sl 1, transfer last 2 sts back to
left-hand needle and psso, place K st back onto
right-hand needle, P1, C4F, P2.
Next row: K2, P4, K1, P to last 7 sts, K1, P4,
K2.
Next row: P2, K4, P1, sl 1, K1, psso, K to last
9 sts, K1, sl 1, transfer last 2 sts back to left-
hand needle and psso, place K st back onto
right-hand needle, P1, K4, P2.
Next row: K2, P4, K1, P to last 7 sts, K1, P4, K2.
Rep last 4 rows until 34 sts rem and 88 chart
rows have been completed.

Shape neck
Next row (RS): P2, K4, P1, sl 1, K1, psso, turn
and leave rem sts on a holder.
Work each side of neck separately.
Next row: Cast off 4 sts, P2, K2.
Next row: P2, sl 1, K1, psso.
Cast off rem 3 sts.
With RS facing rejoin yarn to rem sts, cast off
centre 16 sts, K1, sl 1 transfer last 2 sts back to
left-hand needle and psso, place K st back onto
right-hand needle, P1, K4, P2.
Next row: K2, P4, K1, P1.
Next row: Cast off 4 sts, K1, sl 1, transfer last 2
sts back to left-hand needle and psso, place K st
back onto right-hand needle, P2.
Cast off rem 3 sts.

FRONT
Work as given for back until 40 sts rem and 82
chart rows have been completed.
Shape front neck
Next row (RS): P2, C4B, P1, sl 1, K1, psso,
K5, turn and leave rem sts on a holder.
Work each side of neck separately.
Keeping patt correct, cast off 3 sts at beg of next
row, then dec 1 st at neck edge on every row
until 2 sts rem.
Work 2 tog.
Fasten off.
With RS facing, rejoin yarn to rem sts, cast off
centre 12 sts, patt to end.
Complete to match other side of neck reversing
all shaping.

SLEEVES (both alike)
Cast on 30 sts using 5mm (US 8) needles.
Work 6 rows in st st beg with a K row.

Next row: P2, (K2, P2) to end.
Next row: K2, (P2, K2) to end.
Rep these 2 rows twice more, inc 1 st at each
end of last row. (32 sts)
Change to 5½mm (US 9) needles and work 74
rows in patt from chart for sleeve and AT THE
SAME TIME, shape sides by inc 1 st, as indicat-
ed, at each end of very 3rd row until there are 74
sts. Take extra sts into patt as they occur.
Shape sleeve top
Cast off 4 sts at beg of next 2 rows.
Next row: K2, sl 1, K1, psso, K to last 4 sts, K1
sl 1, transfer last 2 sts back to left-hand needle
and psso, place K st back onto right-hand needle, K2.
Next row: Purl.
Rep these 2 rows until 10 sts rem ending with a
WS row. Cast off.

MAKING UP
Press all pieces as described on the information
page.
Join raglan seams using backstitch.
Join side and sleeve seams using backstitch.
Neaten all ends on knotted edge detail.
Neckband
With RS facing and 5mm (US 8) circular needle,
pick up and K 10 sts from top of left sleeve, 13
sts down left front neck, 12 sts across centre, 13
sts up right front neck, 10 sts from top of right
sleeve, 7 sts down right back neck, 16 sts from
centre back and 7 sts up left back neck. (88 sts)
Work 8 rounds in K2, P2 rib, then 6 rounds in st
st (every round knit).
Cast off.
Press seams.

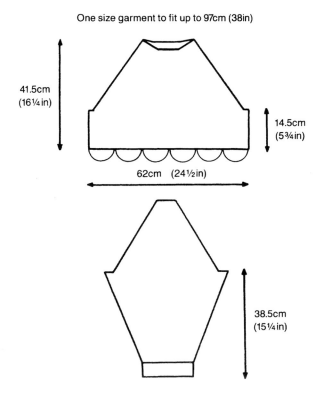

One size garment to fit up to 97cm (38in)

41.5cm
(16¼ in)

14.5cm
(5¾ in)

62cm (24½ in)

38.5cm
(15¼ in)

KEY

□ K on RS, P on WS

• P on RS, K on WS

◩ Slip 1, K1, p.s.s.o

◪ K1, slip 1, transfer last 2 sts back
to left-hand needle and p.s.s.o, place
K st back onto right-hand needle

▨ K onto front and back of st

◺ C4B slip next 2 sts onto cable
needle and hold at back, K2,
then K2 from cable needle

◿ C4F slip next 2 sts onto cable
needle and hold at front, k2,
then K2 from cable needle

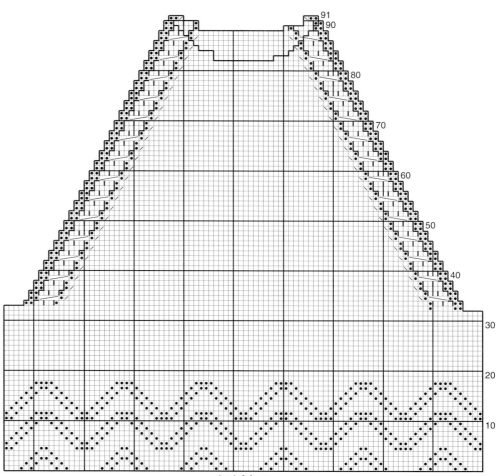

back & front

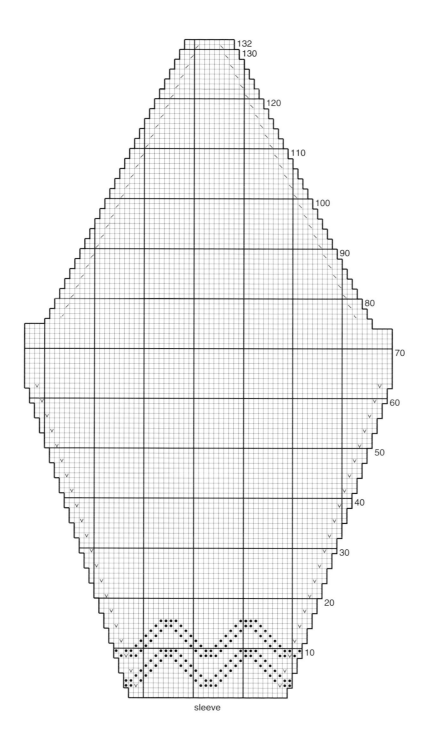

sleeve

Traditional Texture

KATE BULLER

However complicated a cable design looks, the cabling itself is always based on the same simple principle—a set of stitches is placed on a double pointed needle, held at the back or front of the work, then transferred to the knitting a few stitches farther on. When the stitches are held to the back, the cable crosses to the right; when stitches are held to the front, the cable crosses to the left. Cables are usually worked on the right side rows of a stocking stitch panel with reverse stocking stitch on either side.

SIMPLE CABLES
CROSSING TO THE RIGHT USING 6 STITCHES (C6B)

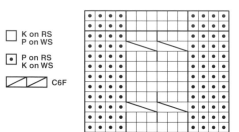

☐ K on RS
P on WS

⊡ P on RS
K on WS

▧ C6B

1. On right side (knit) row, work to the position of the cable panel, slip the next 3 stitches onto a cable needle and hold at the back of the work.

2. Knit the next 3 stitches pulling the yarn tightly to close up the gap.

3. Push the 3 stitches on the cable needle to the left hand side and knit these stitches off the cable needle. Continue until the next cable row is reached.

CROSSING TO THE LEFT USING 6 STITCHES (C6F)

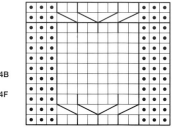

☐ K on RS
P on WS

⊡ P on RS
K on WS

▧ C6F

Work as for crossing a cable to the right, but hold the cable needle to the front instead of the back.

ALTERNATIVE SIMPLE CABLES
Cable variations are made by altering the number of stitches to be cabled, the direction of the cross, and/or the number of rows between cabling rows.

From left to right:
C4F: 4-stitch cable crossed to the left every 4th row.
C6B: 6-stitch cable crossed to the right every 6th row.
C6F: 6-stitch cable crossed to the left every 8th row.
C8B: 8-stitch cable crossed to the right every 10th row.

DOUBLE CABLES
Another cable variation is made by placing 2 sets of simple cables together in a panel and crossing the cables to the left and right. As with simple cables, varying the number of stitches used and the number of rows between the cables will result in different looks.

HORSESHOE CABLE

WORKED OVER 8 STITCHES.
This cable is made up of 2 simple cables worked over 4 stitches each, the first set crossed to the right, the second set crossed to the left.
Foundation Row (WS): P8.

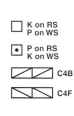

☐ K on RS
P on WS

⊡ P on RS
K on WS

▧ C4B

▧ C4F

Row 1 (RS) (Cable Row): Sl next 2 sts onto cable needle and hold at back, K2, then K2 from cable needle (C4B), sl next 2 sts onto cable needle and hold at front, K2, then K2 from cable needle (C4F).
Rows 2, 4, 6, and 8: P8.
Rows 3, 5, and 7: K8.

PLAITED CABLE

WORKED OVER 9 STITCHES.
A little more sophisticated than the Horseshoe, but just as easy to work. The centre set of 3 stitches are alternately crossed to the left, then to the right, with the outer three stitches on each side.

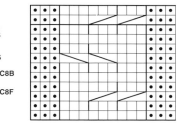

☐ K on RS
P on WS

⊡ P on RS
K on WS

▧ C8B

▧ C8F

Row 1 (RS): K9.
Rows 2, 4, and 6: P9.
Row 3: Sl next 3 sts onto cable needle and hold at front, K3, then K3 from cable needle (C6F), K3.
Row 5: K9.
Row 7: K3, sl next 3 sts onto cable needle and

hold at back, K3, then K3 from cable needle (C6B).

TRAVELLING STITCHES

Many traditional Aran designs use a combination of cables in conjunction with these travelling stitches. By crossing two knit stitches with a purl stitch, the raised pattern can be moved across the knitted fabric.

CROSSING 2 STITCHES TO THE RIGHT (CR2R)

1. Slip a purl stitch onto the cable needle and hold at the back of the work.

2. Knit the next 2 sts.

3. Purl the stitch off the cable needle.

Crossing 2 stitches to the left (Cr2L)
Slip the 2 knit stitches onto the cable needle and hold at the front of the work, purl the next stitch, then knit the 2 stitches from the cable needle.

BOBBLES

Bobbles are often used in Aran knitting and combined with cables or travelling stitches for intri-cate designs. Bobbles are worked by making a number of stitches out of one, working a few rows of stocking stitch, then decreasing back to one.

HOW TO MAKE A BOBBLE

1. On a right-side row, in this case the background is reverse stockinette, knit to the position of the bobble. Work into the front, back, front, back, and front of the next stitch forming 5 new stitches. Drop the original st off the left-hand needle.

2. Turn and purl 5 sts, turn and knit 5 sts.

3. To decrease, turn and purl 2 sts together, purl 1, then purl the remaining 2 sts together. Turn, slip the next stitch, knit 2 together, then pass the slipped stitch over to complete the bobble.

DIAMOND AND BOBBLE PANEL

Use travelling stitches with bobbles to create a typical Aran stitch pattern.

Panel of 17 stitches
Foundation Row (WS): K6, P2, K1, P2, K6.
Row 1 (RS): P6, sl next 3 sts onto cable needle and hold at back, K2, then sl purl st from cable needle back to left-hand needle and purl it, K2 from cable needle, P6.
Row 2: K6, P2, K1, P2, K6.

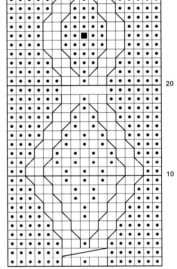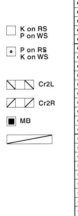

☐	K on RS P on WS
•	P on RS K on WS
Cr2L	
Cr2R	
■	MB

Row 3: P5, Cr2R, K1, Cr2L, P5.
Row 4 and all following WS rows: K all K sts and P all P sts.
Row 5: P4, Cr2R, K1, P, K1, Cr2L, P4.
Row 7: P3, Cr2R, (K1, P1) twice, K1, Cr2L, P3.
Row 9: P2, Cr2R, (K1, P1) 3 times, K1, Cr2L, P2.
Row 11: P2, Cr1L, (P1, K1) 3 times, P1, Cr2R, P2.
Row 13: P3, Cr2L, (P1, K1) twice, P1, Cr2R, P3.
Row 15: P4, Cr2L, P1, K1, P1, Cr2R, P4.
Row 17: P5, Cr2L, P1, Cr2R, P5.
Row 19: As row 1.
Row 21: P5, Cr2R, P1, Cr2L, P5.
Row 23: P4, Cr2R, P3, Cr2L, P4.
Row 25: P4, K2, make bobble, P2, K2, P4.
Row 27: P4, Cr2L, P3, Cr2R, P4.
Row 29: As row 17.
Row 30: As row 4.
Rep rows 1 to 30.

Oversized Cable Sweater

ERIKA KNIGHT

Rowan Chunky Chenille

s	m	l		
10	10	11	x	100gm

(photographed in Aubergine 356)

NEEDLES

1 pair 3¾mm (no 9) (US 5)
1 pair 4½mm (no 7) (US 7)
Cable needle

TENSION

16 sts and 24 rows to 10cm measured over reverse stocking stitch using 4½mm (US 7) needles

SPECIAL ABBREVIATIONS

C8F slip next 4 sts onto a cable needle and hold at front of work, K4, then K 4 from cable needle.
C8B slip next 4 sts onto a cable needle and hold at back of work, K4, then K4 from cable needle.
C5L slip next 4 sts onto a cable needle and hold at front of work, P next st, then K 4 from cable needle.
C5R slip next st onto a cable needle and hold at back of work, K4, then P next st from cable needle.

STITCH NOTE

Double cable (worked over 28 sts and 30 rows and referred to in pattern as Cable 28)
Row 1: K4, P6, K8, P6, K4.
Row 2: P4, K6, P8, K6, P4.
Row 3: K4, P6, C8B, P6, K4.
Row 4: Work as row 2.
Row 5: C5L, P4, C5R, C5L, P4, C5R.
Row 6: K1, P4, K4, P4, K2, P4, K4, P4, K1.
Row 7: P1, C5L, P2, C5R, P2, C5L, P2, C5R, P1.
Row 8: K2, P4, K2, P4, K4, P4, K2, P4, K2.
Row 9: P2, C5L, C5R, P4, C5L, C5R, P2.
Row 10: K3, P8, K6, P8, K3.
Row 11: P3, C8B, P6, C8B, P3.
Row 12: Work as row 10.
Row 13: P3, K8, P6, K8, P3.
Row 14: Work as row 10:
Row 15: Work as row 13.
Row 16: Work as row 10.
Row 17: Work as row 11.
Row 18: Work as row 10.
Row 19: P2, C5R, C5L, P4, C5R, C5L, P2.
Row 20: Work as row 8.
Row 21: P1, C5R, P2, C5L, P2, C5R, P2, C5L, P1.
Row 22: Work as row 6.
Row 23: C5R, P4, C5L, C5R, P4, C5L.
Row 24: Work as row 2.
Row 25: Work as row 3.
Row 26: Work as row 2.
Row 27: Work as row 1.
Row 28: Work as row 2.

Row 29: Work as row 1.
Row 30: Work as row 2.
Rep these 30 rows throughout for centre panel.

Double Plait (worked over 17 sts and 10 rows and referred to in patt as Plait 17)
Rows 1, 5, 7 and 9: K17.
Row 2 and every foll alt row: P17.
Row 3: C8B, K1, C8F.
Rep these 10 rows throughout for side panels.

BACK

Cast on 108(112:116) sts using 4½mm (US 7) needles.
Change to 3¾mm (US 5) needles and work 9cm in K2, P2 rib ending with a RS row.
Next row (WS)(inc): Rib 4(6:8), (M1, rib 9) 11 times, M1, rib 5(7:9). (120(124:128) sts) change to 4½mm (US 7) needles and cont in patt as folls:
Row 1: P19(21:23) sts, work row 1 Plait 17, P10, work row 1 Cable 28, P10, work row 1 Plait 17, P19(21:23).
This row sets position of patt.
Cont in patt as set until 154(160:166) charts rows have been completed and work measures 73.5(76:78.5) cm from beg. Place coloured markers at each end of row 92(96:98) to indicate armhole position.

Shape shoulders

Cast off 15(15:16) sts at beg of next 4 rows and 15(16:16) sts at beg of foll 2 rows.
Cast off rem 30(32:32) sts.

FRONT

Work as given for back until 142(148:154) chart rows have been completed and front measures 68.5(71:73.5) cm from beg.

Shape front neck

Patt 55(57:59) sts, turn and leave rem sts on a holder.
Work each side of neck separately.
Dec 1 st at neck edge on every row until 45(46:48) sts rem.
Cont without further shaping until front matches back to shoulder.

Shape shoulder

Cast off 15(15:16) sts at beg of next row and foll alt row.
Work 1 row.
Cast off rem 15(16:16) sts..
With RS facing, rejoin yarn to rem sts, cast off centre 10 sts, patt to end.
Complete to match first side reversing all shaping.

SLEEVES (both alike)

Cast on 48(48:52) sts using 4½mm (US 7) needles.
Change to 3¾mm (US 5) needles and work 7.5cm in K2, P2 rib ending with a RS row.
Next row (WS)(inc): Rib 6(4:8), [M1, rib 12(8:12)] 3(5:3) times, M1, rib 6(4:8). (52(54:56) sts)
Change to 4½mm (US 7) needles and cont in patt as folls:
Row 1: P12(13:14) sts, work row 1 Cable 28,

P12(13:14) sts.
Cont in patt as set until 92(98:104) chart rows have been completed and work measures 45.5(48.5:51) cm from beg. AT THE SAME TIME, shape sides by inc 1 st at each end of 3rd row and every foll 4th row until there are 90(94:100) sts. Work extra sts in reversed stocking stitch as they occur.
Cast off.

COLLAR

Cast on 84(88:92) sts using 4½mm(US 7) needles.
Change to 3¾mm (US 5) needles and work 7.5cm in K2, P2 rib.
Cast off firmly in rib using 4½mm (US 7) needles.

MAKING UP

Press all pieces (very gently) on WS using a warm iron over a damp cloth.
Join both shoulder seams using backstitch.
Set in sleeve top between markers using backstitch.
Join side and sleeve seams using backstitch on main knitting and an edge to edge stitch on ribs.
Join collar seam, then stitch evenly into place around neck edge, placing seam at shoulder seam.
Press seams.

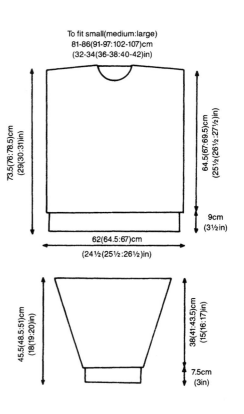

To fit small(medium:large)
81-86(91-97:102-107)cm
(32-34(36-38:40-42)in)

73.5(76:78.5)cm
(29(30:31)in)

64.5(67:69.5)cm
(25½(26½:27½)in)

9cm
(3½in)

62(64.5:67)cm
(24½(25½:26½)in)

45.5(48.5:51)cm
(18(19:20)in)

38(41:43.5)cm
(15(16:17)in)

7.5cm
(3in)

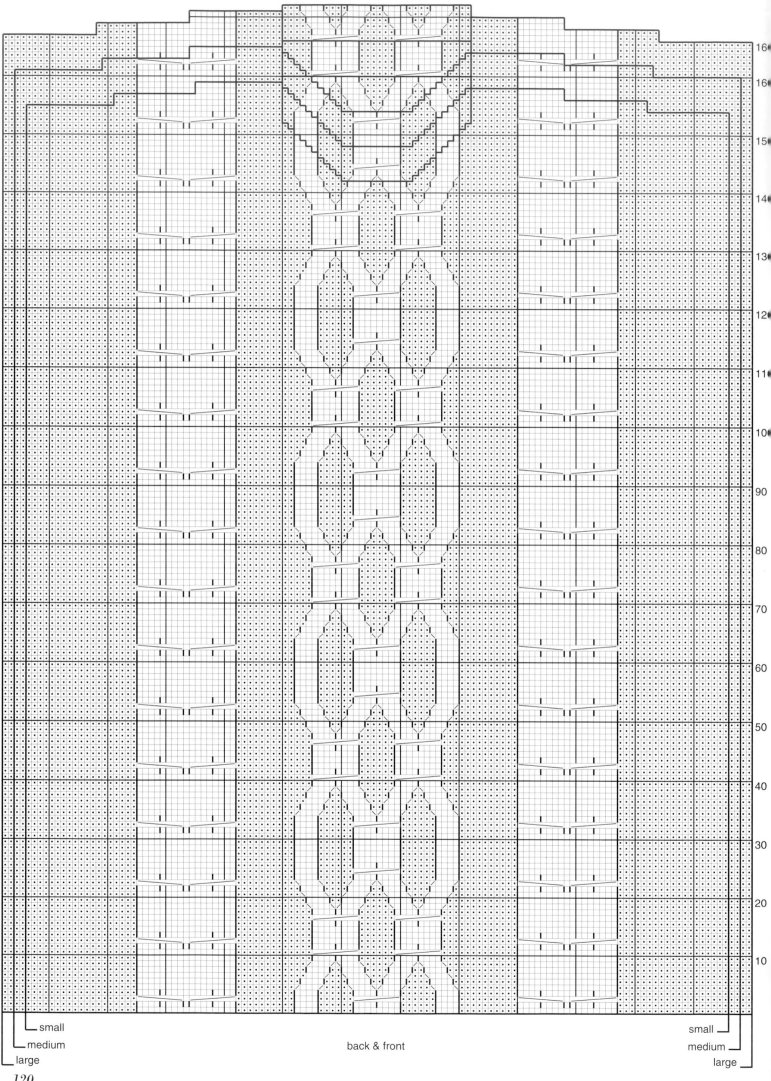

160

160

150

140

130

120

110

100

90

80

70

60

50

40

30

20

10

small

medium

large

back & front

small

medium

large

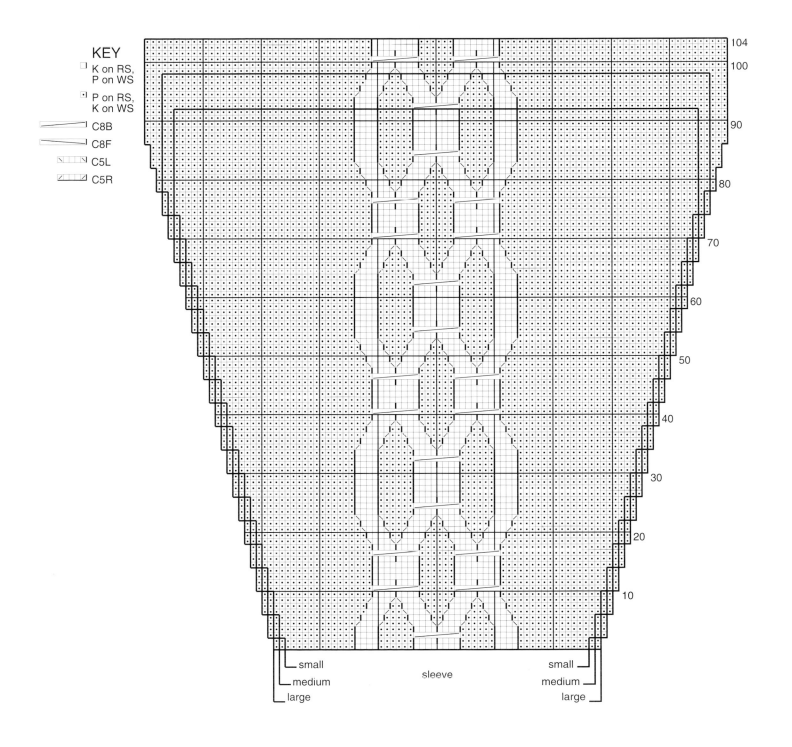

KEY
- ☐ K on RS, P on WS
- ⊡ P on RS, K on WS
- C8B
- C8F
- C5L
- C5R

104
100
90
80
70
60
50
40
30
20
10

small
medium
large

sleeve

small
medium
large

Florida

KIM HARGREAVES

YARN

Rowan True 4 ply Botany
10   x   50gm

NEEDLES

1 pair 2¼mm (no 13)(US 1)
1 pair 3mm (no 11) (US 2)

BUTTONS

5

TENSION

28 sts and 35 rows to 10cm measured over stocking stitch using 3mm (US 2) needles

SPECIAL NOTE

yon	yarn over needle
sl2-p	slip 2 sts purlwise
p2sso	pass 2 slipped stitches over

BACK

Cast on 141 sts using 3mm (US 2) needles.
Work in patt from chart for back setting stitches as folls:

Chart row 1 (RS): Knit.
Chart row 2: Knit.
Chart row 3: K3, (yon, K3, sl2, K1, p2sso, K3, yon, K5) 9 times, yon, K3, sl2, K1, p2sso, K3, yon, K3.
Chart row 4: P4, (yon, P2, sl2-p, P1, p2sso, P2, yon, P7) 9 times, yon, P2, sl2-p, P1, p2sso, P2, yon, P4.

Cont in patt from chart for back until chart row 36 completed.
Cont in st st only until work measures 23cm from beg, ending with a WS row.

Shape armholes

Cast off 8 sts at beg of next 2 rows. (125sts)
Cont without further shaping until work measures 23cm from beg of armhole shaping ending with a WS row.

Shape shoulders and back neck

Cast off 14 sts at beg next 2 rows.
Cast off 14 sts, patt 19, turn leaving rem sts on a holder.

Work each side of neck separately.
Cast off 4 sts, patt to end.
Cast off rem 15 sts.
With RS facing rejoin yarn to rem sts, cast off centre 31 sts, patt to end.
Complete to match first side reversing shaping.

LEFT FRONT

Cast on 70 sts using 3mm (US 2) needles.
Work in patt from chart for left front (do not work motif at end of row 7) until chart row 36 completed and then cont in st st until work measures same as back to armhole ending with a WS row.

Shape armhole and front neck

Cast off 8 sts at beg of next row. (62sts)
Work 9 rows without shaping.
Dec 1 st at end of next row and at same edge on every foll 3rd row until 43 sts rem.
Work without shaping until front matches back to shoulder ending with a WS row.

Shape shoulder

Cast off 14 sts at beg of next row and foll alt row.
Work 1 row.
Cast off rem 15 sts.

RIGHT FRONT

Cast on 70 sts using 3mm (US 2) needles.
Work as for left front foll chart for right front and reversing all shaping.

SLEEVES (both alike)

Cast on 57 sts using 3mm (US 2) needles.
Work 8 rows in patt from chart for sleeve, inc 1 st at each end of row 3 and 7. (61sts)

Cont in stocking st only, inc 1st at each end of every foll 4th row to 129 sts.
Cont without further shaping until sleeve measures 48cm from cast on edge ending with a WS row.
Cast off loosely and evenly.

MAKING UP

Press all pieces as described on the information page.
Join both shoulder seams using backstitch.
Button band (worked in one piece)
Using 2¼mm (US 1) needles cast on 7 sts.
1st row (RS): K1, (K1, P1) twice, K2.
2nd row: K1, (P1, K1) 3 times.
Repeat these two rows until band (when slightly stretched) fits up left front edge to start of neck shaping, up left front slope, across back neck and down right front slope to start of neck shaping.
Slip stitch band into place as you go along.
Mark position of 5 buttons on left front band the first to come 1cm up from cast on edge, the 5th to come 1cm down from start of shaping and rem 3 spaced evenly between.
Complete right front band to match with the addition of 5 buttonholes worked to correspond with markers as folls:
Buttonhole row: Work 3 sts, yon, work 2tog, cont to end.
Cast off.
Slip st into place.
See information page for finishing instructions.

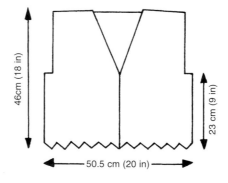

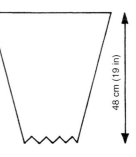

KEY

○	yarn over needle
▲	sl2, K1, p2sso RS, sl2, P1, p2sso on WS
•	K on WS
✓	k2tog on RS, P2tog on WS
↘	sl1, K1, Psso on RS, P2 tog-b on WS

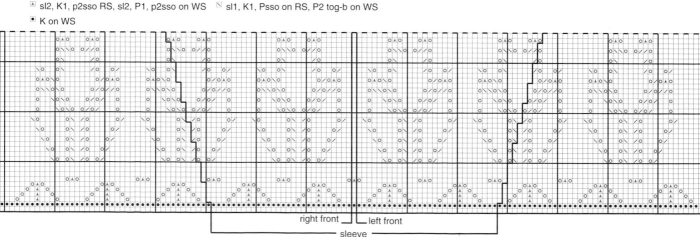

right front   left front

sleeve

Persia
KIM HARGREAVES

YARN
Rowan Magpie, Magpie Tweed, Chunky Chenille, Designer D.K., Light Weight DK and Donegal Lambswool Tweed

JACKET–WRAPOVER (one size)

A	Magpie	Neptune	612	2	x	100gm
B	Lt Wt DK	Brick	78*	4	x	25gm
C	M. Tweed	Squirrel	772	4	x	100gm
D	Magpie	Raven	62	1	x	100gm
E	D.D.K.	Airforce	65*	5	x	50gm
F	D.D.K.	Chestnut	663*	6	x	50gm
G	Magpie	Pumice	301	3	x	100gm
H	Magpie	Dapple	450	3	x	100gm

SWEATER

				s	m	l	
A	Ch. Chenille	Serge	378	2	2	2 x	100gm
B	D.D.K.	Highland	631*	2	2	2 x	50gm
C	M. Tweed	Dolphin	770	2	2	2 x	100gm
D	D.L. Tweed	Storm	468*	2	2	2 x	25gm
E	Magpie	Neptune	612	2	2	2 x	100gm
F	D.D.K.	Chestnut	663*	4	4	6 x	50gm
G	Lt Wt DK	Brick	78*	8	8	8 x	25gm
H	Magpie	Dapple	450	2	2	2 x	100gm

* USE DOUBLE THROUGHOUT

NEEDLES
1 pair 4mm (no 8) (US 6)
1 pair 5mm (no 6) (US 8)

TENSION
18 sts and 23 rows to 10cm measured over patterned stocking stitch using 5mm (US 8) needles

Jacket
BACK
Cast on 109 sts using 4mm (US 6) needles and yarn C.
Work 10 rows in st st beg with a K row.
Next row (RS): Purl to form hemline.
Next row (WS): Purl.
Change to 5mm (US 8) needles and using the INTARSIA technique described on the information page cont in patt from chart for jacket back which is worked entirely in st st beg with a K row. Work until chart row 100 completed.

Shape armhole
Cast off 6 sts at beg next 2 rows.
Dec 1 st at each end of next row and 8 foll alt rows. (79sts)
Work without further shaping until chart row 164 completed.

Shape shoulders and back neck
Cast off 8 sts at beg next 2 rows.
Cast off 9 sts at beg next row, patt 13 sts, turn and leave rem sts on a holder.
Work each side of neck separately.
Cast off 4 sts at beg next row, patt to end.
Cast off rem 9 sts evenly.

With RS facing rejoin yarn to rem sts, cast off centre 19 sts, patt to end.
Complete to match first side reversing all shaping.

POCKET LININGS (make two)
Cast on 26 sts using 4mm (US 6) needles and yarn C.
Work 30 rows in st st beg with a K row.
Leave sts on a holder.

LEFT FRONT
Cast on 61 sts using 4mm (US 6) needles and yarn C.
Work 10 rows in st st beg with a K row.
Next row (RS): Purl to form hemline.
Next row: Purl.
Change to 5mm (US 8) needles and cont from chart for left front until row 40 completed.

Place pockets
Row 41: Patt 9 sts, place next 26 sts on a holder and in place of these patt across sts for first packet lining, patt to end.
Cont in patt from chart until row 78 completed.

Shape front neck and armhole
Dec 1 st at front edge on next and every foll 4th row until there are 26 sts and AT THE SAME TIME, when chart row 100 completed work armhole as given for back.
Cont without further shaping until front matches back to shoulder.

Shape shoulder
Cast off 8 sts at beg next row and 9 sts at beg foll alt row.
Work 1 row.
Cast off rem 9 sts.

RIGHT FRONT
Work as given for left front foll chart for right front and reversing all shaping and pocket position.

SLEEVES (both alike)
Cast on 51 sts using 4mm (US 6) needles and yarn C.
Work 10 rows in st st beg with a knit row.
Next row (RS): Purl to form hemline.
Next row: Purl.
Change to 5mm (US 8) needles and starting at chart row 33, work from chart for sleeve until row 132 completed and AT THE SAME TIME, inc 1 st at each end of 11th row and every foll 3rd row until there are 101 sts.

Shape sleeve head
Cast off 6 sts at beg next 2 rows.
Dec 1 st at each end of next row and foll 7 alt rows. (73sts)
Cast off loosely and evenly.

COLLAR
Cast on 5 sts using 5mm (US 8) needles and yarn G.
Cont in patt from chart for collar until row 116 completed, AT THE SAME TIME, shape sides by inc 1 st at each end of the 3rd row and every foll 3rd row until there are 59 sts.
Now turn chart and work back from row 105 to

row 1 reversing all shaping.
Cast off evenly.

BELT
Cast on 276 sts using 4mm (US 6) needles and yarn C.
Work 21 rows from chart for belt, working 6 st rep across row.
Cast off loosely and evenly.
Fold belt in half with RS together and stitch cast on edge to cast off edge.
Turn to RS. Press flat having seam down centre on reverse side.

MAKING UP
Press all pieces as described on the information page.

Pocket tops
With RS facing, using 4mm needles, place 26 sts from holder onto LH needle.
Work 3 rows in patt from chart.
Change to yarn C and purl 3 rows.
Work 8 rows in st st beg with a K row.
Cast off evenly.

Left front band
With RS facing using 4mm (US 6) needles and yarn C, pick up and K 62 sts from beg of front neck shaping to foldline.
Next row: K to form foldline.
Work 8 rows in st st beg with a K row, AT THE SAME TIME, inc 1 st at neck edge on every row.
Cast off evenly.

Right front band
Work as given for left frontband.
Join both shoulder seams using backstitch.
Turn hem up on WS and slip st into place.
Sew collar neatly into place having centre of collar to centre back. Fold in half and slip st into place on WS.

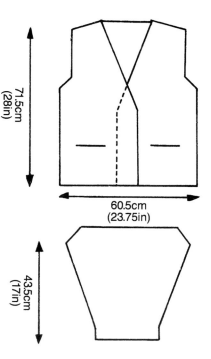

Fold frontband to WS at foldline and slip st into place, mitreing corner at hemline and taking over collar at neck edge.

See information page for finishing instructions.

Sweater

BACK

Cast on 108(114:118) sts using 4mm (US 6) needles and yarn C.

Work 2.5cm in K2, P2 rib inc 1 st at end of last row. (109(115:119)sts)

Change to 5mm (US 8) needles and work from chart for back as given for jacket, until chart row 82(88:94) completed.

Shape armholes

Cast off 5 sts at beg next 2 rows. (99(105:109) sts) *

Cont without further shaping until chart row 146(152:158) completed ending with a WS row.

Shape shoulders and back neck

Cast off 10(11:12) sts at beg next 2 rows.

Cast off 10(11:12) sts, patt 15(16:16) sts, turn and leave rem sts on a holder.

Work each side of neck separately.

Cast off 4 sts patt to end.

Cast off rem 11(12:12) sts.

With RS facing, rejoin yarns to rem sts, cast off centre 29 sts, patt to end.

Complete to match first side reversing shaping.

FRONT

Work as given for back to *.

Cont without further shaping until chart row 126 completed.

Shape front neck

Patt 44(47:49) sts, turn and leave rem sts on a holder.

Work each side of neck separately.

Cast off 3 sts at beg next row, patt to end.

Dec 1 st at neck edge on next 5 rows and foll 5 alt rows. (31(34:36)sts)

Cont without further shaping until front matches back to shoulder.

Shape shoulder

Cast off 10(11:12) sts at beg of next row and foll alt row.

Work 1 row.

Cast off rem 11(12:12) sts evenly.

With RS facing, rejoin yarn to rem sts, cast off centre 11 sts, patt to end.

Complete to match first side reversing all shaping.

SLEEVES (both alike)

Cast on 46 sts using 4mm (US 6) needles and yarn C.

Work 6.5cm in K2, P2 rib, ending with a RS row.

Next row (inc): Rib 5, (M1, rib 9) 4 times, M1, rib 5. (51sts)

Change to 5mm (US 8) needles and starting at chart row 33, cont in patt for sleeve until chart row 132 completed and AT THE SAME TIME, inc 1 st at each end of 3rd row and every foll 4th row until there are 69 sts and then on every foll 3rd row until there are 101 sts.

Cast off loosely and evenly.

MAKING UP

Press all peces as described on the information page.

Join right shoulder seams using back stitch.

Polo neck

With RS facing using 4mm (US 6) needles and yarn C, pick up and K 26 sts down left front neck, 11 sts across centre front, 26 sts up right front neck and 37 sts across back neck. (100sts)

Work 12.5cm in K2, P2 rib.

Cast off loosely in rib.

See information page for finishing instructions.

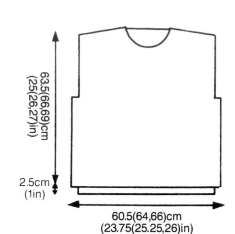

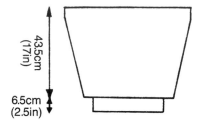

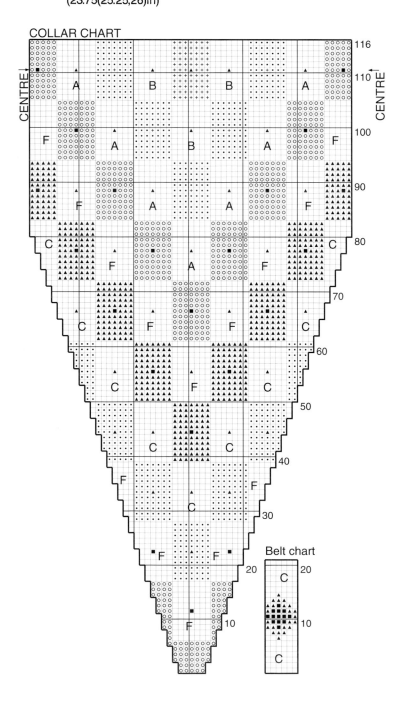

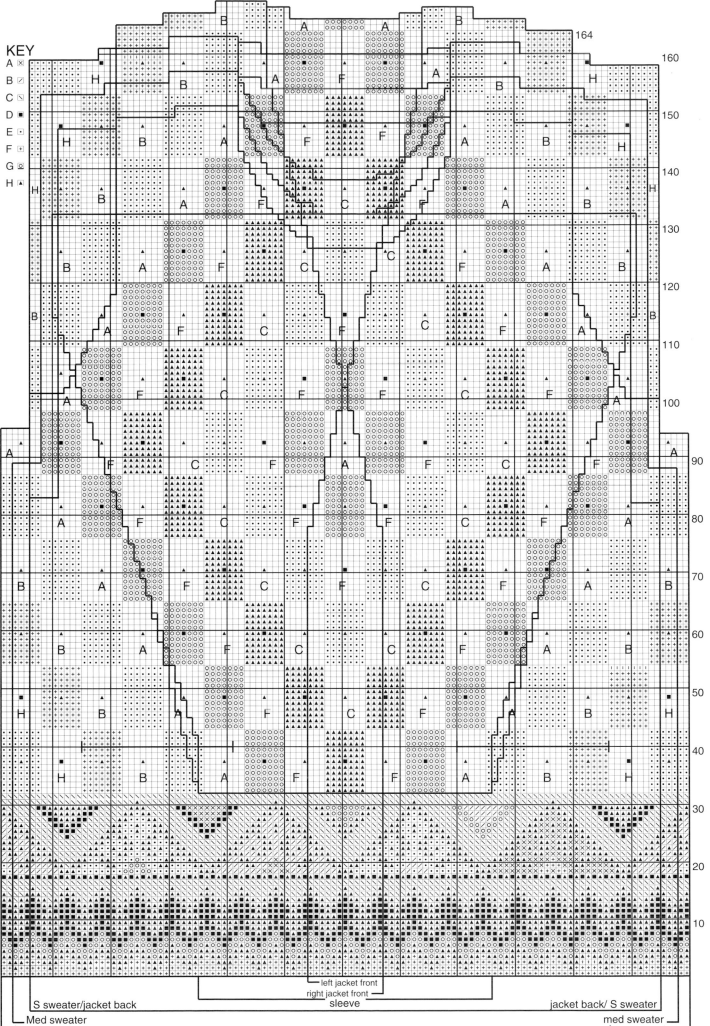

KEY

A ⊠
B ◩
C ◪
D ■
E ⊡
F ⊞
G ⊙
H ▲

160
164
150
140
130
120
110
100
90
80
70
60
50
40
30
20
10

left jacket front
right jacket front
sleeve
S sweater/jacket back
jacket back/ S sweater
Med sweater
Large sweater
med sweater
Large sweater

127

Floating Circles

KAFFE FASSETT

YARN

Rowan Donegal Lambswool Tweed, Light Weight D.K., Kid Silk, and Designer D.K.

Sweater

A	D.L.T	Black 491	12	x	25gm
B	D.L.T	Bramble 484	1	x	25gm
C	D.L.T	Cinnamon 479	1	x	25gm
D	D.L.T	Tarragon 477	1	x	25gm
E	D.L.T	Juniper 482	1	x	25gm
F	D.L.T	Bark 475	1	x	25gm
G	D.L.T	Dolphin 478	1	x	25gm
H	D.L.T	Roseberry 480	1	x	25gm
J	D.L.T.	Leaf 481	1	x	25gm
K	D.L.T.	Pickle 483	1	x	25gm
L	Lt.Wt.DK	Olive 407	2	x	25gm
M	Lt.Wt.DK	Wine 602	1	x	25gm
N	Lt.Wt.DK	Rust 77	1	x	25gm
P	Lt.Wt.DK	Old Rose 94	1	x	25gm
R	Lt.Wt.DK	Forest 73	1	x	25gm
S	Lt.Wt.DK	Ruby 663	1	x	25gm
T	K.Silk	Holly 990	1	x	25gm
U	D.D.K.	Peat 80	1	x	50gm
V	K.Silk	S. Blue 991	1	x	25gm
W	D.L.T	Rainforest 489	1	x	25gm

Waistcoat

A	D.L.T	Black 491	9	9	x	25gm
B	D.L.T	Bramble 484	1	1	x	25gm
C	D.L.T	Cinnamon 479	1	1	x	25gm
D	D.L.T	Tarragon 477	1	1	x	25gm
E	D.L.T	Juniper 482	1	1	x	25gm
F	D.L.T	Bark 475	1	1	x	25gm
G	D.L.T	Dolphin 478	1	1	x	25gm
H	D.L.T	Roseberry 480	1	1	x	25gm
J	D.L.T.	Leaf 481	1	1	x	25gm
K	D.L.T.	Pickle 483	1	1	x	25gm
L	Lt.Wt.DK	Olive 407	2	2	x	25gm
M	Lt.Wt.DK	Wine 602	1	1	x	25gm
N	Lt.Wt.DK	Rust 77	1	1	x	25gm
P	Lt.Wt.DK	Old Rose 94	1	1	x	25gm
R	Lt.Wt.DK	Forest 73	1	1	x	25gm
S	Lt.Wt.DK	Ruby 663	1	1	x	25gm
T	K.Silk	Holly 990	1	1	x	25gm
U	K.Silk	G.Brown 994	1	1	x	25gm
V	K.Silk	S.Blue 991	1	1	x	25gm
W	D.L.T	Rainforest 489	1	1	x	25gm

NEEDLES

1 pair 2¾mm (no 12) (US 2)
1 pair 3¼mm (no 10) (US 3)
2¾mm (no 12) (US 2) circular needle (waistcoat only)

BUTTONS (waistcoat only)

7

TENSION

26 sts and 38 rows to 10cm measured over patterned stocking stitch using 3¼mm (US 3) needles

Sweater

BACK

Cast on 140 sts using 2¾mm (US 2) needles and yarn A and work 5cm in K1, P1 rib ending with a RS row.

Next row (WS)(inc): Rib 7, (M1, rib 9) 14 times, M1, rib 7. (155sts)

Change to 3¼mm (US 3) needles and using the INTARSIA technique described on the information page, cont in patt from chart for back, which is worked entirely in st st beg with a K row, until chart row 228 completed.

Shape shoulders and back neck

Next row: Cast off 17 sts, patt 48, turn leaving rem sts on a holder.
Work each side of neck separately.
Cast off 7 sts, patt to end.
Cast off 17 sts, patt to end.
Cast off 6 sts, patt to end.
Cast off rem 18 sts.
With RS facing rejoin yarns to rem sts, cast off centre 25 sts, patt to end.
Complete to match first side reversing shaping.

FRONT

Work as for back until chart row 198 completed ending with a WS row.

Shape front neck

Next row (RS): Patt 73, turn leaving rem sts on a holder.
Work each side of neck separately.
Cast off 3 sts at beg next row and 2 foll alt rows.
Dec 1 st at neck edge on next 7 rows and 5 foll alt rows. (52sts)
Cont without further shaping until chart row 228 completed ending with a WS row.

Shape shoulder

Cast off 17 sts at beg next row and foll alt row.
Work 1 row.
Cast off rem 18 sts.
With RS facing rejoin yarn to rem sts, cast off centre 9 sts, patt to end.
Complete to match first side reversing shaping.

SLEEVES (both alike)

Cast on 60 sts using 2¾mm (US 2) needles and yarn A, work 5cm in K1, P1 rib, ending with a RS row.

Next row (WS)(inc): Rib 10, (M1, rib 10) 4 times, M1, rib 10. (65sts)

Change to 3¼mm (US 3) needles and work from chart for sleeve until chart row 174 completed and AT THE SAME TIME, inc 1 st at each end of 3rd row and every foll 4th row to 145 sts.
Cast off loosely and evenly.

MAKING UP

Press all pieces as described on the information page.
Join right shoulder seam using back stitch.

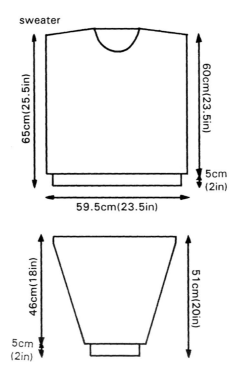

sweater

65cm(25.5in)

60cm(23.5in)

5cm (2in)

59.5cm(23.5in)

46cm(18in)

51cm(20in)

5cm (2in)

Neckband

With RS facing using 2¾mm (US 2) needles and yarn A, pick up and K 36 sts down left front neck, 9 sts across centre front, 36 sts up right front and 51 sts across back neck. (132sts)
Work 3cm in K1, P1 rib.
Change to yarn T, work 1 row in rib.
Cast off loosely and evenly using yarn T.
See information page for finishing instructions.

Waistcoat

Cast on 137(143) sts using 2¾mm (US 2) needles and yarn A and work 8 rows in st st beg with a K row.
Next row (RS): Using yarn J, K across row.
Next row: Using yarn J, K across row to form foldline.
Change to 3¼mm (US 3) needles and yarn A.
Beg at chart row 38 and using the INTARSIA techniques described on the information page, work in patt from chart for back which is worked entirely in st st beg with a K row and AT THE SAME TIME, inc 1 st at each end of 12th row and every foll 12th row to 149(155) sts.
Work until chart row 130 completed ending with a WS row.

Shape armhole

Cast off 4(5) sts at beg next 2 rows.
Dec 1 st at each end of next 11 rows and 2(3) foll alt rows. (115(117)sts)
Cont without further shaping until chart row 228 completed ending with a WS row.

Shape shoulder and back neck

Next row: Cast off 10(11) sts, patt 35 sts, turn, leaving rem sts on a holder.
Work each side separately.
Cast off 7 sts, patt to end.
Cast off 11 sts, patt to end.
Cast off 6 sts, patt to end.
Cast off rem 11 sts.
With RS facing rejoin yarns to rem sts, cast off centre 25 sts, patt to end.
Complete to match first side reversing shaping.

LOWER POCKET LINING (work 2)

Cast on 34 sts using 3¼mm (US 3) needles and yarn A.
Work 36 rows in st st beg with a K row.
Leave sts on holder.

BREAST POCKET LINING (work 1)

Cast on 26 sts using 3¼mm (US 3) needles and yarn A.
Work 18 rows in st st beg with a K row.
Leave sts on a holder.

LEFT FRONT

Cast on 2 sts using 3¼mm (US 3) needles and yarn A.
Beg with a K row, work 38 rows in st st in patt from chart for left front, shaping each side as indicated. (62sts)
Row 39(inc): Cast on 5(8) sts patt to last st, inc in last st. (68(71)sts)
Cont until chart row 130 completed, inc at side edge as indicated and AT THE SAME TIME, when row 78 has been completed, place lower pocket lining as folls: (74(77)sts)

Place lower pocket lining

Row 79: Patt 16(19) slip next 34 sts onto a holder and in place of these K across sts of first pocket lining, patt to end.

Shape armhole and front neck

Cast off 4(5) sts at beg next row, patt to last 2 sts, K2tog.
Work 1 row.
Dec 1 st at armhole edge on next 11 rows and 2(3) foll alt rows and AT THE SAME TIME, dec 1 st at neck edge on every 3rd row until chart row 154 completed.

Place breast pocket lining

Row 155: Keeping front neck shaping correct, patt 10(11) sts slip next 26 sts onto a holder and in place of these K across sts of breast pocket lining, patt to end.
Cont dec every 3rd row to 41(42) sts and then every foll 4th row to 32(33) sts.
Cont without further shaping until chart row 228 completed.

Shape shoulder

Cast off 10(11) sts at beg next row and 11 sts beg foll alt row.
Work 1 row.
Cast off rem 11 sts.

LOWER LEFT FRONT EDGES

With RS facing, using 2¾mm (US 2) needles and yarn J, pick up and knit 39 sts from centre front to lower point, 1 st at centre and 45 sts from point to side edge. (85sts)
Next row: K to form foldline.
Change to yarn A.
Next row: K 38, sl, K2tog, psso, K to end.
Next row: Purl to end.
Next row: K37, sl 1, k2tog, psso, K to end.
Cont dec at centre as before until 79 sts rem.
Cast off.

RIGHT FRONT

Work as given for left front omitting breast pocket, reversing all shaping, placing of lower pocket lining and foll chart for right front.

LOWER RIGHT FRONT EDGES

Work as given for left front, picking sts up as folls:
45 sts from side edge to point, 1 st at centre and 39 sts from point to centre front.

MAKING UP

Press all pieces as described on the information page.
Join together both shoulder seams using back stitch.

Front band (worked in one piece)

With RS facing using 2¾mm (US 2) circular needle and yarn W, pick up and knit 74 sts up right front edge to beg of front neck shaping, 96 sts to shoulder, 50 sts across back neck, 96 sts down left front to beg of shaping and 74 sts to lower edge. (390 sts)
Work 5 rows in patt from chart B working in st st beg with a purl row, rep the patt across row and making buttonholes on row 3 and 4 as folls:
Chart row 3 (buttonholes): Patt 2 sts, (cast off 2 sts, patt 8) 7 times, cast off 2, patt to end.
Chart row 4: Patt across row casting on 2 sts over those cast off on previous row.
Next row (RS): Using yarn W only, K to end.
Next row (WS): K to form fold line.
Change to yarn A and work 7 rows in st st beg with a K row, working buttonholes to correspond with those worked previously on rows 3 and 4.

Armhole edging (both alike)

With RS facing and using 2¾mm (US 2) needles and yarn W, pick up and K 184 sts along armhole edge.
Next row (WS): Purl using yarn W.
Next row: (K2 B, K2 L) to end.
Next row: (P2 L, P2 B) to end.
Next row: Knit using yarn W.
Next row (WS): Purl using yarn W, to form fold line.
Change to yarn A and work 6 rows in st st beg with a K row.
Cast off very loosely.

Lower pocket tops

With RS facing slip 34 sts from holder onto a 2¾mm (US 2) needle. *
Knit across row using yarn W.
Next row: (P2 B, P2 L) to last 2 sts, P2 B.
Next row: (K2B, K2 L) to last 2 sts, P2 B.
Next row: P using yarn W.
Next row (RS): Purl using yarn W, to form foldline.
Change to yarn A and work 6 rows in st st beg with a P row.
Cast off loosely. **

Breast pocket top

With RS facing slip 26 sts from holder onto a 2¾mm (US 2) needle.
Work as for lower pocket tops from * to **.
See information page for finishing instructions.

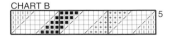

CHART B

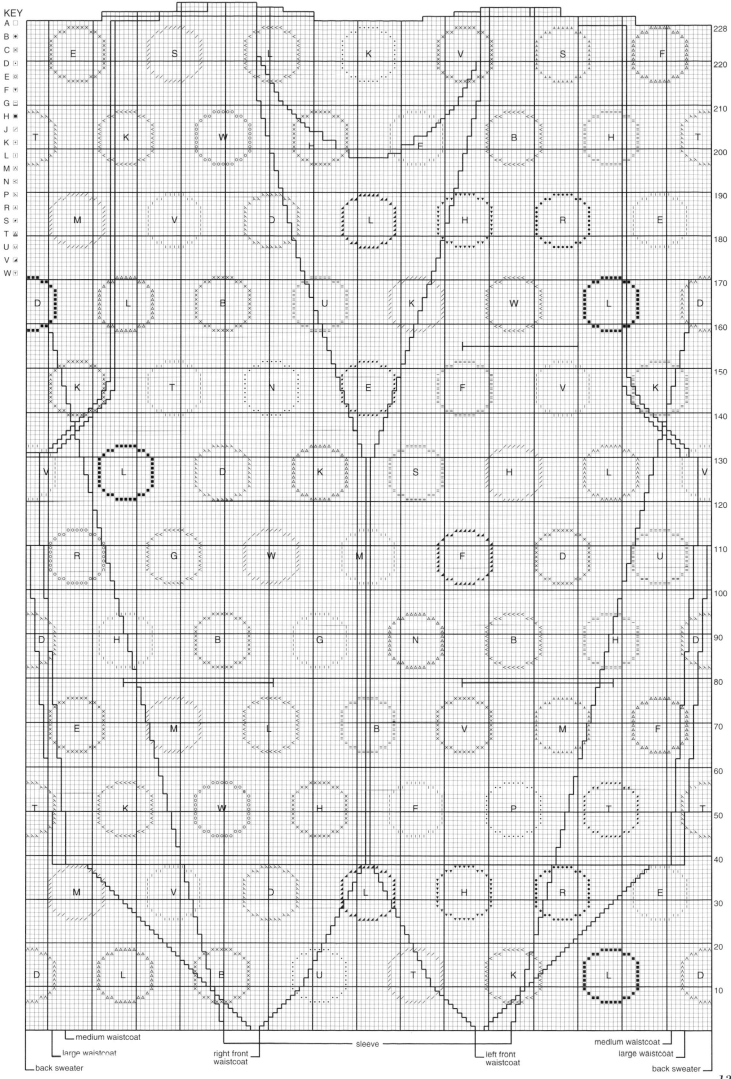

KEY
A □
B •
C ⊠
D ⊡
E ⊙
F ▼
G ⊟
H ▣
J ▥
K ⊞
L ▦
M ◩
N ▨
P ▧
R ▩
S ▤
T △
U ▪
V ◪
W ▽

228
220
210
200
190
180
170
160
150
140
130
120
110
100
90
80
70
60
50
40
30
20
10

└ medium waistcoat
└ large waistcoat
└ back sweater

right front
waistcoat

sleeve

left front
waistcoat

medium waistcoat ┘
large waistcoat ┘

back sweater ┘

131

Frenchie

KIM HARGREAVES

YARNS
Rowan Chunky Chenille

| s | m | l |

SWEATER

8   8   9   x   100gm
(photographed in Raspberry 377)

JACKET

9   10   10   x   100gm
(photographed in Serge 378)

NEEDLES
1 pair 4mm (no 8) (US 6)
1 pair 5mm (no 6) (US 8)

BUTTONS
Jacket only–5

TENSION
16 sts and 24 rows to 10cm measured over stocking stitch using 5mm (US 8) needles

Special abbreviation
MB = make bobble, (K1, P1, K1, P1, K1) into next st, turn K5, turn K5 then slip 2nd, 3rd, 4th and 5th st over 1st.

Note: Getting the tension correct when knitting chenille can be difficult. Knitters often get a bar between each stitch making the knitting too open. This is because the pile does not allow the yarn to re-adjust itself on the needles, so the stitch has to be created in a more precise way. If you run your fingers tips down a length of chenille you will feel the pile is smoother one way than the other, so when knitting you will find it much easier if the pile is going away from your knitting rather than towards it and also unlike knitting fairisle where you spread the stitches out to keep the work elastic, when knitting with chenille keep the stitch just knitted close to the tip of the right hand needle and then work the next stitch close up to it.

Sweater and jacket
BACK
Cast on 84(88:94) sts using 4mm (US 6) needles.
Sweater only
Work 5cm in K2, P2 rib ending with a WS row.
Change to 5mm (US 8) needles and cont in st st beg with a K row until work measures 46(48.5:51)cm from cast on edge ending with a WS row.
Jacket only
Work 5cm in garter st ie knit every row, ending with a WS row.
Change to 5mm (US 8) needles and cont in st st beg with a K row until work measures 7(8.5:10)cm from cast on edge ending with a WS row.
Shape sides
Dec 1 st at each end of next row and every foll 6th row to 68(72:78)sts.

Cont without further shaping until work measures 30(31.5:33.5)cm from cast on edge ending with a WS row.
Inc 1 st at each end of next row and every foll 4th row to 84(88:94)sts.
Cont without further shaping until work measures 46(48.5:51)cm from cast on edge ending with a WS row.

Sweater & Jacket
Shape armhole
Next row (RS): Cast off 5 sts at beg next 2 rows.
Cast off 2 sts at beg next 4 rows.
Dec 1 st at each end of next row and every foll alt row to 56(60:66) sts.
Cont without further shaping until work measures 22.75cm from beg armhole shaping ending with a WS row.

Shape shoulder and back neck
Sweater only
Cast off 4(4:5) sts at beg next 2 rows.
Cast off 4(5:6) sts, knit 8(9:10) sts, turn and leave rem sts on a holder.
Work each side of neck separately.
Cast off 4 sts, P to end.
Cast off rem 4(5:6) sts.
With RS facing rejoin yarn to rem sts, cast off centre 24 sts, K to end.
Complete to match first side reversing shaping.
Jacket only
Cast off 5(6:7) sts at beg next 2 rows.
Cast off 5(6:7) sts, knit 10(10:11) sts, turn and leave rem sts on a holder.
Work each side of neck separately.
Cast off 4 sts, purl to end.
Cast off rem 6(6:7) sts.
With RS facing rejoin yarn to rem sts, cast off centre 16 sts, knit to end.
Complete to match first side reversing shaping.

Sweater & Jacket
SLEEVES (both alike)
Cast on 40 sts using 5mm (US 8) needles.
Work in st st beg with a K row until work measures 7.5cm from cast on edge ending with a WS row.
Inc sides by inc 1 st at each end of next row and every foll 10th row to 56 sts.
Cont without further shaping until work measures 43cm or length required from cast on edge ending with a WS row.

Shape sleeve head
Cast off 5 sts at beg next 2 rows.
Work 2 rows.
Dec 1 st at each end of next row and 6 foll 4th rows and 1 foll alt row. (30sts)
Dec 1 st at each end of next 3 rows.
Cast off 4 sts at beg next 2 rows.
Cast off rem 16sts.

Sweater only
FRONT
Work as given for sweater back until front is 20 rows shorter than back to shoulder shaping ending with a WS row.
Shape front neck
Next row (RS): Knit 22(24:27) sts, turn and leave rem sts on a holder.

Work each side of neck separately.
Cast off 2 sts, P to end.
Dec 1 st at neck edge on next 4 rows and 4 foll alt rows.
(12(14:17)sts)
Cont without further shaping until front matches back to shoulder ending with a WS row.
Shape shoulder
Cast off 4(4:5) sts at beg next row and 4(5:6) beg foll alt row.
Work 1 row.
Cast off rem 4(5:6) sts.
With RS facing rejoin yarn to rem sts, cast off centre 12 sts, K to end.
Complete to match first side reversing shaping.

Jacket only
POCKET LINING (make 2)
Cast on 20 sts using 5mm (US 8) needles and work 11.5(12.5:13.5)cm in st st beg with a K row end with a P row.
Leave sts on a holder.

LEFT FRONT
Cast on 42(44:47) sts using 4mm (US 6) needles

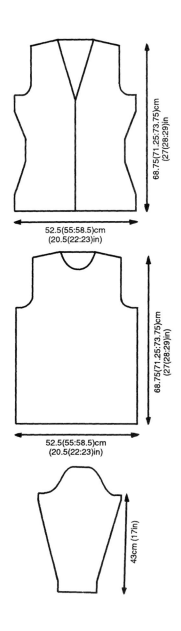

68.75(71.25:73.75)cm
(27(28:29)in)

52.5(55:58.5)cm
(20.5(22:23)in)

68.75(71.25:73.75)cm
(27(28:29)in)

52.5(55:58.5)cm
(20.5(22:23)in)

43cm (17in)

and work 5cm in garter st as given for back ending with a WS row.
Change to 5mm (US 8) needles and cont in st st beg with a K row until work measures 7(8.5:10)cm from cast on edge ending with a WS row.

Shape side edge

Dec 1 st at side edge on next row and every foll 6th row to 34(36:39) sts and AT THE SAME TIME when work measures 16.5(17.5:18.5)cm from cast on edge place pocket as folls:

Place pocket

Next row (RS): Keeping side dec correct K9(11:13) sts, slip next 20 sts onto a holder and replace with 20 sts of first pocket lining, K to end. (34(36:39)sts)
Cont without further shaping until work measures 30(31.5:33.5)cm from cast on edge ending with a WS row.
Inc 1 st at side edge on next row and every foll 4th row to 42(44:47) sts.
Cont without further shaping until front matches back to armhole shaping ending with a WS row.

Shape armhole and front neck

Cast off 5 sts at beg next row.
Work 1 row.
Dec 1 st at neck edge on next row and every foll 4th row to 16(18:21) sts and AT THE SAME TIME shape armhole as given for back as folls:
Cast off 2 sts at beg next row and foll alt row.
Dec 1 st at armhole edge on next row and every foll alt row to 16(18:21) sts.
Cont without further shaping until front matches back to shoulder shaping ending with a WS row.

Shape shoulder

Cast off 5(6:7) sts at beg next row and 5(6:7) beg foll alt row.
Work 1 row.
Cast off rem 6(6:7) sts.

RIGHT FRONT

Work as given for left front reversing all shaping and placing of pocket.

MAKING UP

PRESS all pieces as described on the information page.

Sweater

Join right shoulder seam using back stitch.

Neckband

With RS facing using 4mm (US 6) needles, pick up and K 25 sts down left front neck, 12 sts across centre front, 25 sts, up right front neck and 32 sts across back neck. (94sts)

Work 20cm in K2, P2 rib.
Cast off in rib.

Cuffs

Cast on 35 sts very loosely using 5mm (US 8) needles.
Knit 2 rows.
Row 1 (bobble)(RS): K2, (MB, K1), to last st, K1.
Row 2: Knit.
Row 3 (bobble)(RS): K3, (MB, K1) to last 2 sts, K2.
Row 4: Knit.
Rep these four rows 3 times more.
Knit 2 rows.
Cast off loosely.

Jacket

Join both shoulder seams using back stitch.

Buttonhole band

With RS facing and using 4mm (US 6) needles pick up and knit 67(71:75) sts up right front from cast on edge to beg front neck shaping.
Next row (WS): Knit.
Next row (RS)(buttonhole): K2, [K2tog, (yon) twice, K2tog, K11(12:13)] 4 times, Ktog, (yon) twice, K2tog, K1.
Next row (cast off): Cast off knitwise working into back of each loop made on previous row.

Button band

Work as given for buttonhole band omitting buttonholes.

Cuffs

Work as given for cuffs for sweater.

Collar

Cast on 93 sts very loosely using 5mm (US 8) needles.
Mark centre stitch with a coloured thread.
Knit 2 rows.
Row 3 (bobble)(RS): K2, (MB, K1) to last st, K1.
Row 4 (dec): K2tog, K to last 2 sts, K2tog. (91sts)
Row 5 (bobble)(RS)(dec): K2tog, (MB, K1) to last 3 sts, MB, K2tog. (89sts)
Row 6 (dec): Work as row 4. (87sts)
Row 7 (bobble)(RS)(dec): K2tog, K1, (MB, K1) to last 2 sts, K2tog. (85sts)
Row 8 (dec): K2tog, K to 1 st before marked stitch, K3tog, K to last 2 sts, K2tog. (81sts)
Keeping bobble patt correct cont dec 1 st at each end of every row until 7 rows of bobbles in all completed ending with a RS row. (67sts)
Next row (WS)(dec): Work as given for row 8. (63sts)
Keeping bobble patt correct cont dec 1 st at each end of every row until 11 rows of bobbles in all completed ending with a RS row. (49sts)
This completes the bobble pattern.
Knit 3 rows dec at each end of each row. (43sts)
Cast off very loosely.

Pocket tops

With RS facing using 4mm (US 6) needles slip sts from holder onto left-hand needle and work 6 rows in garter st.
Cast off knitwise.

Belt

Cast on 2 sts using 4mm (US 6) needles and work in garter st shaping end as folls:
Inc 1 st at beg of every row to 7 sts.
Cont without further shaping until belt measures 125cm from cast on edge.
Dec 1 st at beg every row to 2 sts.
Cast off.
Make 2 tassels and attach to both ends.
See information page for finishing instructions.
Slip stitch cast off edge of collar neatly into place starting and ending at top of front bands and matching centre of collar with centre back neck.
Fold cuff in half RS together and join selvedges together using a back stitch seam.
With WS of sleeve and RS of cuff facing join cast on edge of cuff to cast on edge of sleeve using a back stitch seam.
Turn cuff to RS.

Foolish Virgins

KAFFE FASSETT

YARN

Rowan Cotton Glace

A	Black 727	4	x	50gm
B	Gentian 743	2	x	50gm
C	Parade 430	1	x	50gm
D	Corn 791	2	x	50gm
E	Blood Orange 445	1	x	50gm
F	Provence 744	2	x	50gm
G	Sky 749	2	x	50gm
H	Petunia 789	2	x	50gm
J	Terracotta 786	1	x	50gm
M	Pear 780	1	x	50gm
N	Dijon 739	2	x	50gm
O	Matador 742	2	x	50gm
V	Nightshade 746	1	x	50gm
X	Poppy 741	3	x	50gm

NEEDLES

1 pair 3¼mm (no 10) (US 3)
1 pair 3¾mm (no 9) (US 5)
3.00 crochet hook

CLASP FASTENERS

8

TENSION

23 sts and 28 rows to 10cm measured over patterned stocking stitch using 3¾mm (US 5) needles

BACK

Cast on 140 sts using 3¼mm (US 3) needles and yarn B.
Work 8 rows in st st beg with a K row.
Purl one row to form hemline.
Next row (inc): P3, (inc in next st, P11) 11 times, inc in next st, P4. (152sts)
Change to 3¾mm (US 5) needles and using the INTARSIA technique described on the information page work 140 rows in patt from chart for back which is worked entirely in sts st beg with a K row.
Place markers at each end of rows 7 and 43 for pocket position.

Shape shoulders

Cast off 18 sts at beg of next 6 rows.
Cast off rem 44 sts,

LEFT FRONT

Cast on 70 sts using 3¼mm (US 3) needles and yarn B.
Work 8 rows in st st beg with a K row.
Purl one row to form hemline.
Next row (inc): P5, (inc in next st, P11) 5 times, inc in next st, P4, (76sts)
Change to 3¾mm (US 5) needles and work in patt from chart for left front until chart row 121 completed, placing markers at beg of rows 7 and 43 for pocket position.

Shape front neck

Cast off 5 sts at beg of next row, patt to end.

Work one row.
Dec 1 st at neck edge on next 17 rows. (54 sts)

Shape shoulder

Cast off 18 sts at beg of next row and foll alt row.
Work one row.
Cast off rem 18 sts.

RIGHT FRONT

Work as given for left front reversing all shaping and marking side edge for pocket positions.

SLEEVES (both alike)

Cast on 47 sts using 3¼mm (US 3) needles and yarn B.
Work 8 rows in st st beg with a K row.
Purl one row to form hemline.
Next row (inc): P3, (inc in next st, K7) 5 times, inc in next st, P3, (53 sts)
Change to 3¾mm (US 5) needles and work 121 rows in patt from chart for sleeves. AT THE SAME TIME, shape sides by inc 1 st at each end of 5th row and every foll 3rd row until there are 131 sts. Please note that the top right-hand edge of sleeve is shown as a sleeve extension at the side of the chart.
Row 122: 4J, (3A, 3J) 21 times, 1J.
Row 123: 2J, (1A, 1J) 64 times, 1J.
Row 124: Work as row 122.
Cast off loosely and evenly using yarn A.

COLLAR

Cast on 100 sts using 3¼mm (US 3) needles and yarn A.
Then, joining in and breaking off colours as required work 6 rows in patt from chart for collar.

Shape collar

Cast off 4 sts at beg of next 14 rows.
Cast off rem 44 sts.

MAKING UP

Press all pieces as described on the information page.

Right pocket lining

With RS facing, 3¾mm (US 5) needles and yarn A, pick up and K 34 sts between pocket markers on right side back edge.
Purl one row.
Cont in st st, cast on 5 sts at beg of next row. (39sts)
Then dec 1 st at beg of next row and every foll alt row until 24 sts rem.
Cast off.

Left pocket lining

With RS facing, 3¾mm (US 5) needles and yarn A, pick up and K 34 sts between markers on left side back edge.
Work in st st beg with a P row, cast on 5 sts at beg of next row. (39 sts)
Then dec 1 st at beg of next row and every foll alt row until 24 sts rem.
Cast off.

Pocket edgings (both alike)

With RS facing, 3¼mm (US 3) needles and yarn A, pick up and K 34 sts evenly between pocket markers on front side edge.
Knit one row to form foldline.
Work 4 rows in st st beg with a K row.

Cast off loosely and evenly.
Join both shoulder seams using backstitch.
Place markers 28cm below shoulder seam on back and front.
Sew sleeve top between markers using backstitch.
Join sleeve seams and side seams above and below pocket opening.
Fold pocket edgings onto WS of work and catch down.
Catch down pocket linings to WS of front.
Fold all edgings to WS at hemline and slip stitch into place.

Front bands (both alike)

With RS facing, 3¼mm (US 3) needles and yarn B, pick up and K 92 sts evenly along front edge.
Knit one row to form hemine.
Change to 3¼mm (US 3) needles and work 8 rows in st st beg with a K row.
Cast off.
Fold front edgings to WS at hemline and slip stitch into place.
Sew collar into position.

Collar edging

With RS facing and 3.00 crochet hook, join yarn B to collar edge, work 4ch, ** 1dc into next 2 sts, 4ch; rep from ** to end finishing with 2dc, turn and work 5 dc into each 4 ch space to end.
Fasten off.
Sew clasp fasteners into psotion.
Press seams.

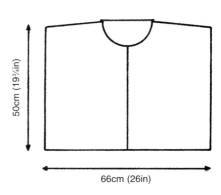

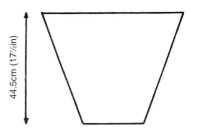

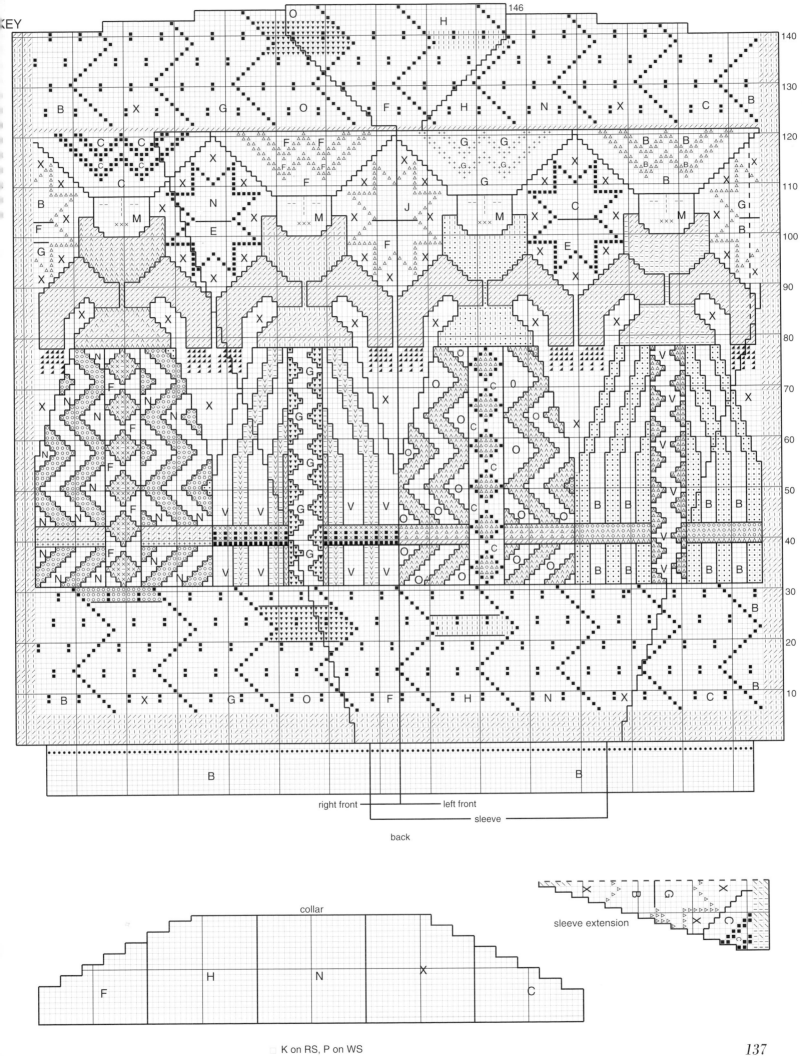

right front — left front

sleeve

back

collar

sleeve extension

□ K on RS, P on WS

• P on RS, K on WS

137

Chequer Flowers

SASHA KAGAN

YARN

Rowan Cotton Glace, Fine Chenille, and 4 ply Cotton

A	Glace	Ecru	725	9	x	50gm
B	F.Chen	Parched	415	1	x	50gm
C	Glace	Shrimp	783	1	x	50gm
D	Glace	Terracotta	786	1	x	50gm
E	Glace	Candy Floss	747	1	x	50gm
F	4 ply Cot.	Straw	110	1	x	50gm
G	Glace	Bleached	726	1	x	50gm
H	Glace	Pear	780	1	x	50gm
J	Glace	Oyster	730	1	x	50gm

NEEDLES

1 pair 3mm (no 11) (US 3)
1 pair 3¾mm (no 9) (US 5)
Circular needle (100cm long) 3mm (no 11) (US 3)
Circular needle (100cm long) 3¾mm (no 9) (US 5)

Buttons

6

TENSION

26 sts and 32 rows to 10cm measured over patterned stocking stitch using 3¾mm (US 5) needles

BACK AND FRONTS (one piece)

Cast on 252 sts using 3mm (US 3) circular needle and yarn A.
Work 3cm in K1, P1 twisted rib (i.e. K into back of every K st).
Change to 3¾mm (US 5) circular needle and using the INTARISA technique described on the information page work in patt from chart which is worked in a mixture of st st and reversed st st, starting and ending where indicated and rep the 56 patt sts 4 times across row.
Work 56 rows in patt.

Divide for right front

Patt 56 sts, turn and work on these sts for right front using ordinary needles. Leave rem sts on circular needle.
Keeping patt correct work 19 rows, thus ending with a WS row.

Shape front neck

Cast off 6 sts at beg of next row and 5 sts at beg of foll alt row.
Work one row, then cast off 2 sts at beg of next row and 3 foll alt rows.
Work one row, then dec 1 st at beg of next row and 4 foll alt rows.
Work 3 rows, then dec 1 st at beg of next row and 3 foll 4th rows. (28sts)
Work 8 rows without further shaping, thus ending with a RS row.
(N.B. Maintain continuity of checks but do not work any more Fair Isle Motifs after 2nd rep of 56 row patt)

Shape shoulder

Cast off 14 sts at beg of next row, patt to end.
Work one row.
Cast off rem 14 sts.
With RS facing, rejoin yarn to rem sts, cast off next 14 sts, patt 112 sts, turn and work on these sts only for back. Leave rem sts on circular needle for left front.
Work 63 rows in patt thus ending with a RS row.
(N.B. Maintain continuity of checks but do not work any more Fair Isle motifs after 2nd rep of 56 row pattern).

Shape shoulders

Cast off 14 sts at beg of next 4 rows.
Cast off rem 56 sts.
With RS facing rejoin yarn to rem sts, cast off first 14 sts, patt to end.
Complete left front to match right front, reversing all shaping and maintaining continuity of patt as set for left front.

SLEEVE (both alike)

Cast on 70 sts using 3mm (US 3) needles and yarn C.
Work one row in K1, P1 twisted rib.
Change to yarn A and cont in twisted rib until work measures 3cm from beg ending with a RS row.

Next row (WS)(inc): Rib 3, (M1, rib 5) 13 times, M1, rib 2. (84sts)
Change to 3¾mm (US 5) needles and working between markers for sleeve work 70 rows in patt from chart and AT THE SAME TIME, shape sides by inc 1 st at each end of 3rd row and every foll 6th row until there are 104 sts.
Take extra sts into patt as they occur.
Cast off loosely and evenly.

BUTTONHOLE BAND

With RS facing, 3mm (US 3) needles and yarn A, pick up and K 74 sts evenly along right front edge.
Work 3 rows in K1, P1 twisted rib.
Next row (buttonholes): Rib 3, (cast off 2, rib 11) 5 times, cast off 2, rib 4.
Next row: Work across row in rib, casting on 2 sts in place of those cast off on previous row.
Work a further 2 rows in twisted rib.
Change to yarn C, rib one row, then cast off using yarn C.

BUTTON BAND

Work as given for buttonhole band omitting buttonholes.

MAKING UP

Press all pieces as described on the information page.
Join both shoulder seams using backstitch.

Neckband

With RS facing, 3mm (US 3) circular needle and yarn A, and beg halfway across top edge of buttonhole band, pick up and K 4 sts from buttonhole band, 61 sts up right side front neck, 56 sts across back neck, 61 sts down left side front neck and 4 sts across top of button band ending halfway across top edge of band. (186 sts)
Work 7 rows in K1, P1 twisted rib.
Change to yarn C and work one row in rib.
Cast off loosely and evenly in rib.
Sew sleeve top into armhole using backstitch.
Join sleeve seams.
Sew on buttons to correspond with buttonholes.
Press seams.

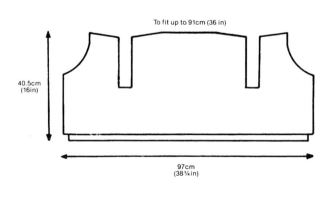

To fit up to 91cm (36 in)

40.5cm (16in)

97cm (38¼in)

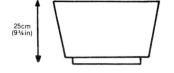

25cm (9¾in)

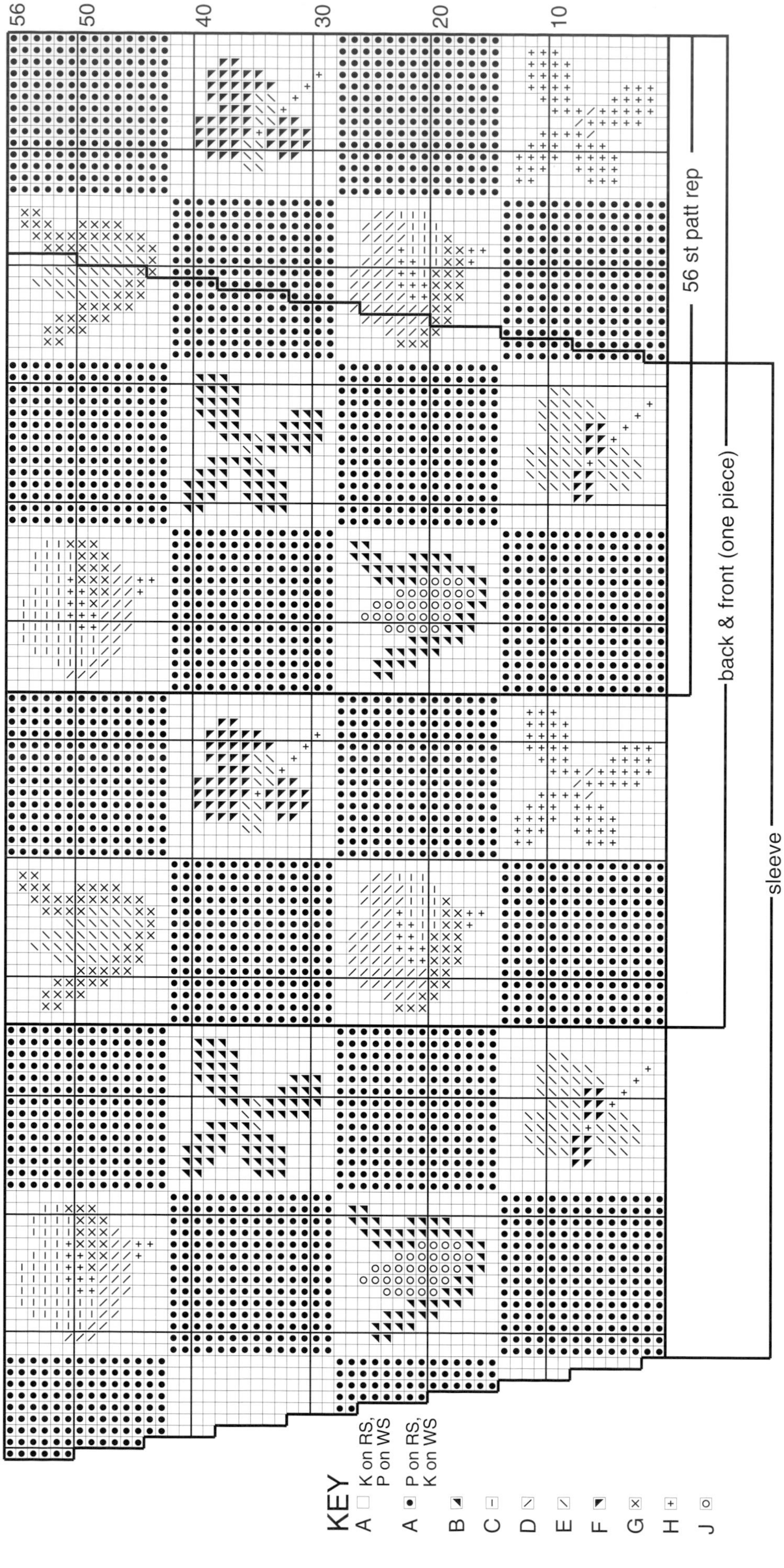

56
50
40
30
20
10

56 st patt rep

back & front (one piece)

sleeve

KEY
A □ K on RS, P on WS
A ● P on RS, K on WS
B ◤
C │
D ╱
E ╲
F ◥
G ✕
H +
J ○

Children's Guernseys
KIM HARGREAVES

YARN
Rowan Cotton Glace

1st	2nd	3rd	4th	5th	6th	7th		
5	6	7	8	9	10	11	x	50gm

NEEDLES
1 pair 3mm (no 11) (US 3)
1 pair 3¾mm (no 9) (US 5)

TENSION
24 sts and 32 rows to 10cm measures over textured pattern using 3¾mm (US 5) needles

Note: This pattern is a basic pattern which can be knitted as a plain guernsey, with a Star motif or with wide rib stitch detail.

BACK
Cast on 80(86:92:98:104:110:116) sts using 3mm (US 3) needles.
Knit 8 rows.
Change to 3¾mm (US 5) needles.
Shirting design
Row 1 (RS): Knit to end.
Row 2: K4, P0(3:6:9:12:1:4), (K2, P12), 5(5:5:5:5:7:7) times, K2, P0(3:6:9:12:1:4), K4.
Rep these 2 rows 4(4:4:5:5:6:6) times more.
Next row (RS): Knit to end.
Next row: P4(7:10:13:2:5:8), (K2, P12), 5(5:5:5:7:7:7) times, P4(7:10:13:2:5:8).
These 2 rows set the patt for the shirting design and are repeated throughout.
Star or plain design
Row 1 (RS): Knit to end.
Row 2: K4, P to last 4 sts, K4.
Rep these 2 rows 4(4:4:5:5:6:6) times more.
All versions
Keeping patt correct for shirting design and working in st st for star or plain design cont until work measures 38.5(41:43.5:46:48.5:51:53.5) from cast on edge ending with a WS row.
Shape shoulders and back neck
Work 28(30:32:34:36:38:40) sts, turn leaving rem sts on a holder.
Work each side of neck separately.
Cast off 4 sts patt to end.
Leave rem sts on a holder.
With RS facing rejoin yarn to rem sts, cast off centre 24(26:28:30:32:34:36) sts, work to end.
Complete to match first side reversing shaping.

FRONT
Shirting or plain design only
Work as for back until front measures 35(37.5:39.5:42:44.5:46:48.5) cm from cst on edge ending with a WS row.
Star design only
Work as for back until front measures 13(14.5:16:17.5:19:20.5:22)cm from cast on edge.
Place star motif
Work 61 rows in patt from chart.

Cont as for back until front measures 35(37.5:39.5:42:44.5:46:48.5)cm from cast on edge ending with a WS row.
All versions
Shape front neck
Work 32(34:36:38:40:42:44) sts, turn leave rem sts on a holder.
Work each side of neck separately.
Cast off 3 sts at beg of next row, work to end.
Dec 1 st at neck edge on next 3 rows and 2 foll alt rows.
Cont without further shaping until front matches back to shoulder ending with a WS row.
Shape shoulders
Leave rem sts on a holder.
With RS facing slip centre 16(18:20:22:24:26:28) sts onto a holder, rejoin yarn and work to end.
Complete to match first side reversing shaping.

SLEEVES (both alike)
Cast on 42(44:48:48:52:52:56) sts using 3mm (US 3) needles.
Knit 8 rows.
Change to 3¾mm (US 5) needles.
Shirting design only
Row 1 (RS): Knit across row inc 1 st at each end of row. (44(46:50:50:54:54:58) sts.
Row 2: P0(1:3:3:5:5:7), (K2, P12) 3 times, K2, P0(1:3:3:5:5:7).
These 2 rows set the patt.
Keeping patt correct inc 1 st at each end of 3rd row and every foll 4th row to 70(76:82:88:94:100:106) sts, taking extra sts into patt as they occur.
Cont without further shaping until sleeve measures 20.5(23:25.5:28:30.5:33:35.5) cm from cast on edge ending with a WS row.
Cast off loosely and evenly.
Star and plain design only
Cont as for shirting design working in st st throughout.

MAKING UP
Press all pieces as described on the information page.
Join right shoulder seam by casting off sts together on the RS.
Neckband
With RS facing, using 3mm (US 3) needles, pick up and knit 14(16:16:16:18:18:18) sts down left front neck, 16(18:20:22:24:26:28) sts across centre front, 14(16:16:16:18:18:18) sts up right front neck and 32(34:36:38:40:42:44) sts across back neck. (76(84:88:92:100:104:108)sts)
Knit 6(6:6:6:8:8:8) rows.
Cast off evenly.
Join left shoulder seam as for right shoulder seam.
See information page for finishing instructions, leaving garter stitch at side seams open to form vents.

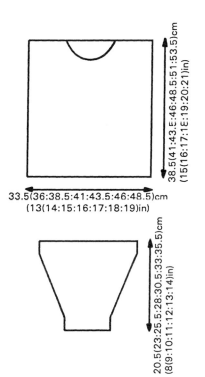

33.5(36:38.5:41:43.5:46:48.5)cm
(13(14:15:16:17:18:19)in)

38.5(41:43.5:46:48.5:51:53.5)cm
(15(16:17:17£:19:20:21)in)

20.5(23:25.5:28:30.5:33:35.5)cm
(8(9:10:11:12:13:14)in)

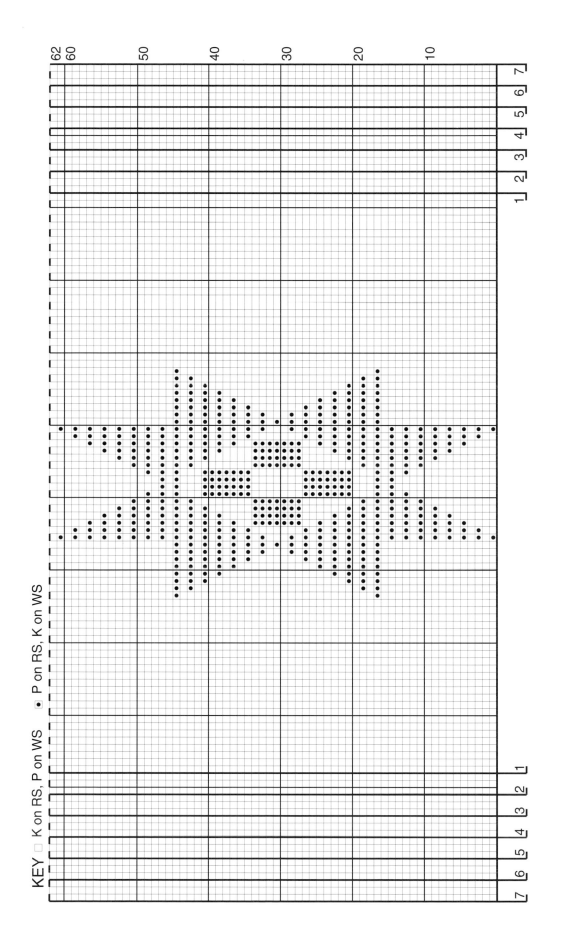

KEY ☐ K on RS, P on WS   ▣ P on RS, K on WS

Heidi

KIM HARGREAVES

YARNS

Rowan Cotton Glace

A	Shrimp	783	4	x	50gm
B	Oyster	730	2	x	50gm
C	Hazel	788	2	x	50gm
D	Lilac wine	440	2	x	50gm
E	Mint	748	2	x	50gm
F	Provence	744	2	x	50gm
G	Dijon	739	2	x	50gm
H	Pear	780	2	x	50gm

NEEDLES

1 pair 2¾mm (no 12) (US 2) needles
1 pair 3¼mm (no 10) (US 3) needles

BUTTONS

5

TENSION

23 sts and 32 rows to 10cm measured over patterned stocking stitch using 3¼mm (US 3) needles

Pattern note: The large dot indicates the texture pattern (P on RS, K on WS) and is always worked in the same colour as used in the appropriate square.

BACK

Cast on 116 sts using 3¼mm (US 3) needles and yarn A.
Joining in and breaking off colours as required work 74 rows in patt from chart for back using the intarsia technique described on the information page, ending with a WS row.

Shape armhole

Cast off 4 sts at beg next 2 rows. (108sts)
Cont in patt from chart until chart row 146 completed ending with a WS row.

Shape shoulders and back neck

Cast off 12 sts at beg next 2 rows.
Cast off 12 sts, patt 17, turn and leave rem sts on a holder.
Work each side of neck separately.
Cast off 4 sts, patt to end.

Cast off rem 13 sts.
With RS facing rejoin yarns to rem sts, cast off 26 sts, patt to end.
Complete to match first side reversing all shaping.

LEFT FRONT

Cast on 58 sts using 3¼mm (US 3) needles and yarn A.
Work 74 rows in patt from chart for left front ending with a WS row.

Shape armhole

Cast off 4 sts at beg next row. (54sts)
Cont without further shaping until chart row 80 completed ending with a WS row.

Shape front neck

Keeping patt correct dec 1 st at end of next row and every foll 4th until 37 sts rem and then for childs size only every foll 4th row to 34 sts. (37sts)
Work until chart row 146 completed.

Shape shoulder

Cast off 12 sts at beg next row and 12 foll alt row.
Work 1 row.
Cast off rem 13 sts.

RIGHT FRONT

Work as given for left front following chart for right front and reversing all shaping.

SLEEVES (both alike)

Cast on 52 sts using 2¾mm (US 2) needles and yarn A.
Work 10 rows in moss st.
Change to 3¼mm (US 3) needles and work 144 rows in patt from chart for sleeve and AT THE SAME TIME shape sides by inc 1 st at each end of 3rd row and every foll 4th row to 74 sts and then every foll 6th row to 104 sts.
Cast off loosely and evenly.

MAKING UP

PRESS all pieces as described on the information page.
Join both shoulder seams using backstitch.

Lace edging

Cast on 12 sts using 3¼mm (US 3) needles and yarn A, work lace edging as folls:
Row 1 (WS): Sl1, K3, yon, K2tog, K2, yon,
K2tog, yon, K2. (13sts)
Row 2: Yon, K2tog, K11.
Row 3: Sl1, K2, (yon, K2tog) twice, K2, yon, K2tog, yon, K2. (14sts)
Row 4: Yon, K2tog, K12.
Row 5: Sl1, K3, (yon, K2tog) twice, K2, yon, K2tog, yon, K2. (15sts)
Row 6: Yon, K2tog, K13.
Row 7: Sl1, K2, (yon, K2tog) 3 times, K2, yon, K2tog, yon, K2. (16sts)
Row 8: Yon, K2tog, K14.
Row 9: Sl1, K2, (K2tog, yon) twice, K2, K2tog, (yon K2tog) twice, K1. (15sts)
Row 10: Yon, K2tog, K13.
Row 11: Sl1, K1, (K2tog, yon) twice, K2, K2tog, (yon K2tog) twice, K1.(14sts)
Row 12: Yon, K2tog, K12.
Row 13: Sl1, K2, K2tog, yon, K2, K2tog, (yon, K2tog) twice, K1. (13sts)
Row 14: Yon, K2tog, K11.
Row 15: Sl1, K1, K2tog, yon, K2, K2tog, (yon, K2tog) twice, K1. (12sts)
Row 16: Yon, K2tog, K10.
Rep rows 1–16 until edging is long enough to fit around bottom edge of garment, leave sts on a holder.
Slip st into place, adjust length, cast off.

Button band

Cast on 5 sts using 2¾mm (US 2) needles and yarn A.
Work in moss st until band fits neatly when slightly stretched up left front from bottom of edging to shoulder and across to centre back neck.
Slip stitch into place adjusting length if necessary.
Cast off.
Mark position of 5 buttons, the 1st to come 1cm up from cast on edge, the 5th 1.5cm below start of front neck shaping, remainder spaced evenly between.

Buttonhole band

Work as given for button band with the addition of 5 buttonholes worked to correspond with markers as folls:
Buttonhole row (RS): Patt 2, yon, patt 2tog, patt 1.
Join bands together at centre back neck.
See information page for finishing instructions.

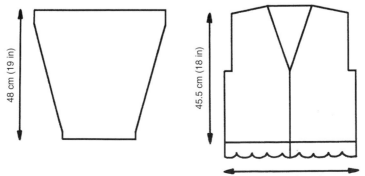

KEY

Using the colour in square

☐ K on RS, P on WS

▣ P on RS, K on WS

right front — left front

sleeve

146

Core

KIM HARGREAVES

YARN

Rowan Denim

s	m	l		
13	14	15	x	50gm

(photographed in Nashville 225)

NEEDLES

1 pair 3¼mm (no 10) (US 3)
1 pair 4mm (no 8) (US 6)

BUTTONS

9

TENSION (before washing)

20 sts and 28 rows to 10cm measured over stocking stitch using 4mm (US 6) needles

Note: Denim will shrink in length when washed for the first time, allowances have been made in this pattern for shrinkage, see size diagram for after washing measurements.

BACK

Cast on 81(85:89) sts using 3¼mm (US 3) needles and work in moss st setting sts as folls:
Row 1 (RS): P1 (K1, P1) to end.
Row 2: Work as given for row 1.
Rep these 2 rows until 10 rows in all completed ending with a WS row.
Change to 4mm (US 6) needles.

Small & large sizes only
Row 1 (RS): P21(23), K2, P1, K33(37), P1, K2, P21(23).
Row 2: K21(23), P2, K1, P33(37), K1, P2, K21(23).
These 2 rows set the stitches.
Rep these 2 rows 3(4) times more.
Next row (RS)(inc): P21(23), K2, P1, M1, K33(37), M1, P1, K2, P21(23). (83(91)sts)
Next row: K21(23), P2, K1, P35(39), K1, P2, K21(23).
Work 6(8) rows on sts as set.
Next row (RS)(inc): P21(23), K2, P1, M1, K35(39), M1, P1, K2, P21(23). (85(93)sts)
Work 7(9) rows on sts as set.
Inc as before at each side of centre st st panel, on next row and 5 foll 8th(10th) rows. (97(105)sts)

Medium size only
Row 1 (RS): P22, K2, P1, K35, P1, K2, P22.
Row 2: K22, P2, K1, P35, K1, P2, K22.
These 2 rows set the stitches.
Rep these 2 rows 3 times more then 1st row again.
Next row (WS)(inc): K22, P2, K1, M1p, P35, M1p, K1, P2, K22. (87sts)
Next row: P22, K2, P1, K37, P1, K2, P22.
Work 7 rows on sts as set.
Next row (RS)(inc): P22, K2, P1, M1, K37, M1, P1, K2, P22. (89sts)
Work 8 rows on sts as set.
Inc as before at each side of centre st st panel,

on next row and 5 foll 9th rows. (101sts)

All sizes
Cont without further shaping until work measures 30.5(33.5:36.5)cm from cast on edge ending with a WS row.

Shape armholes

Cont on sts as set and AT THE SAME TIME shape armhole as folls:
Cast off 4 sts at beg next 2 rows.
Dec 1 st at each end of next 7 rows and 3(4:5) foll alt rows. (69(71:73)sts)
Work 1 row.
Complete armhole shaping and beg moss st yoke
Next row (RS)(dec): P2tog, (K1, P1) to last 3 sts, K1, P2tog. (67(69:71)sts)
Next row: P1, (K1, P1) to end.
Cont in moss st as set until work measures 25cm from beg armhole shaping ending with a WS row.

Shape shoulder

Cast off 6(6:6) sts at beg next 2 rows.
Cast off 6(6:7) sts, patt 10(11:11), turn and leave rem sts on a holder.
Work each side of neck separately.
Cast off 4 sts, patt to end.
Cast off rem 6(7:7) sts.
With RS facing rejoin yarn to rem sts cast off centre 23, patt to end.
Complete to match first side reversing shaping.

LEFT FRONT

Cast on 47(49:51) sts using 3¼mm (US 3) needles.
Work 9 rows in moss st as given for back.
Row 10 (WS): Patt 6 and leave these sts on a holder for front band, patt to end. (41(43:45)sts)
Change to 4mm (US 6) needles.

Row 1 (RS): P21(22:23), K2, P1, work 7 sts in moss st as set, P1, K2, P7(8:9).
Row 2: K7(8:9), P2, K1, moss st 7, K1, P2, K21(22:23).
These 2 row set the sts.
Rep these 2 rows 7(8:9) times more.
Next row (RS)(inc): P21(22:23), K2, P1, M1, moss st 7, M1, P1, K2, P7(8:9). (43(45:47)sts)
Next row: K7(8:9), P2, K1, moss st 9, K1, P2, K21(22:23).
Work 14(16:18) rows on sts as set.
Inc as before at each side of moss st panel on next row and 2 foll 16th(18th:20th) rows. (49(51:53)sts)
Cont without shaping on sts as set until front matches back to beg armhole shaping ending with a WS row.

Shape armhole

Cont on sts as set and AT THE SAME TIME shape armhole as folls:
Cast off 4 sts at beg next row.
Work 1 row.
Dec 1 st at armhole edge on next 7 rows and 3(4:5) foll alt rows. (35(36:37)sts)
Work 1 row.
Complete armhole shaping and beg moss st yoke

Small & large sizes only
Next row (RS)(dec): K2tog, (P1, K1) to last st, P1. (34(36)sts)

Medium size only
Next row (RS)(dec): P2tog, (K1, P1) to end. (35sts)

All sizes
Cont in moss st until work measures 16cm from beg armhole shaping ending with a RS row.

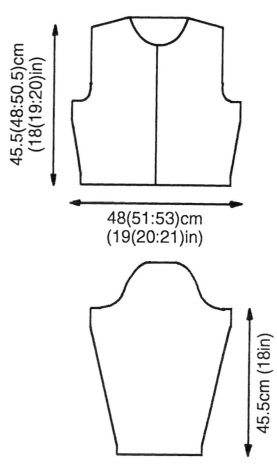

45.5(48:50.5)cm
(18(19:20)in)

48(51:53)cm
(19(20:21)in)

45.5cm (18in)

Shape front neck

Cast off 6 sts at beg next row.

Dec 1 st at neck edge on next 5 rows, 3 foll alt rows and 2 foll 4th rows. (18(19:20)sts)

Work without further shaping until front matches back to shoulder shaping ending with a WS row.

Shape shoulder

Cast off 6(6:6) sts at beg next row and 6(6:7) sts foll alt row.

Work 1 row.

Cast off rem 6(7:7) sts.

RIGHT FRONT

Cast on 47(49:51) sts using 3¼mm (US 3) needles.

Work 6 rows in moss st as given for back.

Next row (RS)(buttonhole): Patt 2, cast off 2, patt to end.

Next row: Patt across row casting on 2 sts over those cast off on previous row.

Work 1 more row in moss st.

Row 10 (WS): Work in patt to last 6 sts, turn and leave rem 6 sts on a holder for front band. (41(43:45)sts)

Change to 4mm (US 6) needles.

Row 1 (RS): P7(8:9), K2, P1, moss st 7, P1, K2, P21(22:23).

Row 2: K21(22:23), P2, K1, moss st 7, K1, P2, K7(8:9).

These 2 rows set the stitches.

Complete as given for left front, work inc each side of moss st panel as given above and reversing all other shaping.

LEFT SLEEVE

Sleeve front

Cast on 38 sts using 4mm (US 6) needles.

Row 1 (RS): (K1, P1) twice, K to end.

Row 2: P to last 5 sts, K1, (P1, K1) twice.

Rep these 2 rows 5 times more ending with a WS row.

Row 13 (RS)(inc): Inc 1 st at end of next row. (39sts)

Work 7 more rows ending with a WS row.

Leave sts on a spare needle.

Sleeve back

Cast on 14 sts using 4mm (US 6) needles.

Row 1 (RS): K to last 4 sts, (P1, K1) twice.

Row 2: K1, (P1, K1) twice, P to end.

Rep these 2 rows 5 times more ending with a WS row.

Row 13 (RS)(inc): Inc 1 st at beg of next row. (15sts)

Work 7 more rows ending with a WS row.

Join back & front sleeve together

Next row (RS): K10 st from sleeve back (5 sts rem), hold front sleeve in front of back sleeve and taking 1 sts from front and 1 st from back together K5, K to end. (49sts)

Work 3 rows in st st.

Inc 1 st at each end of next row and every foll 12th row to 67 sts.

Cont without further shaping until work measures 49cm from cast on edge ending with a WS row. (This allows for shrinkage)

Shape sleevehead

Cast off 4 sts at beg next 2 rows.

Dec 1 st at each end of next 5 rows, 3 foll alt rows and 6 foll 4th rows. (31sts)

Work 1 row.

Dec 1 st at each end of next row, 1 foll alt row.

Dec 1 st at each end of next 3 rows. (21sts)

Cast off 4 sts at beg of next 2 rows.

Cast off rem 13 sts.

RIGHT SLEEVE

Sleeve back

Cast on 14 sts using 4mm (US 6) needles.

Row 1 (RS): K1, (P1, K1) twice K to end.

Row 2: P to last 5 sts, K1, (P1, K1) twice.

Rep these 2 rows 5 times more ending with a WS row.

Row 13 (RS)(inc): Inc 1 st at end of next row. (15sts)

Work 7 more rows ending with a WS row.

Leave sts on a spare needle.

Sleeve front

Cast on 38 sts using 4mm (US 6) needles.

Row 1 (RS): K to last 4 sts, (P1, K1) twice.

Row 2: K1, (P1, K1) twice, P to end.

Rep these 2 rows 5 times more ending with a WS row.

Row 13 (RS)(inc): Inc 1 st at beg of next row. (39sts)

Work 7 more rows ending with a WS row.

Join back & front sleeve together

Next row (RS): K34 st from sleeve front (5 sts rem), hold front sleeve in front of back sleeve and taking 1 sts from front and 1 st from back together K5, K to end. (49sts)

Work 3 rows in st st.

Complete as given for left sleeve.

MAKING UP

Do not press.

Join both shoulder seams using back stitch.

Button band

With RS facing slip sts from holder on left front onto a 3¼mm (US 3) needle and cont in moss st until band fits neatly when slightly stretched up front to beg front neck shaping.

Slip stitch into place.

Cast off.

Mark position of 5 buttons, the first to come opposite buttonhole on right band, the last 1.5cm below cast off edge of band and rem spaced evenly between.

Buttonhole band

Work as for button band with the addition of 4 buttonholes worked to correspond with markers as before.

Collar

Cast on 87 sts using 3¼mm (US 3) needles.

Row 1 (RS): K3, P1, moss st to last 4 sts, P1, K3.

Row 2: K1, P2, K1, moss st to last 4 sts, K1, P2, K1.

Row 3 (RS)(inc): K3, P1, M1, moss st to last 4 sts, M1, P1, K3. (89sts)

Row 4: Work as row 2.

Row 5: Work as row 1.

Row 6 (WS)(inc): K1, P2, K1, M1, moss st to last 4 sts, M1, K1, P2, K1. (91sts)

Rep these 6 rows until 28 rows in all completed ending with a WS row. (105sts)

Cast off in patt.

Left cuff

Cast on 47 sts using 3¼mm (US 3) needles.

Work 6 rows in moss st.

Next row (RS)(buttonholes): Patt 2, cast off 2, patt to end.

Next row: Patt across row casting on 2 sts over those cast off on previous row.

Work 8 more rows.

Cast off evenly in moss st.

Right cuff

Work as given for left cuff reversing buttonhole row as folls:

Buttonhole row (RS): Patt to last 4 sts, cast off 2 sts, patt 2.

Mock pocket tops (Work 2)

Cast on 25 sts using 3¼mm (US 3) needles.

Row 1 (RS): K3, P1, K1, (P1, K1) to last 4 sts, P1, K3.

Row 2: K1, P2, K1, K1, (P1, K1) to last 4 sts, K1, P2, K1.

Rep these 2 rows until 14 rows in all completed.

Next row (RS)(dec): K3, P1, P2tog, patt to last 6 sts, P2tog, P1, K3. (23sts)

Next row (WS)(dec): K1, P2, K1, K2tog, patt to last 6 sts, K2tog, K1, P2, K1. (21sts)

Rep these 2 rows until 11 sts rem ending with a RS row.

Next row (WS)(dec): K1, P2, K1, sl1, K2tog, psso, K1, P2, K1. (9sts)

Next row (RS)(dec): K3, sl1, P2tog, psso, K3. (7sts)

Next row (WS)(dec): K1, P1, sl1, P2tog, psso, P1, K1. (5sts)

Next row (RS)(dec): K1, sl1, K2tog, psso, K1. (3sts)

Next row (WS)(dec): Sl1, K2tog, psso.

Fasten off.

Machine wash all pieces together at the same time, as described on the ball band, before sewing together.

See information page for finishing instructions.

Placing centre of collar to centre back neck, sew cast on edge of collar evenly around neck edge, beg and end halfway across front bands.

With right sides together sew cuffs to sleeves using a backstitch.

Sew mock pocket tops in place at yoke between centre panels on each front as shown in photograph.

Sew on buttons.

Frieze

MARTIN STOREY

YARN

Rowan Magpie and Chunky Cotton Chenille

A	Magpie	Berry 684	6	x	100gm
B	Magpie	Raven 62	1	x	100gm
C	Ch.Chen	Fern 364	4	x	100gm
D	Ch.Chen	Elephant 348	2	x	100gm
E	Magpie	Natural 002	1	x	100gm
F	Magpie	Cloud 507	1	x	100gm

NEEDLES

1 pair 3¾mm (no 9) (US 5)
1 pair 4½mm (no 7) (US 7)

TENSION

18 sts and 26 rows to 10cm measured over patterned stocking stitch using 4½mm (US 7) needles

Special abbreviations

MSB(E) = make small bobble using yarn E: (K1, yf, K1) into next st, turn, P3, turn K3, turn, P3, turn, sl 1, K2tog, psso.
MLB(E) = make large bobble using yarn E: (K1, yf, K1, yf, K1) in next st, turn, P5, turn, K5, turn, P2tog, P1, P2tog, turn, sl 1, K2tog, psso.
T5R = Place next 3 sts onto cable needle and hold at back of work, K2, then P1, K2 from cable needle.
T3B = Slip next st onto cable needle and hold at back of work, K2, then P st from cable needle.
T3F = Slip next 2 sts onto cable needle and hold at front of work, P1, then K2 from cable needle.

BACK

Cast on 107 sts using 3¾mm (US 5) needles,

yarn B, and work 7 rows in moss st.
Next row (WS): Purl to end.
Change to 4½mm (US 7) needles and using the INTARSIA technique described on the information page, work 178 rows in patt from chart which is worked entirely in st st beg with a K row, ending with a WS row.

Shape back neck

Patt 41 sts, turn leaving rem sts on a holder.
Work each side of neck separately.
Dec 1 st at neck edge on next 5 rows. (36sts)
Cast off rem sts.
Slip centre 25 sts onto a holder.
With RS facing rejoin yarn to rem sts, patt to end.
Complete to match first side reversing all shaping.

FRONT

Work as given for back until chart row 162 completed ending with a WS row.

Shape front neck

Patt 48 sts, turn and leave rem sts on a holder.
Work each side of neck separately.
Cast off 4 sts at beg of next row and 2 sts beg foll alt row.
Work 1 row.
Dec 1 st at neck edge on next row and foll 5 alt rows. (36sts)
Cont without further shaping until front matches back to shoulder.
Cast off.
Slip centre 11 sts onto a holder.
With RS facing join yarn to rem sts, patt to end.
Work 1 row.
Complete to match first side, reversing all shaping.

SLEEVES (both alike)

Cast on 43 sts using 3¾mm (US 5) needles and yarn B and work 7 rows in moss st.
Next row (WS): Purl across row.

Change to 4½mm (US 7) needles and work 106 rows in patt from chart for sleeve and AT THE SAME TIME, shape sides by inc 1 st at each end of 3rd row and every foll alt row to 57 sts and then every foll 4th row to 97 sts.
Cast off loosely and evenly.

MAKING UP

Press all pieces as described on the information page.
Join right shoulder seam using backstitch.

Neckband

With RS facing using 3¾mm (US 5) needles and yarn B, pick up and K 30 sts down left front neck, work across sts on holder as folls, (K2, M1) 5 times, K1, pick up and K 31 sts up right front neck and 6 sts down right back neck, work across sts on holder as folls, (K2, M1) 12 times, K1, pick up and K 6 sts up left back neck. (126sts)
Row 1 (WS): K to end.
Row 2: * P2, T5R, P2, rep from * to end.
Row 3: * K2, P2, K1, P2, K2, rep from * to end
Row 4: * P1, T3B, P1, T3F, P1, rep from * to end.
Row 5: * K1, P2, K3, P2, K1, rep from * to end.
Row 6: * T3B, P3, T3F, rep from * to end.
Row 7: * P2, K5, P2, rep from * to end.
Row 8: K2, * P2, MSB(E), P2, C4B, rep from * ending last rep K2 instead of C4B.
Row 9: Work as row 7.
Row 10: * T3F, P3, T3B, rep from * to end.
Row 11: Work as row 5.
Row 12: * P1, T3F, P1, T3B, p1, rep from * to end.
Row 13: Work as row 3.
Row 14: Work as row 2.
Cast off loosely and evenly in patt.
See information page for finishing instructions.

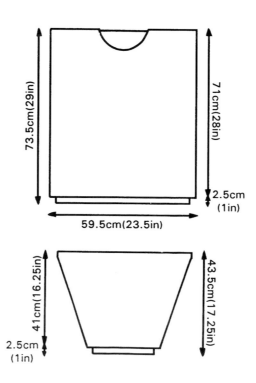

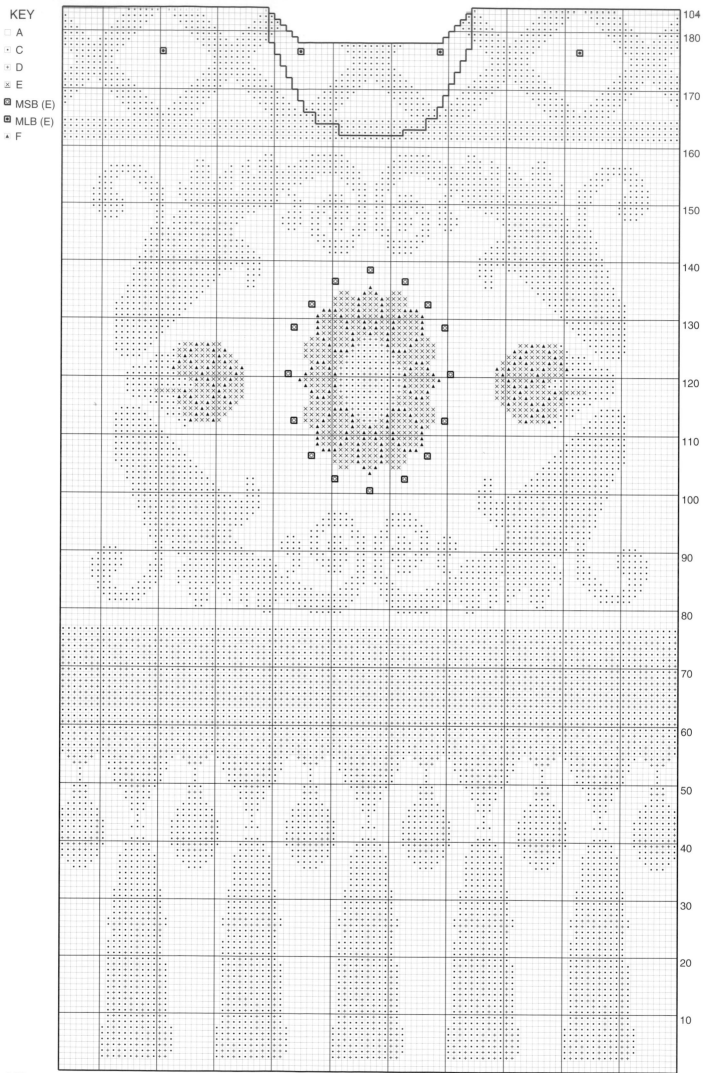

Back and front

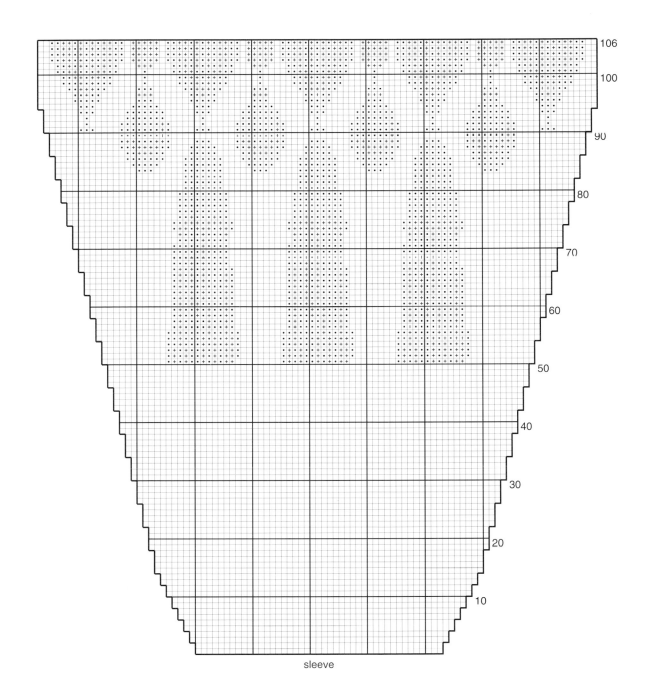

sleeve

The Finishing Touch

SUE HORAN

Much time and money is spent knitting a Rowan sweater, so it is important to get a really good result when it comes to working the neckband.

If a neckband is badly knitted, with stitches unevenly picked up, you will never be totally satisfied with the finished garment. This is especially important on a plain sweater knitted in a simple stitch like stocking stitch, when any uneven stitches will be very apparent. It is important, too, to pick up the correct number of stitches round a neckline. If you are following a pattern, the instructions will give you the exact number of stitches to knit up, but if you are working a design of your own, it is worth taking a little more care when picking up stitches for the neckband. Take care not to pick up too many, or too few, stitches. Too many stitches will give a frilled look, too few will give a neck opening that probably won t fit over your head. If the neckband is not right, don t be afraid to pull the whole thing back and start again.

SHAPING UP

When shaping the neck at the knitting stage, try to ensure that the edge remains as neat as possible. This will make picking up the neckband stitches much easier. When casting off in groups for a round neckline, stitches should be cast off in pattern and the first stitch of each group should be slipped. This gives a sloping edge, rather that a step, to each cast off group.

For a 'V' neckline, a neater edge will be achieved on a plain stitch if the shaping is worked one or two stitches in from the edge. This is called 'fully-fashioned' shaping.

TIP

When working a neckband, always use needles one or two sizes smaller than those used for knitting the garment. This gives a firmer, more elastic band. When casting off, use a needle one size larger that the ones you have been using. This will make sure the neckband isn't too tight to fit over your head.

Most knitting patterns give instructions for knitting the neckbbands on two needles. To do this, the right shoulder seam is joined first, leaving a long, straight edge to be picked up for the neckband. Before starting, check the pressing instructions on the ball band. If the yarn can be pressed, pin out the knitted pieces to the correct shape, and steam or press carefully. Join the right shoulder seam and press it on the wrong side. After the neckband is completed, the left shoulder seam and the two edges of the band are joined together and pressed. (In our photos we have shown only the front neckbands for simplicity.)

Another method is to join both shoulder seams, and to pick up around the neckline using a circular needle. The band is then knitted in the round. This method eliminates the need to join a seam after knitting, but means that knitters need a complete set of circular needles in different sizes.

PICKING UP STITCHES

To pick up the stitches that will form a new row along a neckline, first pin out the pieces and steam or press them, then join the right shoulder seam. With the right side facing, beginning at the shoulder edge, insert the needle through the edge of the knitting and loop the yarn over the needle. Draw a loop through to make a new stitch. Repeat along neckline edge until the required number of stitches have been picked up. Insert the needle through the centre of the stitch when picking up cast-off groups. When you get to the stitches that have been held on a stitch holder, simply knit them off the holder.

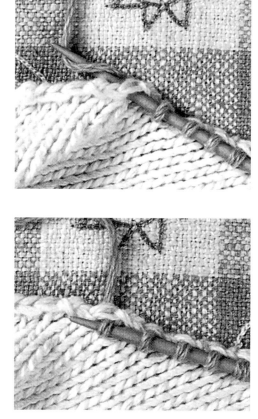

PICKING UP A ROUND NECKBAND

It is very important that the stitches are picked up evenly around the neck edge, and that the correct number are picked up at each side of the neckline. To ensure even spacing, use pins to divide the neck into equal sections and pick up the same number of stitches from each section as you go.

KNITTING A ROUND NECKBAND

Round neckbands of more than a few rows are usually finished with a ribbed border, as these are the most flexible. If the pick-up row isn't as tidy as you would like, knit the first row, then continue in rib for the rest of the band. The knit row will help hide any irregular stitches. When measuring the depth of the band, remember that the band will stretch out after casting off, so always work two more rows than you think you need. Always cast off in rib.

To knit a modern, stylish neckband, work the neckband in rib for the required depth, then work about eight rows of stocking stitch (one row knit, one row purl). Cast off loosely. Allow the stocking stitch to roll gently on to the right side of the sweater.

PICKING UP A 'V' NECKBAND

When picking up the stitches for the neckband, it is important that they are evenly spaced around the neck edge. Again, the easiest way to ensure this is to divide the neck edge into equal sections with pins. If sixty stitches are needed for each side of the neck, divide each side into six equal sections with pins. Ten stitches must be picked up from each section and these stitches should be spaced evenly.

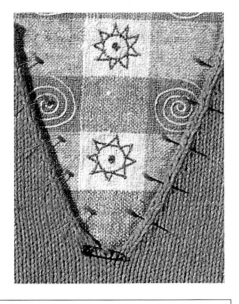

TIP

For a really professional finish, the neckband on a cable or Aran-style sweater looks much neater if any ribbed stitches on the front and back follow through into the neckband rib.

KNITTING THE BAND

For a ribbed 'V' neckband, pick up stitches evenly down the left front edge. At the centre front, either knit the centre front stitch or pick up and knit one stitch. Fasten a safety pin through

this stitch. Pick up the stitches up the right front of the neck and knit the stitches from the back neck holder. Make sure you have an odd number of stitches for the back neck. (You may need to pick up and knit an extra stitch to achieve this.)

Next row (Wrong side) P1 [K1, P1] to within 2 stitches before centre front stitch, K2 together, P centre front stitch from safety pin and move pin up to new centre front stitch, K2 together through back of loops, [P1, K1] to end.

Next row (Right side) Work in rib as set to within two stitches before centre front stitch, K2 together through back of loops, K centre front stitch from safety pin and move pin up to centre front stitch, K2 together, rib as set to end. Repeat these two rows until neckband is required depth, ending with a wrong-side row. Cast off

evenly in rib, decreasing at each side of centre front stitch as before.

For a contrast band, pick up the stitches in the main colour. Change to the contrast colour and purl the following row, decreasing purlwise at each side of centre front stitch.

For a simple 'V' neckband, pick up the stitches down the left front edge of the neck. Work straight in rib for as many rows as you need and cast off evenly in rib. Work the right front edge and the back neck together in the same way. To finish, overlap the ends at the centre front and sew the sides of neckband to the neck shaping on the front. A button can be sewn to the centre front if required.

Many knitting patterns these days give instructions for different types of bands—moss stitch, 2-colour rib and Fair Isle are only a few of these. As these need to be reduced in tension to stop them becoming too wide, follow the instructios carefully until you have enough experience to experiment with different types of bands yourself. But once you have a little experience, there is no limit to the creative ways you can finish off a plain neck.

Dancing Horses

DEBBIE JENKINS

YARN

Rowan Magpie, Magpie Tweed, Chunky Chenille and Designer D.K.

A	Magpie	Cloud	507	7	x	100gm
B	Mag.Twd	Squirrel	772	2	x	100gm
C	Magpie	Natural	002	2	x	100gm
D	Magpie	Dapple	450	1	x	100gm
E	Magpie	Cork	309	1	x	100gm
F	D.D.K	*Highland	628	2	x	50gm
G	CH.Chen	Aubergine	356	1	x	100gm
H	Ch.Chen	Maple	380	1	x	100gm
J	Ch.Chen	Fern	364	1	x	100gm
L	Ch.Chen	Tide	385	1	x	100gm

* USE DOUBLE THROUGHOUT

NEEDLES

1 pair 4mm (no 8) (US 6)
1 pair 4½mm (no 7) (US 7)

BUTTONS

5

TENSION

18 sts and 25 rows to 10cm measured over patterned stocking stitch using 4½mm (US 7) needles

BACK

Cast on 104(108) sts using 4mm (US 6) needles and yarn A.
Work 13 rows in K1, P1 rib.
Next row (inc): Rib 4 sts, [M1, rib 19(11)] 5(9) times, M1, rib 5. (110(118)sts)
Change to 4½mm(US 7) needles and using the INTARSIA technique , except for fairisle bands, cont in patt from back until chart row 156 completed, placing a contrast marker at each end of row 87 for sleeve position.

Shape shoulders

Cast off 36(40) sts at beg of next 2 rows.
Cast off rem 38 sts.

POCKET LININGS (make 2)

Cast on 28 sts using 4mm (US 6) needles and yarn A.
Work 30 rows in st st, ending with a WS row.
Leave st on a holder.

LEFT FRONT

Cast on 52(56) sts using 4mm (US 6) needles and yarn A.
Work 13 rows in K1, P1 rib.
Next row (inc): Rib 9(8), [M1, rib 17(20)] twice, M1, rib 9(8). (55(59)sts)
Change to 4½mm (US 7) needles cont in patt from chart A for left front until chart row 30 completed.

Place pocket

Row 31: Patt 13(17) sts, slip next 28 sts onto a holder and in place of these patt across sts of first pocket lining, patt to end.
Cont from chart A until chart row 58 completed.
Now cont working from chart B.
Work until chart row 94 completed, placing a contrast marker on row 87 for sleeve position.

Shape front neck

Dec 1 st at neck edge on next row and 3 foll 4th rows and then every foll 3rd row until 36(40)sts rem.
Cont without further shaping until front matches back to shoulder.
Cast off loosely and evenly.

RIGHT FRONT

Work as given for left front foll charts for right front and reversing all shaping and pocket position.

SLEEVES (both alike)

Cast on 40 sts using 4mm (US 6) needles and yarn A.
Work 15 rows in K1, P1 rib.
Next row (inc): Rib 1 [M1, rib 1, M1, rib 2] 13 times. (66sts)
Change to 4½mm (US 7) needles and cont from chart C for sleeve until chart row 102(104) completed and AT THE SAME TIME, shape sides by inc 1 st at each end of the 5th row and every foll 4th row until there are 108 sts.
Cast off loosely and evenly.

COLLAR AND FRONT BANDS (worked in one piece)

Cast on 11 sts using 4mm (US 6) needles and yarn A.
Row 1: Sl 1, (K1, P1) 4 times, K2.
Row 2: Sl 1, (P1, K1) 5 times.
Rep last 2 rows once more
*Next row (buttonhole): Sl 1, K1, P1, K1, cast off 3 sts, P1, K2.
Next row: Sl 1, P1, K1, P1, cast on 3 sts, P1, K1, P1, K1.
Rep 1st and 2nd rows 10 times.*
Rep from * to * 3 times more.
Rep 2 buttonhole rows once more.

Work 6 rows in rib.
Next row: Sl 1, rib to last 2 sts, inc into next st, K1.
Next row: Inc into 1st st, rib to end.
Rep last 2 rows 8 times more. (29sts)
Cont to sl 1st stitch on RS edge, inc 1 st at end of next row and every foll 4th row until there are 41 sts.
Work 75 rows in rib marking the ends of rows 18 and 57 at the shaped edge of collar with a contrast thread.
Cont to sl 1st stitch on RS edge, dec at shaped edge on next and every foll 4th row to 29sts and then every foll alt row to 11 sts.
Work 100 rows without shaping.
Cast off.

MAKING UP

Press all pieces as described on the information page.

Pocket tops (both alike)
With RS facing using 4mm (US 6) needles and yarn B, K across sts from holder.
Next row: (K1, P1) to end.
Next row: (K1 yarn H, P1 yarn B) to end.
Next row: (K1 yarn B, P1, yarn J) to end.
Work 2 rows in rib using yarn B.
Cast off evenly in rib.
Join both shoulder seams using back stitch.
Slip collar neatly into place matching coloured markers with shoulder seams.
See information page for finishing instructions.

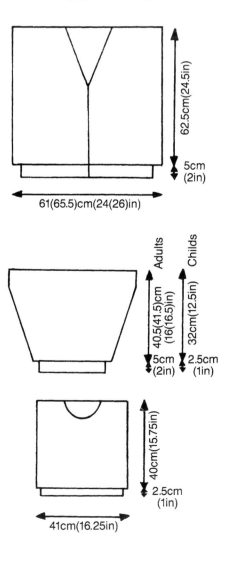

CHART B

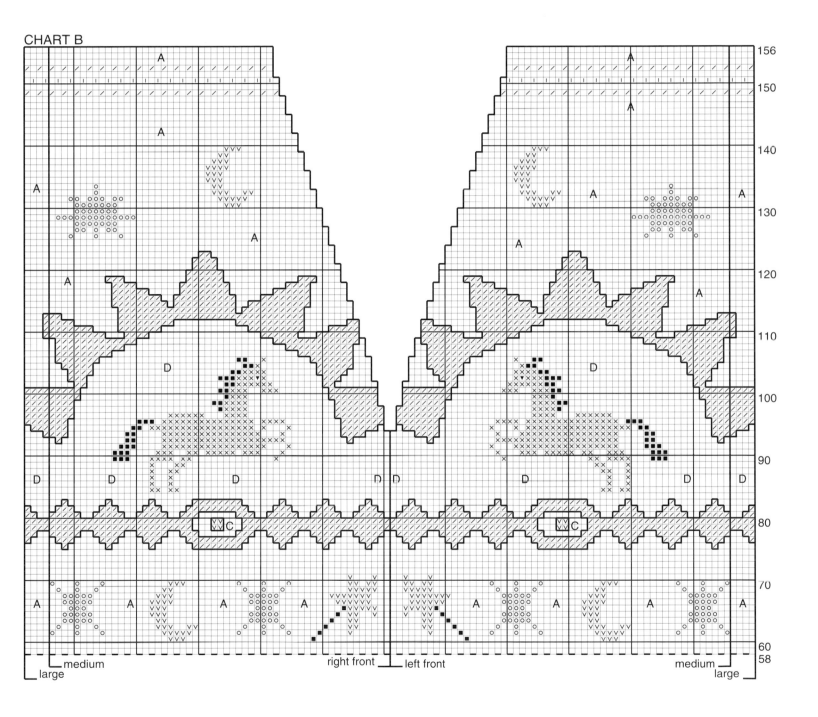

CHART C

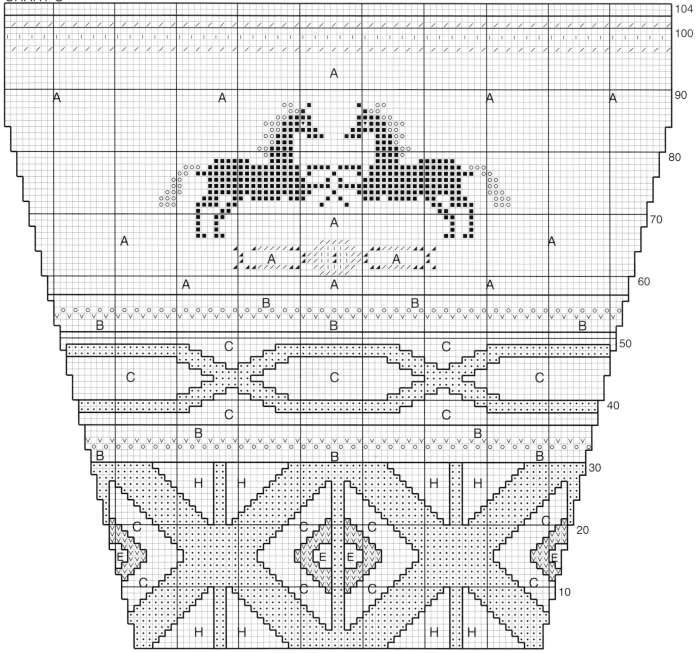

sleeve

Hannah

KIM HARGREAVES

YARN

Rowan Cotton Glace

			s	m	l	
A	Glace	Ecru	725	7	8	8 x 50gm
B	Glace	Oyster	730	2	2	2 x 50gm
C	Glace	Provence	744	1	1	1 x 50gm
D	Glace	Nightshade	746	1	1	1 x 50gm
E	Glace	Airforce	442	1	1	1 x 50gm
F	Glace	Wine	790	1	1	1 x 50gm
G	Glace	Bloom	784	1	1	1 x 50gm
H	Glace	Dijon	739	1	1	1 x 50gm
J	Glace	Corn	791	1	1	1 x 50gm

NEEDLES

1 pair 2¾mm (no 12) (US 2)
1 pair 3¼mm (no 10) (US 3)

BUTTONS

7(8:8)

TENSION

27 sts and 33 rows to 10cm measured over patterned stocking stitch using 3¼mm (US 3) needles

BACK

Cast on 133(139:147) sts using 2¾mm (US 2) needles and yarn A work in moss st as folls:
Row 1: K1, (P1, K1) rep to end.
Rep this row until work measures 2cm ending with a WS row.
Change to 3¼mm (US 3) needles and using the INTARSIA techniques described on the information page work 58(66:76) rows in patt from the chart for back, which is worked in a mixture of st st and moss st, beg with a K row.

Shape armholes

Cast off 8 sts at beg next 2 rows. (117(123:131) sts)
Cont without further shaping until chart row 138(146:156) completed.

Shape shoulders and back neck

Cast off 12(13:15) sts at beg next 2 rows.
Cast off 13(14:15) sts at beg next row, patt 17(18:19) sts, turn and leave rem sts on a holder.
Work each side separately.
Cast off 4 sts at beg of next row, work to end.
Cast off rem 13(14:15) sts.
With RS facing rejoin yarn to rem sts, cast off centre 33 sts, patt to end.
Complete to match first side reversing all shaping.

LEFT FRONT

Cast on 67(70:74) sts using 2¾mm (US 2) needles and yarn A.
Work 2cm in moss st ending with a WS row.
Change to 3¼mm (US 3) needles and foll chart for left front cont in patt until chart row 58(66:76) completed ending with a WS row.

Shape armhole

Cast off 8 sts patt to end. (59(62:66) sts)
Cont without further shaping until chart row 103(111:121) completed ending with a RS row.

Shape front neck

Cast off 6sts at beg of next row and 3 sts beg foll 2 alt rows.
Dec 1 st at neck edge on next 2 rows and foll 3 alt rows.
Work 3 rows.
Dec 1 st at neck edge on next row and 3 foll 4th rows. (38(41:45) sts)
Cont without further shaping until front matches back to shoulder ending with a WS row.

Shape shoulder

Cast off 12(13:15) sts at beg next row and 13(14:15) foll alt row.
Work 1 row.
Cast off rem 13(14:15) sts.
Right front
Work as given for left front and foll chart for right front, reversing all shaping.

SLEEVES (both alike)

Cast on 65 sts using 2¾mm (US 2) needles and yarn A.
Work 2cm in moss st as for back ending with a WS row.
Change to 3¼mm (US 3) needles and work in patt from chart for sleeve and AT THE SAME TIME, shape sides by inc 1 st at each end of 3rd and every foll 4th row to 129 sts.
Cont without further shaping until chart row 150 completed.
Cast off loosely and evenly.

MAKING UP

PRESS all pieces as described on the information page.
Join both shoulder seams using back stitch.

Button band

Cast on 5 sts using 2¾mm (US 2) needles and yarn A.
Work in moss st until band fits to beg of neck shaping when slightly stretched, leave sts on a holder, slip st into place.
Mark position of 6(7:7) buttons, the 1st, 3rd, 5th and 0(7th:7th) to come in line with centre of horizonal moss st bands the others to be spaced evenly between.

Buttonhole band

Work as for button band with the addition of 6(7:7) buttonholes working buttonholes to correspond with markers as folls:
Buttonhole row: Patt 2, yrn to make a st, K2tog, patt 1.
Leave sts on a holder.
Slip st buttonhole band into place.

Neckband

With RS facing and using 2¾mm (US 2) needles and yarn A, patt across 5 sts on buttonholeband, pick up and knit 46 sts up right front neck, 41 sts across back neck and 46 sts down left front neck, patt across 5 sts on button band. (143 sts)
Work 7 rows in moss st working button hole in line with others on row 4.
Cast off evenly in moss st.
See information page for finishing instructions.

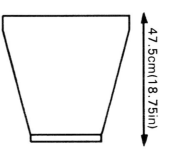

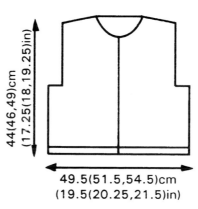

47.5cm(18.75in)

44(46,49)cm (17.25(18,19.25)in)

49.5(51.5,54.5)cm (19.5(20.25,21.5)in)

Indian Summer 1

KIM HARGREAVES

YARN

Rowan 4 ply Cotton and Cotton Glace

A	4ply	Black	101	2	x	50gm
B	4ply	Magenta	106	2	x	50gm
C	Glace	Kiwi	443	1	x	50gm
D	4ply	Cobolt	108	1	x	50gm
E	4ply	Straw	110	1	x	50gm
F	Glace	Provence	744	2	x	50gm
G	4ply	Racey	107	2	x	50gm
H	4ply	Vine	103	2	x	50gm
J	Glace	Parade	430	3	x	50gm
L	Glace	Fiesta	437	3	x	50gm
M	4ply	Blaze	105	2	x	50gm

NEEDLES

1 pair 2¼mm (no 13) (US 1)
1 pair 2¾mm (no 12) (US 2)
1 circular needle 2¼mm (no 13) (US 1)

BUTTONS

9

TENSION

32 sts and 41 rows to 10cm measured over patterned stocking stitch using 2¾mm (US 2) needles

BACK

Cast on 187 sts using 2¼mm (US 1) needles and yarn A.
Work 2.5cm in twisted rib as follows:
Row 1 (RS): P1b, * K1b, P1b, rep from * to end.
Row 2: K1b, * P1b, K1b, rep from * to end.
Change to 2¾mm (US 2) needles and using the INTARSIA and FAIR ISLE techniques described on the information page, cont in patt for back which is worked entirely in st st beg with a K row.
Cont in patt from chart until row 114 completed.

Shape armholes

Cast off 8 sts at beg of next 2 rows.
Cont without further shaping until chart row 208 completed ending with a WS row.

Shape shoulders and back neck

Cast off 20 sts at beg of next 2 rows.
Cast off 20 sts at beg next row, patt 25 sts, turn and leave rem sts on a holder.
Work each side of neck separately.
Cast off 4 sts patt to end.
Cast off rem 21 sts.
With RS facing rejoin yarn to rem sts and cast off centre 41 sts, patt to end.
Complete to match other side reversing all shaping.

LEFT FRONT

Cast on 93 sts using 2¼mm (US 1) needles and yarn A.

Work 2.5cm in K1, P1 twisted rib, ending with a WS row.
Change to 2¾mm (US 2) needles and cont in patt from chart for left front until chart row 114 completed ending with a WS row.

Shape front neck and armhole

Cast off 8 sts at beg next row, patt to last 2 sts, K2tog.
Keeping armhole edge straight, dec 1 st at neck edge on every foll 4th row, 21 times, then on foll 2 alt rows. (61sts)
Cont without further shaping until front matches back to shoulder.
Cast off 20 sts at beg of next row and foll alt row.
Work 1 row.
Cast off rem 21 sts.

RIGHT FRONT

Work as given for left front following chart for right front and reversing all shaping.

SLEEVES (both alike)

Cast on 73 sts using 2¼mm (US 1) needles and yarn A.
Work 2.5cm in K1, P1 twisted rib ending with a WS row.
Change to 2¾mm (US 2) needles and foll chart for sleeve, work until row 188 completed and AT THE SAME TIME, shape sides by inc 1 st at each end of the 3rd row and every foll 4th row until there are 121 sts, and then every foll 6th row until there are 145 sts.
Cast off evenly.

MAKING UP

Press all pieces using a warm iron over a damp cloth.
Join both shoulder seams using back stitch.
Front band (knitted in one piece)
With RS facing using 2¼mm (US 1) circular needle and yarn M, pick up and K 102 sts up right front to beg neck shaping, 84 sts up right front to shoulder, 55 sts across back neck, 84 sts down left front neck to beg shaping and 102 down left front to cast on edge. (427 sts)
Mark the 101 sts up from bottom of right front for start of button holes.
Joining in yarn H, work 4 rows in patt from chart for front band as folls:
Row 1 (WS): P1H, (P5M, P1H) rep the 6 st patt rep across row, until marker is reached (101 sts on left-hand needle), now keeping patt correct make buttonholes as folls, (cast off 3, patt 9) 8 times, cast off 3, patt 2.
Row 2(RS): Patt across row following row 2 of chart, and casting on 3 sts over those cast off on previous row.
Work 2 more rows in patt from chart.
Next row (WS): Using yarn H, K across row to form foldline.
work 4 more rows in st st, working buttonholes on 3rd and 4th row to correspond with those worked previously.
Cast off loosely.
See information page for finishing instructions.

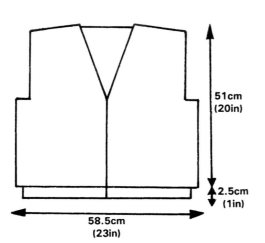

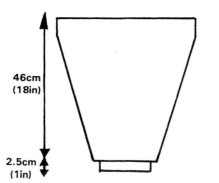

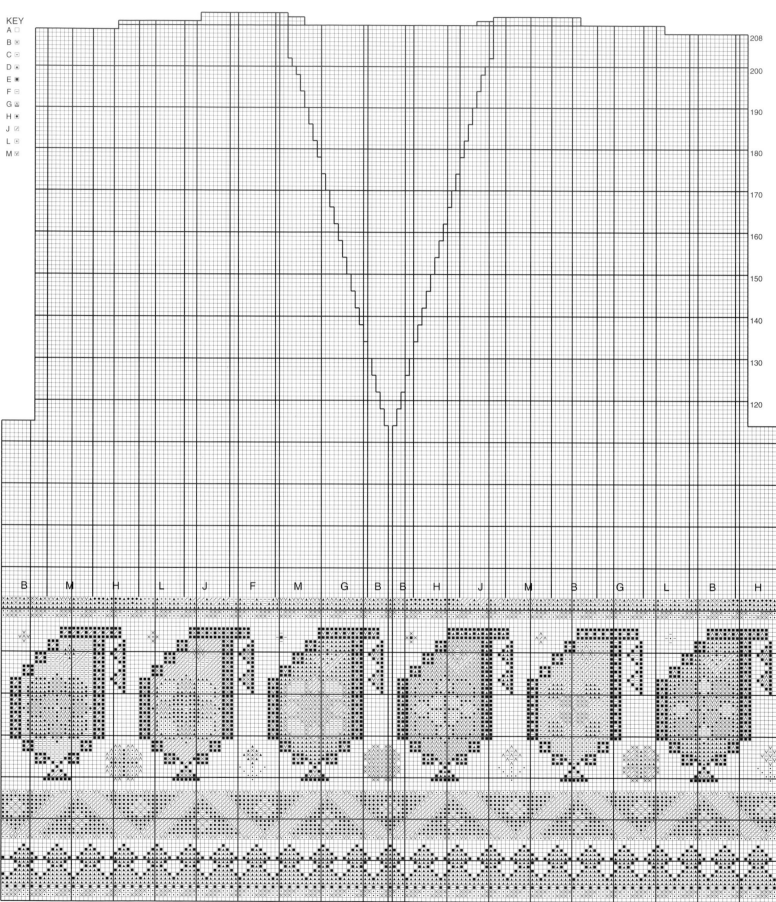

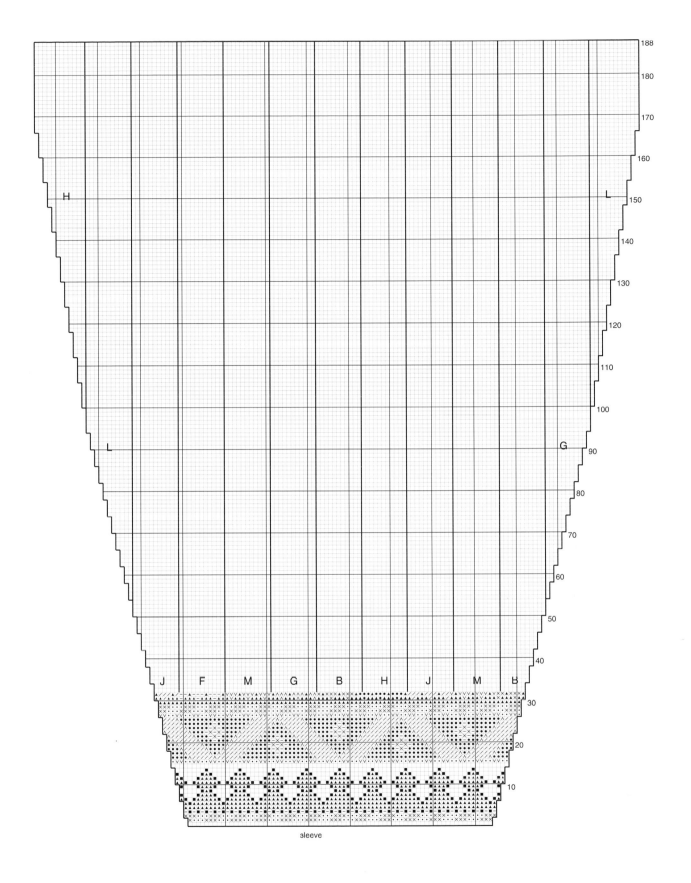

sleeve

neckband chart

4

6st rep

Indian Summer 2

KIM HARGREAVES

YARN

Rowan Light Weight D.K.

A	Black	62	4	x	25gm
B	Wine	602	4	x	25gm
C	Rose	70	3	x	25gm
D	Rust	77	3	x	25gm
E	Grass	404	1	x	25gm
F	Forest	606	4	x	25gm
G	Pine	91	4	x	25gm
H	Purple	99	2	x	25gm
J	Petrol	54	1	x	25gm
L	Blue	53	4	x	25gm
M	Gold	11	2	x	25gm

NEEDLES

1 pair 2¾mm (no 12) (US 2)
1 pair 3¼mm (no 10) (US 3)
Circular needle 2¾mm (no 12) (US 2)—80cm long

BUTTONS

8

TENSION

27 sts and 37 rows to 10cm measured over patterned stocking stitch using 3¼mm (US 3) needles

BACK

Cast on 157 sts using 2¾mm (US 2) needles and yarn A.
Work 2.5cm in twisted rib as folls:
Row 1: P1b, * K1b, P1b, rep from * to end.
Row 2: K1b, * P1b, K1b, rep from * to end.
Change to 3¼mm (US 3) needles and using the INTARSIA and FAIR ISLE techniques described on the information page, cont in patt for back which is worked entirely in st st beg with a K row, working background of border in yarn A.

Cont in patt from chart until row 102 completed.

Shape armholes

Cast off 7 sts at beg next 2 rows. (143 sts)
Cont without further shaping until chart row 188 completed.

Shape shoulders and back neck

Cast off 17 sts at beg of next 2 rows.
Cast off 17 sts at beg next row, patt 22 sts, turn and leave rem sts on a holder.
Work each side of neck separately.
Cast off 4 sts, patt to end.
Cast off rem 18 sts.
With RS facing rejoin yarn to rem sts, cast off centre 31 sts, patt to end.
Complete to match other side reversing all shaping.

LEFT FRONT

Cast on 78 sts using 2¾mm (US 2) needles and yarn A.
Work 2.5cm in K1, P1, twisted rib, ending with a WS row.
Change to 3¼mm (US 3) needles and cont in patt from chart for left front until chart row 102 completed.

Shape front and armhole

Cast off 7 sts at beg next row, patt to last 2 sts, K2tog.
Keeping armhole edge straight, dec 1 st at neck edge on every foll 4th row until 52 sts rem.
Cont without further shaping until front matches back to beg shoulder shaping.
Cast off 17 sts at beg of next and foll alt row.
Work 1 row.
Cast off rem 18 sts.

RIGHT FRONT

Work as given for left front following chart for right front and reversing all shaping.

SLEEVES (both alike)

Cast on 59 sts using 2¾mm (US 2) needles and yarn A.

Work 2.5 cm in K1, P1 twisted rib ending with a WS row.
Change to 3¼mm (US 3) needles and foll chart for sleeve for cardigan, work until row 160 completed and AT THE SAME TIME, shape sides by inc 1 st at each end of the 3rd row and every foll 4th row until there are 121 sts and then every foll 6th row to 125 sts.
Cast off evenly.

MAKING UP

Press all pieces as described on the information page.
Join both shoulder seams.

Front band (knitted in one piece)

With RS facing using 2¾mm (US 2) circular needle and yarn D, pick up and K 90 sts up right front to beg of neck shaping, 70 sts up right front to shoulder, 38 sts across back neck, 70 sts down left front neck to beg shaping and 90 sts down left front to cast on edge. (358 sts)
Mark the 89th st up from cast on edge of right front, for start of button holes.
Joining in yarn B, work 4 rows in patt from chart for front band as folls:
Chart row 1 (WS): P1B, (P5D, P1B) rep the 6 st patt rep across row, until marker is reached, (89 sts on LH needle), now keeping patt correct make buttonholes as folls, (cast off 3, patt 9) 7 times, cast off 3, patt 2.
Chart row 2 (RS): Patt across row casting on 3 sts over those cast off on previous row.
Work 2 more rows in patt from chart.
Next row (WS): Using yarn B, K across row to form foldline.
Work 4 more rows in st st using yarn B, working buttonholes on 3rd and 4th rows to correspond with those worked previously.
Cast off loosely.
See information page for finishing instructions.
Fold front band to wrong side at foldline, slip stitch into place.

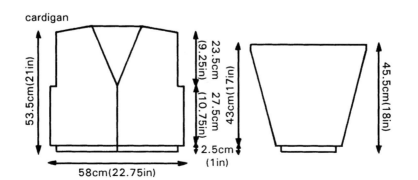

cardigan

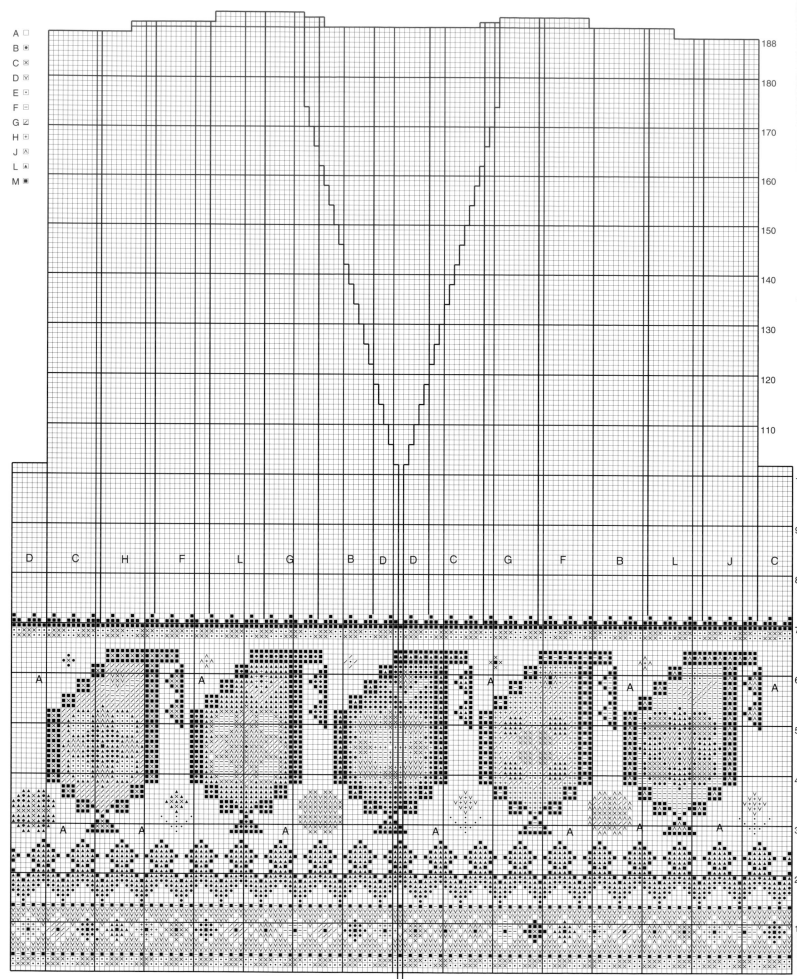

right front —— left front

Back

170

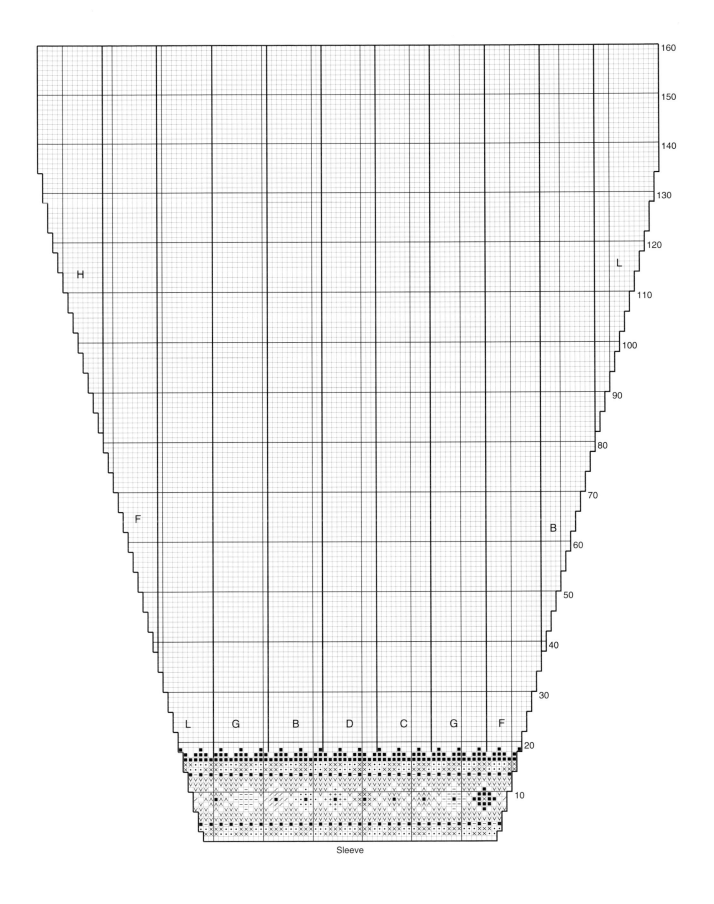

160

150

140

130

120

L

H

110

100

90

80

70

F

B

60

50

40

30

L   G   B   D   C   G   F

20

10

Sleeve

Front band
chart

Beastly Sweater

EDY LYNGAAS

YARN

Rowan Designer D.K. & D.K. Tweed

			med	large	x-large	
A	D.D.K	Black	62	13	14	14	x 50gm
B	D.D.K	Petrol	685	1	1	1	x 50gm
C	D.D.K	Maroon	637	1	1	1	x 50gm
D	DK.twd	Hare	853	1	1	1	x 50gm
E	D.D.K	Blue	696	1	1	1	x 50gm
F	D.D.K	Purple	636	1	1	1	x 50gm

NEEDLES

1 pair 3¼mm (no 10)(US 3)
1 pair 4mm (no 8)(US 6)
Set of 4 double-pointed 3¼mm (no 10) (US 3)

TENSION

22 sts and 30 rows to 10cm measured over patterned stocking stitch using 4mm (US 6) needles

BACK

Cast on 118(126:132) sts using 3¼mm (US 3) needles and yarn A.

Work 2-colour rib patt as folls:
Row 1 (RS): K2B, (P2A, K2B) to last 0(0:2) sts, P0(0:2)A.
Row 2: K0(0:2)A, (P2B, K2A) to last 2 sts, P2B.
Work a further 16 rows in rib as set, keeping all floats on WS of work.
Change to 4mm (US 6) needles and using the INTARSIA technique described on the information page cont in patt from chart which is worked entirely in st st beg with a K row.
Work 124 rows in patt from chart.
Then cont in yarn A only, work in moss stitch as folls:
Row 1: (K1, P1) to end.
Row 2: (P1, K1) to end.
These 2 rows form the moss stitch patt.
Cont in moss stitch as set until work measures 66(67:68.5)cm from beg ending with a WS row.

Shape shoulders

Cast off 9(11:12) sts at beg of next 2 rows.
Cast off 10(11:12) sts at beg of next row, patt 19(20:21) sts, turn and leave rem sts on a holder.
Work each side of neck separately.
Cast off 9 sts at beg of next row, patt to end.
Cast off rem 10(11:12) sts.
With RS facing, rejoin yarn to rem sts, cast off centre 42 sts, patt to end.
Complete second side to match first side, reversing all shaping.

FRONT

Work as given for back until front is 18 rows shorter than back to start of shoulder shaping.

Shape front neck

Patt 44(48:51) sts, turn and leave rem sts on a holder.
Work each side of neck separately.
Cast off at neck edge on next row and foll alt rows 4 sts once, 3 sts twice, 2sts once and 1 st 3 times. (29(33:36)sts)
Work 4 rows without further shaping.

Shape shoulder

Cast off 9(11:12) sts at beg of next row and 10(11:12) sts at beg of foll alt row.
Work one row.
Cast off rem 10(11:12) sts.
With RS facing, rejoin yarn to rem sts, cast off centre 30 sts, patt to end.
Complete second side to match first side reversing all shaping.

SLEEVES (both alike)

Cast on 58(62:62) sts using 3¼mm (US 3) needles and yarn A.
Work 18 rows in 2-colour rib as given for medium size back.
Change to 4mm (US 6) needles and cont in patt from chart for sleeve and AT THE SAME TIME, shape sides by inc 1 st at each end of 1st row and every foll 4th row until there are 110(114:114) sts, then every foll 5th row until there are 124(128:128) sts.
Work a further 10 rows in patt.
Cast off loosely and evenly.

MAKING UP

Press all pieces as described on the information page.
Join both shoulder seams using back stitch.
Place markers 28(29:29)cm below shoulder seam on back and front.
Set in sleeves between markers using backstitch.
Join side and sleeve seams.

Neckband

With RS facing, 3¼mm (US 3) set of 4 double-pointed needles and yarn A, pick up and K 9 sts down right side back neck, 42 sts across centre back, 9 sts up left side back neck, 23 sts down left side front neck, 30 sts across centre front and 23 sts up right side front neck. (136sts)
Knit 2 rounds using yarn D.
Knit 2 rounds using yarn C.
Join in yarns A and B and work 5 rounds in 2-colour rib as given for back, working first round knitwise, then rem 4 rounds in K2, P2 rib.
Cast off in rib using yarn A. (N.B. It is important to cast off evenly and carefully. This is not an elastic rib, so it must go comfortably over the head, whilst not being too sloppy).
Press seams.

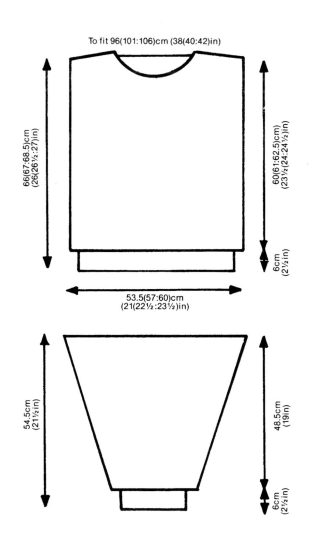

To fit 96(101:106)cm (38(40:42)in)

66(67:68.5)cm (26(26½:27)in)

60(61:62.5)cm (23½(24:24½)in)

6cm (2½in)

53.5(57:60)cm (21(22½:23½)in)

54.5cm (21½in)

48.5cm (19in)

6cm (2½in)

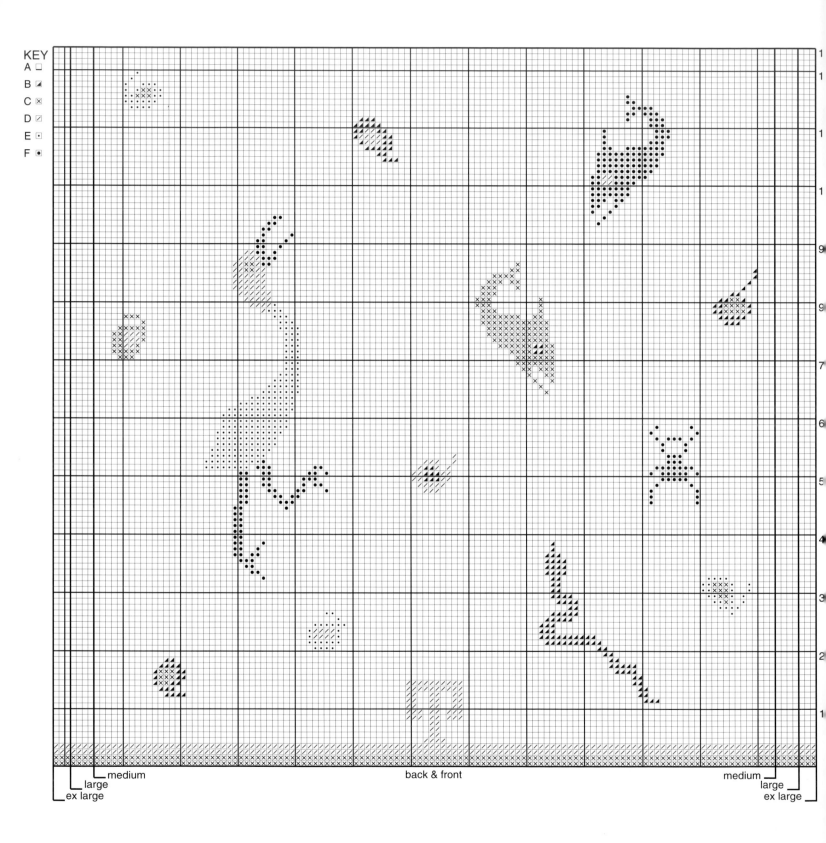

KEY
A ☐
B ◩
C ⊠
D ☑
E ⊡
F ⊙

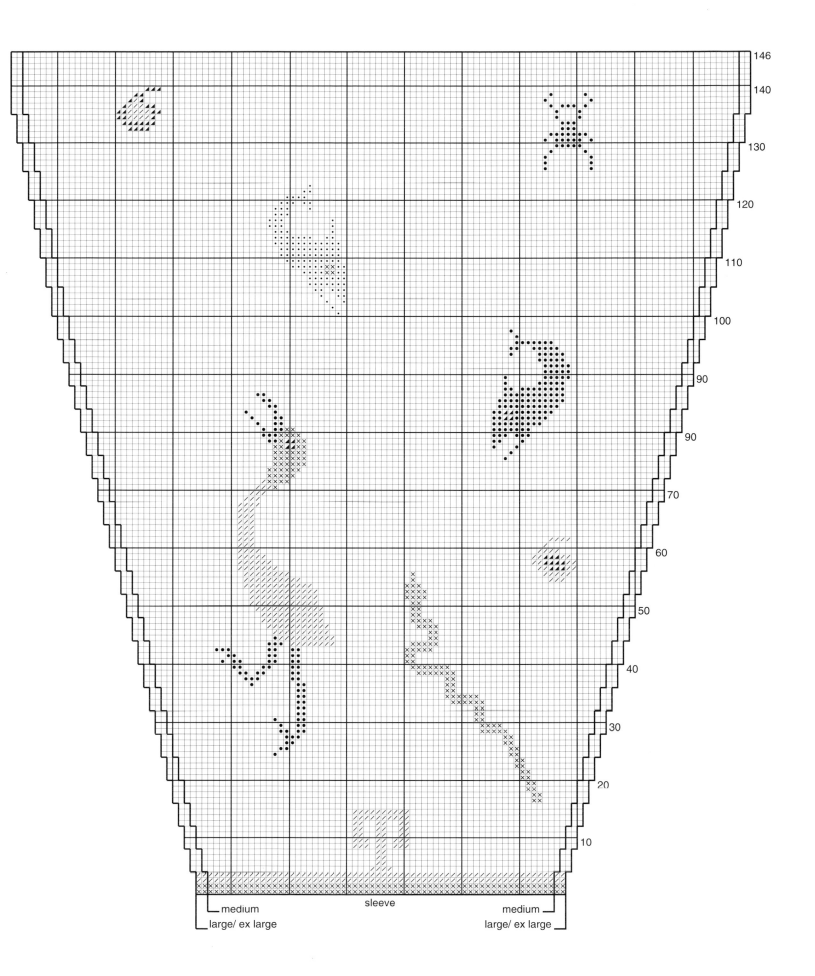

146
140
130
120
110
100
90
90
70
60
50
40
30
20
10

medium — medium
large/ ex large —— large/ ex large
sleeve

Kilim Jacket

KAFFE FASSETT

YARN

Rowan Kid Silk, Donegal Lambswool, Lightweight DK and Designer DK

A	DDK	Stone	693	1	x	50gm
B	DLT	Nutmeg	470	2	x	25gm
C	Lt Wt DK	Custard	008	2	x	25gm
D	Kid Silk	Turnip	997	4	x	25gm
E	Lt Wt DK	Pear	664	1	x	25gm
F	DLT	Oatmeal	469	3	x	25gm
G	DLT	Rye	474	4	x	25gm
H	DLT	Mist	466	4	x	25gm
J	DDK	S.Blonde	163	2	x	50gm
K	DDK	Sage	162	2	x	50gm
L	DLT	Blue Mist	476	2	x	25gm
M	DLT	Cinnamon	479	2	x	25gm
N	Lt Wt DK	Ice Blue	422	4	x	25gm
O	DLT	Eau D.Nil	458	2	x	25gm
P	Kid Silk	P.Pourri	996	3	x	25gm
R	DLT	D.Rose	462	3	x	25gm
S	DLT	Mulberry	459	3	x	25gm
T	Lt Wt DK	Pink	148	2	x	25gm
U	Lt Wt DK	Porridge	613	1	x	25gm
V	DLT	Pepper	473	1	x	25gm
W	DLT	Dragonfly	488	2	x	25gm
Y	Kid Silk	Smoke	998	7	x	25gm
Z	DLT	Dolphin	478	5	x	25gm
a	DLT	Pickle	483	5	x	25gm
b	DLT	Storm	468	3	x	25gm

NEEDLES

1 pair 5mm (no 6) (US 8)
1 pair 6mm (no 4) (US 10)

BUTTONS

6

TENSION

16 sts and 20 rows to 10cm measured over patterned stocking stitch using 6mm needles

Note: The finer yarns are used in combination e.g. YY–use 2 strands of yarn Y, FGH–use one strand of yarn F, one strand of yarn G and 1 strand of yarn H. For the combinations of yarns denoted by symbols on the chart, please refer to the chart key.

BACK

Cast on 92 sts using 5mm (US 8) needles and yarns ZZa, work 17 rows in K1, P1 rib in the following colour sequence:
1 row ZZa, 2 rows SZa, 2 rows LRV, 2 rows NPY, 2 rows BBC, 1 row BBS, 3 rows YYa, 1 row KO, 1 row Za, 2 rows RSa.
Next row (WS)(inc): Using yarns ZZZ, rib 4 (M1, rib 3) 29 times, rib 1. (121 sts)
Change to 6mm (US 10) needles and using the INTARISA technique described on the information page cont in patt from chart for back which is worked entirely in st st beg with a K row.
Work 134 rows in patt, marking each end of rows 12 and 46 for pocket openings, ending with a WS row.

Divide for neck

Patt 52 sts, turn and leave rem sts on a holder.
Work each side of neck separately.
Cast off 4 sts beg next row, patt to end.
Cast off rem 48 sts.
With RS facing rejoin yarns to rem sts, cast off centre 17 sts, patt to end.
Work 1 row.
Complete to match first side reversing all shaping.

LEFT FRONT

Cast on 46 sts using 5mm (US 8) needles and yarns ZZa.
Work 17 rows in K1, P1 rib in colour sequence as given for back.
Next row (WS)(inc): Using yarns ZZZ, rib 3 (M1, rib 3) 14 times, rib 1. (60 sts)
Change to 6mm (US 10) needles and work 91 rows in patt from chart for left front, marking position of pocket opening on side edge as for back.

Shape front neck

Next row (WS): Cast off 4 sts patt to end.
Work 3 rows.
Dec 1 st at beg next row and every foll 4th row until 48 sts remain.
Cont without further shaping until front matches back to shoulder ending with a WS row.
Cast off.

RIGHT FRONT

Work as given for left front, foll chart for right front and reversing all shaping.

SLEEVES (both alike)

Cast on 37 sts using 5mm (US 8) needles and yarns ZZa.
Work 17 rows in K1, P1 rib as given for back.
Next row (WS)(inc): Using yarns ZZZ, rib 1, (M1, rib 2) 18 times. (55 sts)
Change to 6mm (US 10) needles and work 72 rows in patt from chart for sleeve and AT THE SAME TIME shape sides by inc 1 st at each end of 3rd row and every foll 3rd row to 97 sts, taking extra sts into patt as they occur.
Cast off loosely and evenly.

MAKING UP

PRESS all pieces as described on the information page.
Join both shoulder seams using backstitch.
Pocket edgings
With RS facing 5mm needles and yarns YZa, pick up and knit 30 sts evenly between markers on side edge of front.
Knit 1 row to form foldline.
Work a further 4 rows in st st beg with a K row.
Cast off loosely and evenly.
Work other side to match.

Left pocket lining

With RS facing using 6mm (US 10) needles and yarns YZa, pick up and knit 31 sts evenly between markers on left side edge of back and cont in st st beg with a purl row and AT THE SAME cast on 8 sts at beg of first row and dec 1 st at end of 5th row and every foll alt row until 24 sts rem.
Cast off evenly.

Right pocket lining

Work as given for left pocket lining reversing all shaping.

Buttonhole band

With RS facing, 5mm (US 8) needles and yarns ZZa, pick up and knit 81 sts evenly along right front edge for a womens jacket, left front edge for a mans.
Next row (WS)(buttonhole): P1, (P2tog, yo, P2tog, P11) 5 times, P2tog, yo twice, P2tog, P1.
Next row: Knit across row Knitting into front and back of yo on previous row.
Next row (WS): Knit to form foldline.
Work a further 8 rows in st st beg with a knit row and work buttonholes on rows 2 and 3 to

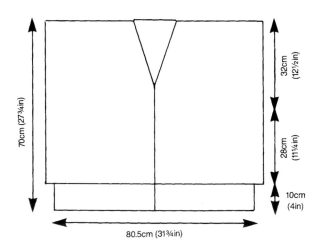

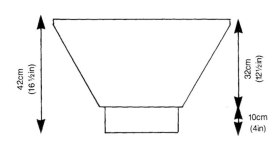

correspond with those made previously.
Cast off loosely and evenly.

Buttonband

Work as given for buttonhole band omitting buttonholes.
Fold front bands to WS along foldline and slip st loosely into place.
Collar
Cast on 133 sts using 5mm (US 8) needles and yarns ZZa.
Cont in K1, P1 rib in colour sequence below and AT THE SAME TIME shape collar by casting off 4 sts at beg of 7th row and every foll row until 17sts rem.

Colour sequence

1 row ZZa, 2 rows SZa, 2 rows LRV, 2 rows NPY, 2 rows BBC, 1 row BBS, 3 rows YYa, 1 row KO, 1 row Za, 2 rows RSa, 3 rows ZZZ, 2 rows PYZ, 3 rows NPY, 3 rows MOZ, 2 rows Zaa, 1 row JMa, 4 rows Ybb, 2 rows GRS.
Cast off using GRS.
Attach shaped collar neatly to neckline, matching centre of collar to centre back neck and cast on edge of collar and foldlines of front bands in one continuous line. Place markers 30cm down from shoulder seam on back and fronts.
Set in sleeve between markers.
Join sleeve seams and side seams above and below pocket markers.
Fold pocket edgings to WS along foldline and slip st loosely into place.
Slip st pocket linings loosely to WS of Jacket fronts.
Sew on buttons to correspond with buttonholes.
Press seams.

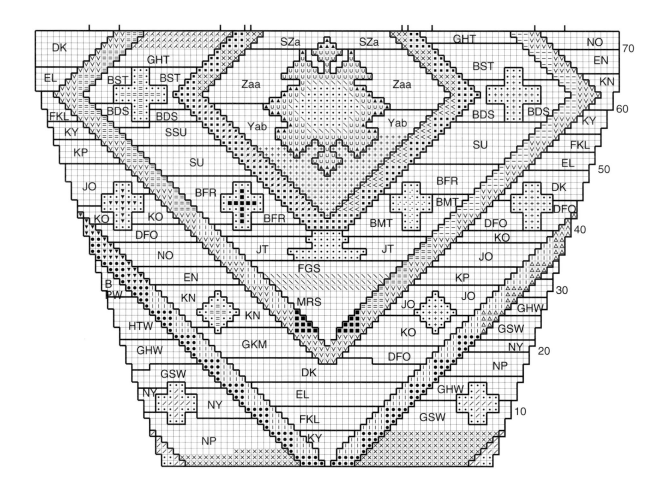

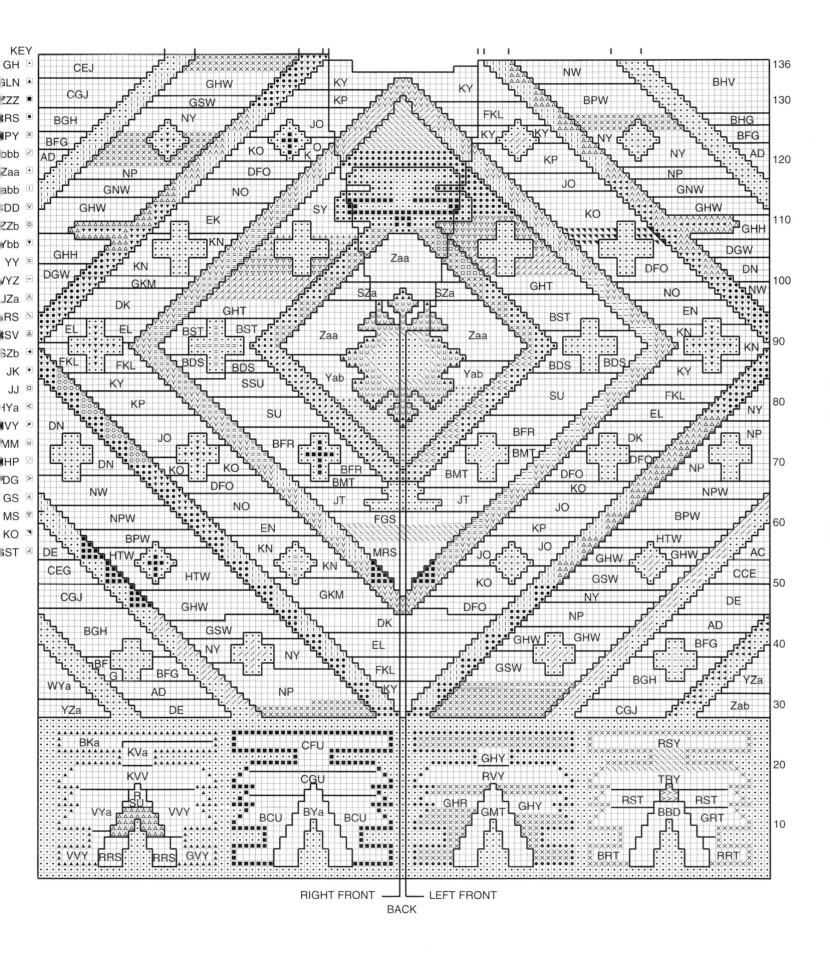

RIGHT FRONT ⎯⎯ ⎯ LEFT FRONT

BACK

Tex

KIM HARGREAVES

YARN

Rowan Denim and Handknit D.K. Cotton

JACKET

Denim	Nashville	225	22	23 x	50gm

WAISTCOAT

A	Denim	Nashville	225	12	x	50gm
B	Hk.DK	Icewater	239	3	x	50gm

BUTTONS

Jacket	10
Waistcoat	5

NEEDLES

1 pair 3¼mm (no 10) (US 3)
1 pair 4mm (no 8) (US 6)

The denim yarn will shrink when washed so the knitting will be longer by approx 1/5th of the finished garment after washing. The tension is before washing

TENSION (before washing)
20 sts and 28 rows to 10cm measured over pattern using 4mm (no 8) (US 6) needles

Jacket with textured yoke

BACK
Cast on 113(123) sts using 3¼mm (US 3) needles.
Work 10 rows in garter st, i.e. knit every row.
Change to 4mm (US 6) needles and cont in st st beg with a K row and AT THE SAME TIME, shape sides by inc 1 st at each end of 11th row and every foll 10th row to 127(137) sts.
Cont without further shaping until work measures 40(42.5)cm from cast on edge ending with a WS row.

Textured yoke
Cont in patt from chart, until chart row 92(102) completed ending with a WS row.

Shape shoulders and back neck
Cast off 15(17) sts at beg next 2 rows.
Cast off 15(17) sts, patt 20(21), turn leaving rem sts on a holder.
Work each side separately.
Cast off 4 sts, patt to end.
Cast off rem 16(17) sts.
With RS facing rejoin yarn to rem sts, cast off centre 27 sts, patt to end.
Complete to match first side reversing shaping.

POCKET LINING (make two)
Cast on 24(28) sts using 4mm (US 6) needles and work 30 rows in st st beg with a K row.
Leave sts on a holder.

LEFT FRONT

Cast on 62(67) sts using 3¼mm (US 3) needles.
Work 4 rows in garter st.
Next row (buttonhole): K to last 5 sts, cast off 2, K3.
Next row: Knit to end casting on 2 sts over

those cast off on previous row.
Work 3 more rows in garter st.
Next row (WS): K6 sts and leave these on a holder, K to end. (56(61)sts)
Change to 4mm (US 6) needles and cont in st st beg with a knit row until front matches back to beg of yoke and AT THE SAME TIME, inc 1 st at side edge on 11th row and every foll 10th row to 63(68) sts.

Textured yoke
Cont from chart until chart row 22 completed.

Place pocket
Work 16(20) sts, slip next 24(28) sts onto a holder and in place of these work across sts from first pocket lining, work to end.
Cont as for back until front is 15 rows shorter than back to beg shoulder shaping ending with a RS row.

Shape front neck
Keeping patt correct cast off 4 sts at beg next row and 2 foll alt rows.
Dec 1 st at neck edge on next 3 rows and 2 foll alt rows. (46(51)sts)
Cont without further shaping until front matches back to beg shoulder shaping.

Shape shoulder
Cast off 15(17) sts at beg next row and foll alt row.
Work 1 row.
Cast off rem 16(17) sts.

RIGHT FRONT

Work as for left front reversing all shaping and position of pocket.

LEFT SLEEVE

Cuff
Cast on 61 sts using 3¼mm (US 3) needles and work 6 rows in garter st.
Next row (buttonhole): K3, cast off 2 sts, knit to end.
Next row: Knit across row casting on 2 sts over those cast off on previous row.
Work 4 more rows in garter st.

Divide for placket
Change to 4mm (US 6) needles, K43 sts, turn leaving rem sts on a holder for back sleeve.

Front sleeve
Next row (WS): Inc into first st, P to last 4 sts, K4. (44sts)
Next row: Knit to last st, M1, K1. (45sts)
Next row: Purl to last 4 sts, K4.
Next row: Knit to end.
Rep last 2 rows once more, then P row again.
Keeping 4 edge sts in garter st as set, inc 1 st at end of next row and every foll 6th row to 34 rows st st completed, ending with a WS row. (50sts)
Leave sts on a holder.
Break yarn.

Back sleeve
With RS facing and using 4mm (US 6) needles, rejoin yarn to rem sts, inc in first st, K to end. (19sts)
Next row (WS): K4, P to end.
Next row: K1, M1, K to end.
Cont until 33 rows st st completed working 4 edge sts in garter st and inc every 6th row as before, ending with a RS row. (25sts)
Next row (WS): Cast off 4 sts, P to end. (21sts)

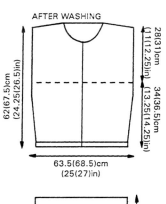

AFTER WASHING

28(31)cm (11(12.25)in)
34(36.5)cm (13.25(14.25)in)
62(67.5)cm (24.25(26.5)in)
63.5(68.5)cm (25(27)in)

43(46)cm (17(18)in)
3cm (1.25in)

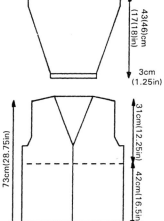

73cm(28.75in)
31cm(12.25in)
42cm(16.5in)
55.5cm(22in)

Next row: K across 21 sts of back sleeve, K across 50 sts of front sleeve. (71sts)
Cont in st st inc every 6th row as before to 101 sts.
Cont without further shaping until sleeve measures 51(54)cm or length required from top of band.

RIGHT SLEEVE
Cuff
Cast on 61 sts using 3¼mm (US 3) needles and work 6 rows in garter st.
Next row (buttonhole): K to last 5 sts, cast off 2, K3.
Next row: Knit across row casting on 2 sts over those cast off on previous row.
Work 4 more rows in garter st.
Divide for placket
Change to 4mm (US 6) needles, K18, turn, leaving rem sts on a holder for front sleeve.
Back sleeve
Next row (WS): Inc into first st, P to last 4 sts, K4. (19sts)
Next row (inc): Knit to last st, M1, K1. (20 sts)
Next row: Purl to last 4 sts, K4.
Next row: Knit to end.
Rep last 2 rows once more, then P row again.
Keeping 4 edge sts in garter st as set, inc 1 st at end of next row and every foll 6th row, cont until 33 rows st st completed, ending with a RS row.
Row 34: Purl to last 4 sts, cast off 4 sts. 21sts.
Break yarn, leaving rem sts on a holder.
Front sleeve
With RS facing and using 4mm (US 6) needles, rejoin yarn to rem sts, inc in first st K to end. (44sts)
Next row: K4, P to end.
Next row (inc): K1, M1, K to end.
Keeping 4 edge sts in garter sts and inc every 6th row cont until 34 rows st st completed ending with a WS row. (50sts)
Next row (RS): K across sts for front sleeve, K across sts for back sleeve (71sts)
Complete as for left sleeve.

Waistcoat with striped yoke
BACK
Cast on 111 sts using 3¼mm (US 3) needles and work 10 rows in garter st, i.e. knit every row.
Change to 4mm (US 6) needles.
Row 1 (RS): Knit to end.
Row 2: K5, P to last 5 sts, K5.
Rep these two rows until work measures 15cm from cast on edge. ***
Cont in st st until work measures 49cm from cast on edge ending with a WS row.
Striped yoke
Joining in and breaking off colours as required cont in patt from chart which is worked entirely in st st beg with a K row, until chart row 28 completed, end with a WS row.
SHAPE ARMHOLE
Cast off 6 sts at beg next 2 rows.
Dec 1 st at each end of next 4 rows and 5 foll alt rows. (81sts)
Cont in patt from chart until chart row 102 com-

pleted ending with a WS row.
Shape shoulders and back neck
Cast off 8 sts at beg next 2 rows.
Cast off 8 sts, patt 13, turn leaving rem sts on a holder.
Work each side of neck separately.
Cast off 4 sts, patt to end.
Cast off 9 rem sts.
With RS facing rejoin yarn to rem sts, cast off centre 23 sts, patt to end.
Complete to match first side reversing shaping.

LEFT FRONT
Cast on 60 sts using 3¼mm (US 3) needles and work 9 rows in garter st.
Next row (WS): K5, leave these sts on a holder for front band, K to end. (55sts)
Change to 4mm (US 6) needles.
Row 1: Knit to end.
Row 2: P to last 5 sts, K5.
Rep these 2 rows until work matches back to ***.
Cont in st st until front matches back to beg yoke.
Striped yoke
Joining in and breaking of colours as required cont in patt from chart until chart row 17 completed ending with a RS row.
Shape front neck
Dec 1 st at neck edge on next row and every foll 5th row to 25 sts and AT THE SAME TIME, when front matches back to beg armhole shaping, shape armhole as folls:
Shape armhole
Cast off 6 sts at beg next row.
Work 1 row.
Dec 1 st at armhole edge on next 4 rows and 5 foll alt rows.
Cont without further shaping until front matches back to beg shoulder shaping ending with a WS row.
Shape shoulder
Cast off 8 sts at beg next row and foll alt row.
Work 1 row.
Cast off rem 9 sts.

RIGHT FRONT
Work as for left front reversing all shaping.

MAKING UP
Join both shoulder seams and side seams using back stitch.
Jacket only
Pocket tops (both alike)
Slip sts from holder onto 3¼mm (US 3) needle.
Rows 1 and 2: Knit to end.
Work 4 more rows in st st beg with a K row.
Cast off.
Turn hem to inside and slip st into place.
Button band
Slip 6 sts from holder of right front onto a 3¼mm needle and work in garter st until band fits neatly up to beg neck shaping when slightly stretched.
Slip st into place.
Mark position of 6 buttons, the first to come opposite buttonhole made on left front band, the

last to come 1cm from top of band and other 4 spaced evenly between.
Buttonhole band
Work as for button band with the addition of 5 buttonholes worked to correspond with button markers and worked as folls:
Buttonhole row: K2, cast off 2, K2.
Next row: Knit to end, casting on 2 sts over those cast off on previous row.
Collar
Cast on 100 sts using 3¼mm (US 3) needles.
Knit 2 rows.
Next row (inc): K2, M1, K to last 2 sts, M1, K2.
Knit 3 rows.
Rep the last 4 rows until 42 rows in all completed.
Cast off loosely and evenly.
Slip st collar neatly into place starting and ending halfway across front bands and matching centre back collar to centre back neck.
DO NOT SEW SLEEVE INTO GARMENT UNTIL AFTER WASHING
Waistcoat only
Buttonband and collar
Slip 5 sts from holder on left front onto a 3¼mm (US 3) needle and cont in garter st until bands fits neatly when slightly stretched up front to beg front shaping, ending with a RS row.
Shape collar
Next row (WS): K1, M1, K to end.
Knit 3 rows.
Rep the last 4 rows until 24 sts on needle, ending at straight edge of work.
Cast off 8 sts, now cast on 8 sts using the cable method as folls: replace st on RH needle onto LH needle, * insert point of RH needle between 1st and 2nd st on LH needle, yon, bring loop through and place loop onto LH needle, thus one st cast on, rep from * 7 times more. (24sts)
Cont without further shaping until collar fits neatly up to left front to shoulder seam and across to centre back neck.
With shaped edge of collar to front edge slip stitch collar and band into place, adjusting length if necessary.
Cast off.
Mark position of 5 buttons, the first to come opposite top of side vent, the last to come 1.5cm below start of front neck shaping and other 3 spaced evenly between.
Buttonhole band and collar
Work as for button band with the addition of 5 buttonholes worked to correspond with button markers as folls:
Buttonhole row: K2, yon, K2tog, K1.
Armhole edging (both alike)
Cast on 4 sts using 3¼mm (US 3) needles and work in garter st until bands fits around armhole edge when slightly stretched.
Cast off.
Slip st into place.
Join armhole edging and side seam above side vents.
Jacket and waistcoat
See ball band for washing instructions
See information page for finishing instructions.

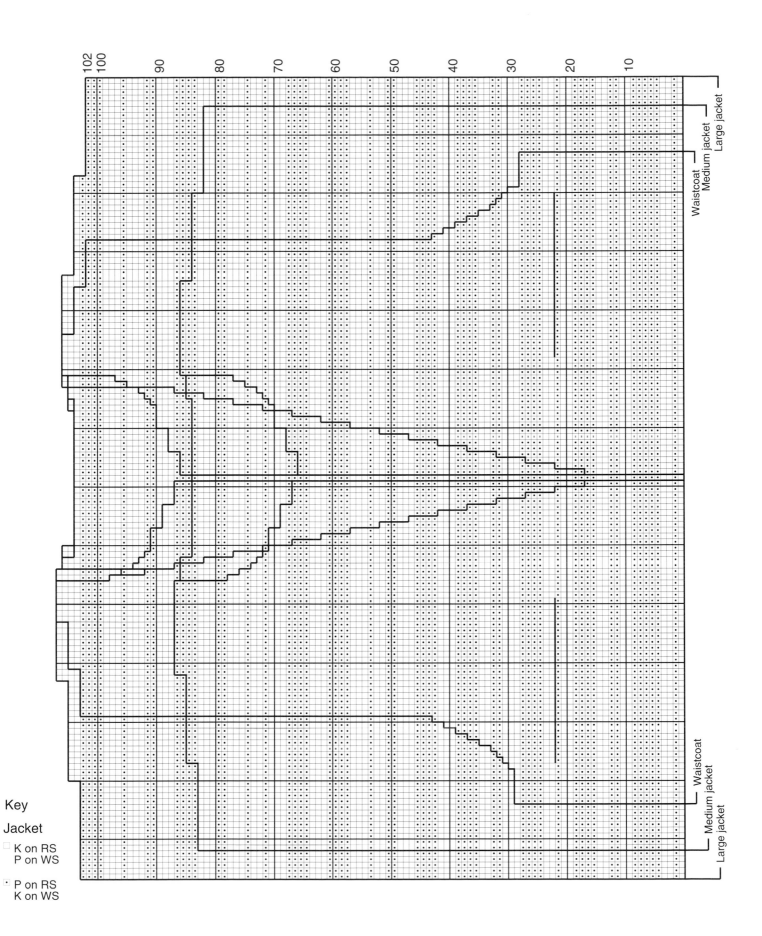

Key

Jacket

☐ K on RS
P on WS

⊡ P on RS
K on WS

Waistcoat

☐ A

⊡ B

Picking Up The Pieces

GAIL ABBOTT

A piece of knitting need not be ruined because you have dropped a stitch or worked some stitches in the wrong colour. Follow our guide to correcting your mistakes and your finished knitting will be as perfect as you could wish

Most problems are caused when we rush blindly ahead without noticing that a stitch has been dropped or a colour wrongly knitted. Carefully checking each row before starting the next is always a good plan, as any problems can be rectified before too may rows have been worked above the mistake. A dropped stitch is easily picked up if it is only one row down. However, if you leave it to work its way down the knitting, especially if you are knitting a complicated Fair Isle or intarsia piece, the problem can be much more difficult to sort out. When you are knitting from a chart and see too late that one or two stitches have been worked in the wrong colour, it is better to wait until the whole piece is finished before correcting the mistake with Swiss darning.

DROPPED STITCHES

When a stitch slips off the end of the needle unnoticed and the you carry on, the stitch is left hanging in the middle of the row. This is why it is a good idea to check the last row you have worked before starting the next. If you notice a dropped stitch, it can be easily picked up on the way back along the next row.

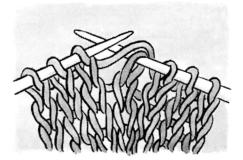

To pick up a knit stitch

Slip the right-hand needle through the stitch from front to back, picking up the horizontal strand above it at the same time. Keep the strand behind the stitch—don't let it jump over the stitch to the front. Slip the left-hand needle through the dropped stitch from back to front.

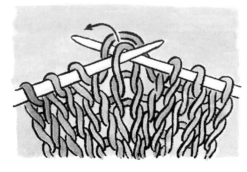

Lift the stitch over the strand behind it and off the needle. The strand of yarn is pulled through the stitch by the right-hand needle, forming a new stitch. This new stitch can be slipped back onto the left-hand needle and knitted as normal.

To pick up a purl stitch

Slip the right-hand needle through the dropped stitch from back to front, picking up the horizontal strand above it. This time, keep the strand in front of the stitch, don't let it slip behind.

Slip the left-hand needle through the dropped stitch from front to back. Lift the stitch over the strand and off the needle. The right-hand needle will pull the strand through the stitch to form a new stitch. Slip this onto the left-hand needle and purl it as normal.

To pick up a stitch a few rows down

When you are knitting with a smooth yarn, such as Cotton Glace or Nice Cotton, you'll find that a dropped stitch can quickly run down a few rows, forming a 'ladder' of strands above it. Always pick up these stitches with the right side (or knit side) of the work facing you. Hold the stitch (or stitches if there are more than one) on a safety pin to stop it running down even farther as soon as you spot it.

Using a medium-sized crochet hook, slip the hook through the rogue stitch from front to back. Keep the crochet hook pointing upwards slightly so that the stitch doesn't fall off, and insert it under the strand immediately above the stitch. Pull this first strand through the stitch. Continue working up the 'ladder', picking up the strands one by one until all the strands have been picked up and one stitch is left on the hook. Insert the left-hand needle through the stitch from front to back and continue the work as before.

If you have continued to knit a few rows above a dropped stitch, the knitting may have become too tight to successfully pick up the stitch using a crochet hook method. There will not be enough spare yarn to rectify 'ladders', so the only solution is to unravel the rows using either of the methods shown at right.

UNRAVELLING ROWS

When knitting in colour, or in a textured stitch, you may need to return to a mistake made on a previous row in order to successfully correct it. There are two methods for doing this.

Unravelling a single row—one stitch at a time

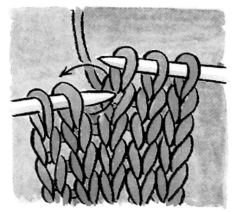

On a knit stitch, insert the left-hand needle through the centre of the loop below the first stitch on the right-hand needle. Do this from front to back. Pull the loop upwards slightly so that the stitch above drops off the end of the right-hand needle and pull the yarn free of the loop. Continue right along the row in the same way.

On a purl stitch, the same method is used.

Unravelling a few rows

If a mistake is discovered a few rows back, you may find that unravelling more than one row stitch by stitch takes too long. The only thing to be done here is to take the work off the needles and unravel the yarn. Mark the row below the mistake with a coloured marker or safety pin first, and don't forget to mark the number of rows you intend to pull back on your pattern if you are in the middle of any increasing or decreasing.

Using a smaller-sized needle than the ones you are knitting with, pick up the loops along the marked row, taking the needle through the stitches from front to back as shown here.

Gently pull the yarn and wind it into a ball as you pull it free of the original stitches. When unravelling knitting worked in two or more colours, wind the different colours separately. Yarns with texture, like chenille, the tweeds and kid silk, will need extra care as the stitches will need to be gently eased apart in places. The mistake will fall away with the unravelled yarn, and you can continue knitting from your pattern as before.

TIP

Unravelled yarn can be re-knitted if it has only recently been knitted for the first time. If the yarn has been knitted up for some time before being pulled out you may find it is too crinkly to re-knit. To re-use a large amount of unravelled, crinkly

yarn, compress the ends of a wire coat-hanger and wind the unravelled yarn onto this. Hang the yarn over a steaming kettle or pan of boiling water—it will miraculously straighten for re-winding and re-knitting.

SWISS DARNING

The best way to correct mistakes in a Fair Isle or intarsia pattern is to keep a careful eye on the work as you knit, unravelling any rows with mistakes, and re-knitting them as described above. However, with a really complicated pattern, even the most careful knitter might miss one or two stitches, or work them in the wrong colour or even in the wrong place. Swiss darning is a method for working on top of incorrect stitches after the work has been cast off, and before it is blocked out or pressed. Swiss darning can be used for reworking single stitches, or for small blocks of colour.

Swiss darning on a horizontal row

Use a tapestry needle threaded with the correct coloured yarn, and weave in the end on the

wrong side of the work. Working from right to left, bring the needle through the base of the first stitch to be covered with the new colour. Now take the needle under the stitch above and back through the base of the first stitch. The first stitch will be completely covered and appears in the new colour. Continue along the row for as many stitches as required.

Swiss darning on a vertical row

Thread a needle and weave in the end as before. Working from bottom to top, bring the nee-

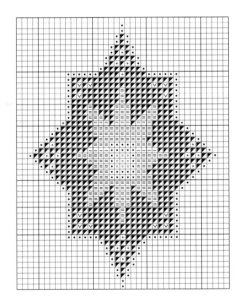

dle out through the base of the first stitch and cover it in the same way. Now take the needle through the base of the stitch above and continue covering stitches in a vertical row.

TIP

Less experienced knitters can use Swiss darning when working a complicated intarsia pattern to fill in the smaller, fussy bits. For example, knit the broader shapes of colour like the centre square and the outer and inner star as shown on this chart. Swiss darn the outlines shown by the symbol • and the details shown by the symbols ◆ and V.

With these recovery methods, there is no need for even the most inexperienced knitters to leave mistakes to in their work. All your finished knitwear will be as perfect as possible, and only you will ever know that there was a problem to solve.

Illustrations by John Batten

Information Page

TENSION

Obtaining the correct tension is perhaps the single factor that can make the difference between a successful garment and a disastrous one. It controls both the shape and size of an article, so any variation, however slight, can distort the finished look of the garment. No one wants to spend hours and hours making a "skinny rib" when they really want a "sloppy Joe". Different designers feature in our books and it is **their** tension, given at the **start** of each pattern, that you must match. Within each pattern there may be different tensions given, for instance, if either **intarsia** or **Fair Isle** techniques **and stocking stitch** are used in the same design. We strongly advise that you knit a square in pattern and/or stocking stitch (depending on the pattern instruction) of perhaps 5 to 10 more stitches and 5 to 10 more rows than those given in the tension note. Place the finished square on a flat surface and measure the central area. If you have too many stitches to 10cm (4 in), try again using larger needles; if you have too few stitches to 10cm, try again using smaller needles. Once you have achieved the correct tension, your garment will be knitted to the measurements given in the pattern. For more information on tension, see 'Knitting Workshop' on page 00.

All ribs should be knitted to a firm tension; for some knitters it may be necessary to use a smaller needle. In order to prevent sagging in cuffs and welts, we suggest you use a "knitting-in" elastic.

SIZE NOTE

The instructions are given for the smallest size. Where there is more than one size, the figures in brackets are for the larger sizes. If there is only one set of figures, it refers to all sizes. For ease in reading charts it may be helpful to have the chart enlarged and outline the size you intend to knit.

CHART NOTE

Many of the patterns in the book are worked from charts. Each square on a chart represents a stitch and each line of squares a row of knitting. When working from the charts, read odd rows (k) from right to left and even rows (p) from left to right, unless otherwise stated. Each colour used is given a different symbol or letter and these are shown in the **materials** section or in the **key** alongside the chart of each pattern.

KNITTING WITH COLOUR

There are two main methods of working colour into a knitted fabric: intarsia and Fair Isle techniques. The first method produces a single thickness of fabric and is usually used where a colour is only required in a particular area of a row and does not repeat in pattern across the row, as in the Fair Isle technique.

Intarsia: The simplest way to do this is to cut short lengths of yarn for each motif or block of colour used in a row. Then, joining in the various colours at the appropriate point on the row, link one colour to the next by twisting them around each other where they meet on the wrong side to avoid gaps. All ends can then either be darned along the colour join lines as each motif is completed, or they can be "knitted in" to the fabric as each colour is worked into the pattern. This is done in much the same way as "weaving in" yarns when working the Fair Isle technique and does save time darning in ends. It is essential that the tension is noted for intarsia, as this may vary from the stocking stitch if both are used in the same pattern.

Fair Isle Knitting: When two or three colours are worked repeatedly across a row, strand the yarn not in use loosely behind the stitches being worked. If you are working with more than two colours, treat the "floating" yarns as if they were one yarn and always spread the stitches to their correct width to keep them elastic. It is advisable not to carry the stranded or "floating" yarns over more than three stitches at a time, but to weave them under and over the colour you are working. The "floating" yarns are therefore caught at the back of the work. For more information on knitting with colour, see 'Colour Works' on page 74.

PRESSING

After working for hours knitting a garment, it seems a great pity that many garments are spoiled because so little care is taken in the pressing and finishing. After darning in all the ends, block each piece of knitting. Press each piece, except ribs, gently, using a warm iron over a damp cloth. Take special care to press the edges as this will make the sewing up both easier and neater. For more information, see 'All Blocked Out' on page 55.

FINISHING INSTRUCTIONS

When stitching the pieces together, match the colour patterns very carefully. Use a back stitch for all main knitting seams and an edge to edge stitch for all ribs unless otherwise stated. Join left shoulder seam using back stitch and neckband seam (where appropriate) using an edge to edge stitch.

Sleeves

Set-in sleeves: Ease sleeve head into armhole using back stitch.

Square set-in sleeve: Set sleeve head into armhole, the straight sides at top of sleeve, to form a neat right-angle to cast-off stitches at armhole on back and front, using back stitch.

Straight cast-off sleeve: Place centre of cast-off edge of sleeve to shoulder seam. With back stitch, sew in sleeve using markers as guidelines where applicable.

Slip stitch pocket edgings and linings into place. Sew on buttons to correspond with buttonholes. After sewing up, press seams and hems. *Ribbed welts, neckbands, and any areas of garter stitch should not be pressed.*

ABBREVIATIONS	
K	knit
P	purl
st(s)	stitch(es)
inc	increas(e)(ing)
dec	decreas(e)(ing)
st st	stocking stitch (1 row K, 1 row P)
garter st	garter stitch (K every row)
beg	begin(ning)
foll	following
folls	follows
rem	remain(ing)
rev	revers(e)(ing)
rep	repeat
alt	alternate
cont	continue
patt	pattern
tog	together
mm	millimetres
cm	centimetres
in(s)	inch(es)
RS	right side
WS	wrong side
psso	pass slip stitch over
tbl	through back of loop
sl	slip
M1	make one stitch by picking up horizontal loop before next stitch and knitting into back of it
M1P	make one stitch by picking up horizontal loop before next stitch and purling into back of it
yon	yarn over needle
yfwd	yarn forward
yrn	yarn round needle
B.Cr	back cross: slip next st onto a cable needle, hold at back of work, K2, then P1 from cable needle
F.Cr	front cross: slip next 2 sts onto a cable needle, hold at front of work, P1, then K2 from cable needle
LT	left twist: knit into back of second stitch, then knit into back of first stitch, slip both stitches off needle
RT	right twist: K2tog leaving stitches on left hand needle, then insert right hand needle from the front between the 2 stitches just worked and knit first stitch again, then slip both stitches off needle together
C4F	cable 4 front: slip next 2 sts onto cable needle and hold at front of work, K2 sts, then K2 from cable needle
C4B	cable 4 back: slip next 2 sts onto cable needle and hole at back of work, K2 sts, then K2 from cable needle
K1b	knit into back of stitch
P1b	purl into back of stitch
LH	left-hand needle
RH	right-hand needle
ch	chain
dc	double crochet
T3B	slip next st onto cable needle and hold at back of work, K2 sts, then P1 st from cable needle
T3F	slip next 2 sts onto cable needle and hold at front of work, P1, then K2 sts from cable needle

STOCKISTS

Stockists designated as 'Rowan at . . .' are Rowan dedicated shops or departments, many offering professional help and mail order facilities

Australia

Distributor: Coats Spencer Crafts, Level 1 , 382 Wellington Road, Mulgrave North, Victoria, Australia 3170. Tel : 61 39561 2288

Canterbury–Rowan at Sunspun, 185 Canterbury Road VIC 3126. Tel (03) 9830 1609 Mail Order.

Lindfield–Rowan at Greta's Handcrafts Centre, 321 Pacific Highway, Lindfield NSW 2070. Tel (02) 9416 2489

Malvern–Wondaflex Yarncraft Centre, 1353 Malvern Road, VIC 3144. Tel (03) 9822 6231

Montrose–Montrose Wool & Craft, Shop 6/926-930, Mt Dandenong Tourist Road, VIC 3765. Tel (03) 9728 6437

Canada

Distributor: Diamond Yarn, 9697 St Laurent, Montreal, Quebec H3L 2N1 Tel (514) 388-6188 / Diamond Yarn (Toronto), 155 Martin Ross, Unit 3, Toronto, Ontario M3J 2L9. Tel (416) 736-6111

Alberta

Calgary–Gina Brown Holdings, 17, 6624 Centre Sr S.E.,T2C 0C6. Tel (403) 225-2200

Calgary–Fiber Hut. No1-2614 4th Street N W, T2M 3A1. Tel (403) 230-3822

Edmonton–Knit & Purl, 10412-124 Street, T5N 1R5. Tel (403) 482-2150

Edmonton–Wool Revival, 6513-112 Avenue, T5W 0P1. Tel (403) 471-2749

St Albert–Burwood House, 205 Carnegie Drive T8N 5B2. Tel (403) 459-4828

British Columbia

Chilliwack–Country Craft Creations, 46291 Yale Road East, V2P 2P7. Tel (604) 792-5434

Duncan–The Loom, R.R. #7,V9L 4W4 Tel (250) 746-5250

Prince George–House of Wool, 1282 N.Nechako Road, V2K 1A6 Tel (250) 562-2803

Richmond–Rowan at Craft Cottage, 7577 Elmbridge Way, V6X 2Z8 Tel (604) 278-0313

Richmond–Imagine Craft Co Ltd, 1835-4311 Hazelbridge Way, V6X 3V7. Tel (604) 270-9683

Sidney–Rowan at In Sheep's Clothing, 9711 Fifth Street, V8L 2W9 Tel (250) 656-2499

Vancouver–Knit & Stitch, 2419 Marine Drive, V7V 1L3. Tel (604) 922-1023

Victoria–Boutique de Laine, 2530 Estevan Ave, V8R 2S7 Tel (250) 592-9616

Victoria–Greatest Knits, 1294 Gladstone Ave, V8T 1G6 Tel (250) 386-5523

Manitoba

Winnipeg–Rowan at Ram Wools, 143 Smith Street, R3C 1J5 Tel (204) 942-2797–Mail Order Available

Nova Scotia

Dartmouth–Fleece Artist, 1174 Mineville Road, B2Z 1K8 Tel (902) 462-0602

Ontario

Ancaster–Rowan at The Needle Emporium, 420 Wilson St. East, L9G 4S4. Tel 01 800 667-9167 Mail Order Service

Belleville–Classic Wool Shop, 169 Albert St, K8N 3N5 Tel (613) 966- 6595

Carleton Place–Real Wool Shop, 142 Franktown Road, Box 130. K7C 3P3 Tel (613) 257-2714

Dundas–Rena's Yarns, 6 Sydenham Street. L9H 2T4 Tel (905) 627-2918

Haliburton–Marty's Custom Knits, Box 857, Highland Street, KOM 1SO. Tel (705) 457-3216

Kemptville–Your Creation (Jill Andrew), 3767 Mapleshore Drive. K0G 1J0 Tel (613) 826-3261

Kingston–Rowan at The Wool Room, 2-313 University Avenue, K7L 3R3. Tel (613) 544-9544 or Tel Toll Free 1 800 449-5868

Oakville–The Wool Bin, 236 Lakeshore Road East, L6J 1H8 Tel (905) 845-9512

Orillia–Imaginit 2000, 3493 Bayou Road, R R No 3, L3V 6H3 Tel (705) 689-8676

Oshawa–Rowan at Alexandra's 35 Division Street, L1G 5L8

Tel (905) 723-7148

Ottawa–Claire's Knitting Place, 1243 Wellington Street, K1Y 3A3 Tel (613) 724-6622

Ottawa–Woolaine, 1200 St Laurent, Ste. 403A, K1K 3B8. Tel (613) 745-3094

Ottawa–Your Creation (Jill Andrew), 3767 Mapleshore Drive (Kemptville). K0G 1J0 Tel (613) 826 3261

Pembroke–Jane's Wool Studio, 128 Pembroke St. W. K8A 5M8 Tel (613) 735-2288

Perth–The Knitting Studio, 2-63 Gore St. E. K7H 1H8. Tel (613) 267-4839

Richmond Hill–Rowan at The Hill Knittery, 10720 Yonge St L4C 3C9 Tel (905) 770-4341 Mail Order Service Email: thehillknittery@cheerful.com

Toronto–Rowan at Celtic Fox, 1721 Bayview Ave, M4G 3C1. Tel (416)487-8177 or TOLL FREE (888) 329-3334 Fax (416) 487-9534

Toronto–Rowan at Passionknit Ltd., 3467 Yonge Street, M4N 2N3 Tel (416) 322-0688 or Fax (416) 864 0984

Toronto–Rowan at Romni Wools Ltd, 658 Queen St. West M6J 1E6 Tel (416) 368-0202 Mail Order Service available

Toronto–(The) Wool Mill, 2170 Danforth Avenue, M4C 1K3 Tel (416) 696-2670

Toronto–Village Yarns, 4895 Dundas Street West, M9A 1B2 Tel (416) 232-2361

Toronto–(The) Yarn Boutique, 1719A Bloor Street West, M6P 1B2 Tel (416) 760-9129

Toronto–Studio Limestone, 16 Fenwick Ave, M4K 3H3 Tel (416) 469-4018 (Mail Order Only)

Quebec

Montreal–A la Tricoteuse, 779 Rachel Est, H2J 2H4 Tel (514) 527-2451

Quebec City–Indigo Inc., 155 Rue St. Paul, G1K 3W2 Tel (418) 694-1419

St Lambert–Saute Mouton, 20 Webster, J4P 1N8. Tel (514) 671-1155

St Elie d'Orford–Entrepot St Elie, 128 Chemin Dion, J0B 2SO Tel (819) 569-7065

Westmount–Brickpoint Studios, 317-319 Victoria Avenue, H3Z 2L6 Tel (514) 489-0993

Saskatchewan

Saskatoon–Prairie Lily Weavers, #7 1730 Quebec Avenue, S7K 1V9 Tel (306) 665 2771 Fax (306) 343-9095 Mail Order Service available

European Stockists

Austria

Wien–Rowan at Wolle & Knopfe–Riki Sauberer, Josefstadter Str. 14, A-1080 Tel 1/40 35 735 Email: WOLLE@eunet.at

Belgium

Distributor: Pavan, Koningin Astridlaan 78, B9000 Gent Tel (09) 221 8594

Antwerpen–Rowan at Lana, Anselmostraat 92, 2018 Tel (03) 238 70 17

Brugge–Stikkestek, Walweinstraat 3, 8000 Tel (050) 34 03 45

Bruxelles–Art et Fil, Rue du Bailli 25. Tel (02) 647 64 51

Gent–Rowan at Pavan, Kon. Astridlaan 78, 9000 Tel (09) 221 85 94

Hasselt–Brelboetiek Hilda, Herkenrodesingel 2, Tel (011) 25 50 71

Leuven–Rowan at Twolwinkeltje, Parijsstraat 25. Tel (016) 22 75 48

St-Niklaas–Rowan at 't Wolleken, Ankerstraat 28, 9100 Tel (03) 777 64 15

Vorselaar–Rowan at 't Allegaartje, Kuiperstraat 22a, Tel (014) 51 64 73

Wilsele–Rowan at D. Yarns, P Van Langendoncklaan 17, Tel (016) 20 13 81

Denmark

Distributor: Ruzicka, Hydesbyvej, DK-4990 Sakskobing Tel (45) 54 70 78 04 Fax (45) 54 70 78 03 Email nis@ruzicka.dk

Aabenraa–Garn Cafe, Storegade 6, 6200, Tel 74 62 07 22

Aalborg–Rowan at Design Vaerkstedet, Boulevarden 9, 9000 Tel 98 12 07 13

Aalborg–Fruens Ting, Gravensgade 13, 9000 Tel 98 13 11 12

Aarhus C–Marianne Isager, Volden 19, 8000, Tel 86 19 40 44

Fano–Kunstladen-Fano, Postvej 29, Rindby, 6270 Tel 75 16 35 04

Frederikssund–Rowan at Mode Ide Strik, Falkenborggaarden 2, 3600 Tel 42 31 23 85

Horsens–Rowan at Stokværket, Smedetorvet 3, 8700 Tel 66 16 01 31

Kobenhavn K–Rowan at Sommerfuglen, Vandkunsten 3, 1057 Tel 33 32 82 90

Kobenhavn K–Rowan at Uldstedet, Fiolstræde 13, 1171 Tel 33 91 17 71

Koge–Garnladen, Torvet 23, 4600 Tel 53 66 30 50

Lyngby–Rowan at Uldstedet, Gl Jernbanevej 7, 2800 Tel 42 88 10 88

Naestved–Butik Unik, Kindhestegade 11, 4700, Tel 53 73 52 07

Nykobing F–Betty Garn, Skolegade 8, 4800 Tel 54 85 05 35

Nykobing M–Nikoline, Blaamunkeveg 12, 7900 Tel 97 72 44 74

Odense C–Rowan at Flensted, Ramsherred 4, 5000 Tel 66 12 70 44

Odense C–Tante Groen, Vestergade 7, 5000 Tel 66 13 24 48

Randers–Gitte Garn, Sct. Mortensgade 1, 8900 Tel 86 41 93 11

Ringkobing–Garn, Stof & Hobby Shoppen, Herningvej 16, 6950 Tel 97 32 60 48

Roskilde–Rowan at Garnhokeren, Karen Olsdatterstraede 9, 4000 Tel 42 37 20 63

Vejle–Arne S. Hansen, Vestergade 45 , 7100 Tel 75 82 02 49

Eire

Dublin

Rowan at Needle Craft Ltd, 27/28 Dawson Street, 2. Tel: +3531 6772493 Fax: +3531 6771446 Email: ncraft@iol.ie Mail Order Access/Visa

Co. Wicklow–The Wool Shop, 71 Main Street, Bray. Tel/Fax: +3531 2760029

Co. Meath–Singer Sewing & Wool Centre, Unit 12, Navan Shopping Centre, Navan. Tel: +3531 2760394 Fax: +353 1 4621546

Kilkenny–Singer Sewing Centre, 64 High Street. Tel: +353 1 5621344

Faroe Islands

Distributor: Ruzicka, Hydesbyvej, DK-4990 Sakskobing Tel 54 70 78 04 Fax 54 70 78 03

Torshavn–Hespan, Smyrilsvegur 16, 100 Tel 18 737

Greenland

Distributor: Ruzicka, Hydesbyvej, DK-4990 Sakskobing Tel 54 70 78 04 Fax 54 70 78 03

Nuuk–Unik APS, Box 166, Aqqusinersuaq 6, 3900 Tel 2 40 96

France

Distributor: Elle Tricote, 52 Rue Principale, 67300 Schiltigheim Tel 03 88 23 03 13

Annecy–Rowan at Od'a'laine, 3 rue Joseph Blanc, 74000. Tel 04 50 51 38 46

Besancon–La Pastourelle, 4 rue Delavelle, 25000. Tel 03 81 80 96 51

Cadenet–Mylene Creations, 14 rue Victor Hugo, 84160 Tel 04 90 77 16 09

Paris (7)–Rowan at Le Bon Marche, 115 rue du Bac, 75007. Tel 01 44 39 80 00 Fax 01 44 39 80 50 Paris(18)–Mme Ceresa, 4 rue Saint Isaure, 75018. Tel 01 42 51 62 37

Ramonville–Rowan at Le Sabot des Laines, 15 avenue d'Occitanie, 31520. Tel 05 61 73 14 38

Saint Dié–Tricot Conseil, 11 rue d'Amerique, 88100. Tel 03 29 56 76 16

Saint-Pierre Reunion–Fath Creation, 10 rue Marius et Ary Leblond, 97410. Tel 02 62 96 18 78

Sarzeau–Rowan at Les Chemins Buissonniers, 1 Place Marie le Franc, 56370 Tel 02 97 48 08 30 Strasbourg–Rowan at Elle Tricote, 4 rue de Paques 67000 Tel 03 88 23 03 13 Fax 03 88 23 01 69

Thonon les Bains–Rowan at Au Vieux Rouet, 7 rue Ferdinand Dubouloz, 74200. Tel 04 50 71 07 33

Toulon–D'un Fil a L'Autre, 53 rue Jean Jaurès, 83000. Tel 04 94 92 63 76

Tours–Floral Street, 77 rue de la Scellerie, 37000 Tel 02 47 61 38 97 Fax 02 47 61 38 97

Germany

Distributor: Wolle & Design, Wolfshovener Strasse 76, 52428 Julich-Stetternich. Tel 02461/54735

Aachen–Rowan at Martin Gorg Wolle, Annastrasse 16, 52005 Tel 0241/4705913

Adelsdorf/Aisch–Rowan at 'LanArt' Susanne Wettendorf, Hohenstrasse 3, 91325 Tel 09195/50515 Ahrweiler–Dat Laedche, Niederhut Str. 17, 53747 Tel 02641/4464

Augsburg–Rowan at Die Mascher–Gertrud Egger, Ludvigstr 4, 86152 Tel 0821/3495607

Bielefeld-Babenhausen–Rowan at Woll-Deele–Reinhild Uffmann, Babenhauser Str. 70, 33619. Tel 0521 887909

Detmold–Die Spindel, Unter der Wehme 5, 32756 Tel 05231/33882

Hamburg–Woll-Eule–Ilse Jalloul, Frahmredder 7, 22393 Tel 040/6012920

Hamburg–Pur-Pur-Woll, Hellkamp 9, 20255 Tel 040/4904579

Hannover–Rowan at Textilwerkstatt–Minke Heijstra, Friedenstr. 1, 30175. Tel 0511 818001

Itzehoe–Allerhand von Hand–E Seligmann, Oelmuhlengang 2, 25524 Tel 04821/2807

Juelich–Rowan at Wolle & Design–R Kaufmann, Wolfshovener Str. 76, 52428 Tel 02461/54735

Keil–Wolkhaufhaus Markmann, Schonberger Str. 32-34, 24148. Tel 0431/723096

Langen–Rowan at Wollwerkstatt–Petra Schoeder, Wassergasse 24, 63225 Tel 06103/22772

Pforzheim Buchenbronn–Wollwerkstatt–M Weinmann, Pforzheimer Str. 8, 75180 Tel 07231/71416

Schallstadt–Rowan at Senfkorn–A & C Bienger, Erlenweg 16, 79227 Tel 07664/978787

Stuttgart Rowan at Strick Art–Silvia Grosse, Alexanderstr 51, 70182 Tel 0711/245218

Velbert–Rowan at mit Nadel & Faden–Barbel Hoppe-Abe, Bahnhofstr 21, 42551 Tel 02051/50712

Wenden–Handarbeiten–B Klur, Severinusstr. 2, 57482 Tel 02762/1351

Holland

Distributor: de Afstap, Oude Leliestraat 12, 1015 AW Amsterdam Tel 020-6231445

Bergen–Finlandia (Vo Haring), Kleine Dorpsstraat 26, 1861 KN. Tel 072-5894642

Bilthoven–Handwerken zonder Grenzen (Henr. Beukers), Nachtegaallaan 18a, 3722 AB. Tel 030-2280930

Zuidlaren–Ryahuis (Lucy van Zanten), Telefoonstraat 26, 9471 EN. Tel 050-4092618.

Italy

Rivoli–Victoriana, Via Fratelli Piol 14, (TO) Tel 011 95 32 142

Luxembourg

Esch/Alzette–Woll-Stuff, Monique Kohnen, Place Hotel de Ville 12, 4138. Tel 548937

Norway

Distributor: Ruzicka, Hans Aanrudsvei 48, N–0956 Oslo Tel : 47 22 25 26 92

Aasgaardstrand–Rowan at Eie's Paletten, Grev Wedelsgt 46, 3155 Tel 33 04 88 80

Elverum–Husfliden, St Olausgt 2, 2400 Tel 62 41 13 90

Kristiansand S–Jonnas Garn & Gaver, Skippergt. 18, 4611. Tel 38 07 03 95

Oslo–Rowan at Husfliden, Mollergt. 4, 0179 Tel 22 42 10 75

Oslo–Colours, Observatoriegt 25, 0252. Tel 22 44 42 60

Sauland–Rett & Vrang, 3692. Tel 35 02 33 66

Ski–Rowan at Eureka, Postbox 357, 1400 Tel 64 86 55 40

Stavanger–Olga Evensens Eftf, Laugmannsgt 4, 4006 Tel 51 89 42 66

Sweden

Distributor: Wincent, Norrtulsgaten 65, 11345 Stockholm Tel (08) 673 70 60

Ahus–P-Persson and Co, Gamia Skeppsbron 10, 29631 Tel (044) 240121

Goteborg–Nypan, Ekiandagatan 16, 41255 Tel (031) 201037

Gustavsberg–Garnplatten Gustavsbergshaven, Odelbergsv 9A, 13440 Tel (08) 510 310 38

Helsingborg–Irmas Hus, Nedra Langvinkelsgatan 15, 25220 Tel (042) 142767

Karlskrona–Cikoria, Amiralitetstorget 27, 37130 Tel (0455) 842 60

Malmo–Irmas Hus, Kalendegatan 13, 21135 Tel (040) 6110800

Orebo–Min Garnbod, Fredsgatan 11, 70362 Tel (019) 6115557

Stockholm -Rowan at Wincent, Norrtulsgaten 65, 11345 Tel (08) 673 70 60

Uppsala–Yll & Tyll, Bredgrand 7c, 75320 Tel (018) 105190

Varnamo–Donegal, Storgatsbacken 6, 33000 Tel (0370) 12590

Switzerland

Zurich–Vilfil, Klosbachstrasse 10, Beim Kreuzplatz, 8032 Tel 01 383 99 03

Hong Kong

Distributor: East Unity Company Limited, Room 902, Block A, Kailey Industrial Centre, 12 Fung Yip Street, Chai Wan Tel (852) 2869 7110

Iceland

Distributor: Rowan at Storkurinn, Kjorgardi, Laugavegi 59, ICE -101. Tel 551 82 58

Akranes–Handradinn, Kirkjubraut 3, 300 Akranes Tel 431 5500

Akureyri–Handid, Skipagata 16, 600 Akureyri Tel 462 4088

Reykjavik–Kjorgardi, Laugavegur 59, 101 Reykjavik Tel 551 8258 Fax 562 8252

Skrinan–Eyrarvegur 27, 800 Selfoss Tel 482 3238

Japan

Distributor: Diakeito Co Ltd, 2-3-11 Senba-Higashi, Minoh City, Osaka 562 Tel 0727 27 6604

New Zealand

Distributor: c/o Coats Spencer Crafts, Level 1 , 382 Wellington Road, Mulgrave North, Victoria, Australia 3170. Tel : 61 39561 2288

Auckland Alterknitives, PO Box 47 961. Tel : 64 937 60337

United Kingdom Stockists

Bath and North East Somerset

Bath–Rowan at Stitch Shop, 15 The Podium, Northgate. Tel: 01225 481134 Mail Order Mastercard/Visa/American Express

Bath–Number Three, 3 Saville Row. Tel no: 01225 427876 Fax: 01225 427976 Mail Order Mastercard/Visa

Bristol

Bristol–Rowan at John Lewis, Cribbs Causeway. Tel: 0117 959 1100

Bedfordshire

Leighton Buzzard–Rowan at Bah Bah's, Peacock Mews. Tel: 01525 376456 Mail Order

Berkshire

Windsor–Caleys, 19 High Street. Tel: 01753 863241

Reading–Rowan at Heelas, Broad Street. Tel: 01189 575955

South Ascot–South Ascot Wools, 18 Brockenhurst Road. Tel: 01344 628327

Buckinghamshire

Aylesbury–Beatties, 27 Friars Square. Tel: 01296 399996 Mastercard/Visa

Milton Keynes–Rowan at John Lewis, Central Milton Keynes. Tel: 01908 679171

Cambridgeshire

Cambridge–Rowan at Robert Sayle, St Andrews Street. Tel: 01223 361292

Peterborough–John Lewis, Queensgate Centre. Tel: 01733 344644

Cheshire

Altrincham–Rowan at Creative Knitting, 27A Oxford Road. Tel: 0161 941 2534 Mail Order Mastercard/Visa 24 Hr Ansphone

Cheadle–John Lewis, Wilmslow Road. Tel: 0161 491 4914

Cornwall

Penzance–Iriss, 66 Chapel Street. Tel: 01736 66568

St. Ives–Antiques, Buttons & Crafts, 3A Tregenna Hill. Tel: 01736 793713

WADEBRIDGE–Rowan at Artycrafts, 41 Molesworth Street. Tel: 01208 812274

Cumbria

Carlisle–Pingouin, 20 Globe Lane. Tel: 01228 20681

Cockermouth–Silkstone, 12 Market Place. Tel: 01900 821 052 Fax: 01900 821 051 Mail Order Mastercard/Visa

Grasmere–Mainly British Crafts, 1 Broadgate Tel: 01539 435553

Penrith Rowan at Indigo, 7 Devonshire Arcade. Tel: 01768 899917 Mail Order Mastercard/Visa

Devon

Braunton–Woolcrafts, 19 Cross Tree Centre. Tel: 01271 815075

Plymouth–Rowan at Dingles, 40-46 Royal Parade. Tel: 01752 266611 Mail Order Mastercard/Visa

Tavistock–Knitting Image, 9 Pepper Street. Tel: 01822 617410

Totnes–Sally Carr Designs, The Yarn Shop, 31 High Street. Tel: 01803 863060

Dorset

Bridport–Harlequin, 76 West Street. Tel: 01308 456449

Christchurch–Honora, 69 High Street. Tel: 01202 486000

Sherborne–Hunters of Sherborne, 4 Tilton Court, Digby Road. Tel: 01935 817722

Wimborne–Rowan at The Walnut Tree, 1 West Borough. Tel: 01202 840722

Durham

Darlington–Rowan at Binns, 7 High Row. Tel: 01325 462606 Mail Order Mastercard/Visa

Barnard Castle–Castle Fabrics & Crafts, 3 Market Place. Tel: 01833 638412 Mail Order

Essex

Maldon–Peachey Ethknits, 6/7 Edwards Walk. Tel: 01621 857102 Mail Order Mastercard/ Visa

Gloucestershire

Cheltenham–Rowan at Cavendish House, The Promenade. Tel: 01242 521300 Mail Order Mastercard/Visa

Cirencester–Ashley's Wool Specialist, 62 Dyer Street. Tel: 01285 653245 Mail Order

Hampshire

Alresford–Designer Knits, The Gable House, New Farm Road. Tel: 01962 733499

Basingstoke–Pack Lane Wool Shop, 171 Pack Lane, Kempshott. Tel: 01256 323644

Lymington–Leigh's, 56 High Street. Tel: 01590 673254

Southampton–Tyrrell & Green, Above Bar. Tel: 01703 227711

Southsea–Knight & Lee, Palmerston Road. Tel: 01705 827511

Twyford–Riverside Yarns, Cockscombe Farm, Watley Lane. Tel: 01962 714380

Winchester–C & H Fabrics, 8 High Street. Tel: 01962 843355

Hertfordshire

Boreham Wood–The Wool Shop, 92 Shenley Road. Tel: 0181 905 2499 Also Mail Order

Harpenden–In Stitches, 12 Leyton Road. Tel: 01582 769011 Mastercard/Visa/Amex

Potters Bar–Institches, 37-39 The Broadway, Darkes Lane. Tel/Fax: 01707 652 963

Watford–Rowan at Trewins, The Harlequin, High Street. Tel: 01923 244266

Welwyn Garden City–Rowan at John Lewis, Tel: 01707 323456

Kent

Canterbury–C & H Fabrics, 2 St. George's Street. Tel: 01227 459760

Herne Bay–Patricia's Wool Shop, 100 Sea St. Tel: 01227 362991

Maidstone–C & H Fabrics, 68 Week Street. Tel: 01622 762054

Rochester–Rowan at Francis Iles, 73 High Street. Tel: 01634 843082 Mail Order Mastercard/Visa

Romney Marsh–Woodfall Wools, 'Retreat', Dungeness Road, Dungeness. Tel: 01797 321708–Mail Order Only

Sandwich–Stitches, 30 St. Peters Street. Tel/Fax: 01304 614702 Mail Order/Accepts credit cards

Tunbridge Wells–C & H Fabrics, 113/115 Mount Pleasant. Tel: 01892 522618

Lancashire

Accrington–Sheila's Wool Shop, 284 Union Road, Oswaldtwistle. Tel: 01254 875525 Email: sheilaswool-shop@compuserve.com

St Anne's On Sea–Rowan at Kathleen Barnes, 22 The Crescent. Tel/Fax: 01253 724194 Mail Order Mastercard/Visa

Leicesterchire

Oakham–Rowan at The Wool Centre, 40 Melton Road. Tel: 01572 757574 Mail Order/Knitting up service available/Mastercard/Visa

Lincolnshire

Boston–Wool & Crafts, 14 Pen Street Tel: 01205 356681

Stamford–Rowan at The Wool Centre, Unit 17 Stamford Walk Tel: 01780 764626 Mail order/Knitting up Service available/Accepts Credit Cards

London–Central

Rowan at Harrods, 87-135 Brompton Road, Knightsbridge, SW1X 7XL. Tel: 0171 730 1234 Mail Order Mastercard/Visa

Rowan at Creativity, 45 New Oxford Street, WC1. Tel: 0171 240 2945 Fax: 0171 240 6030 Mail Order Mastercard/Visa

Rowan at Colourway, 112A Westbourne Grove, W2. Tel: 0171 229 1432 Mail Order Mastercard/Visa 24 Hr Ansphone

Rowan at Liberty, Regent Street, W1. Tel: 0171 734 1234 Mail Order Mastercard/Visa

Rowan at John Lewis, Oxford Street, W1. Tel: 0171 629 7711

Rowan at Peter Jones, Sloane Square, SW1. Tel: 0171 730 3434

Rowan at Selfridges, 400 Oxford Street W1A 1AB. Tel: 0171 318 3856 Mail Order Mastercard/Visa Chiswick–Creations, 29 Turnham Green Terrace. W4 1RS Tel: 0181 747 9697 Mail Order

Debbie Bliss, 365 St John Street, EC1V 4LB Tel: 0171 833 8255

London–North

Rowan at John Lewis, Brent Cross Shopping Centre, NW4. Tel: 0181 202 6535

London–South

Maple Textiles, 199 Maple Road, Penge. Tel: 0181 778 8049

Needles Wool Shop, Thornton Road, East Sheen SW14. Tel: 0181 878 1592

Creations, 79 Church Road, Barnes SW13. Tel: 0181 563 2970 Mail Order

Merseyside

Liverpool–Rowan at George Henry Lee, Basnett Street. Tel: 0151 709 7070

Middlesex

Brentford–Stable of Imagination, Syon Park Garden Centre. Tel: 0181 569 9525

Norfolk

Roughton–Rowan at Sew Creative, Groveland Farm, Thorpe Market Road. Tel: 01263 834021 Mail Order Mastercard/Visa

Norwich–Bonds, All Saints Green. Tel: 01603 660021

Norwich–Traditional Wool Shop, 8 Bridewell Alley. Tel: 01603 761861

Northumberland

Corbridge–The Fabric & Tapestry Shop, Sydgate House, Middle Street. Tel: 01434 632902 Mail Order

Nottinghamshire

Nottingham–Rowan at Jessops, Victoria Centre. Tel: 0115 9418282

Oxfordshire

Burford–Burford Needlecraft Shop, 117 High Street. Tel: 01993 822136 Mail Order Mastercard/Visa

Oxford–Rowan at Rowan–102 Gloucester Green. Tel: 01865 793366 Mail Order Mastercard/Visa 24 Hr Ansphone

Shropshire

Shrewsbury–Rowan at House of Needlework, 11 Wyle Cop. Tel: 01743 355533 (Formerly Osa)

Somerset

Burnham-on-Sea–The Woolsack, 7 College Street. Tel: 01278 784443

Taunton–Hayes Wools, 150 East Reach. Tel: 01823 284768 Mail Order Mastercard/Visa

Yeovil–Enid's, Wool & Craft Shop, Church Street. Tel: 01935 412421

Staffordshire

Newcastle under Lyme–The Spinning Wheel, 40 High Street. Tel: 01782 630484

Suffolk

Bury St Edmunds–Rowan at Jaycraft, 78 St John's Street. Tel: 01284 752982 Mail order/Accepts credit cards

Ipswich–Spare Moments, 13 Northgate Street. Tel: 01473 259876

Surrey

Banstead–Maxime Wool & Craft Shop, 155 High Street. Tel: 01737 352798

Kingston–Rowan at John Lewis, Wood Street. Tel: 0181 547 3000

Guildford–Rowan at Army & Navy, High Street. Tel: 01483 568171 Mail Order Mastercard/Visa

Nr Dorking–Holmcroft Supplies, 186 The Street, Capel. Tel: 01306 711126 Mail Order Mastercard/Visa

East Sussex

Battle–Battle Wool Shop, 2 Mount Street. Tel: 01424 775073

Brighton–Rowan at Colourworks, 22 Gardner Street. Tel: 01273 628860 Mail Order Mastercard/Visa

Brighton–C & H Fabrics, 179 Western Road. Tel: 01273 321671

Eastbourne–C & H Fabrics, 82/86 Terminus Road. Tel: 01323 410503

East Hoathley (Nr Uckfield)–The Wool Loft, Upstairs at Clara's, 9 High Street. Tel: 01825 840339 Mail Order

Forest Row–Village Crafts, The Square. Tel: 01342 823238

Lewes–Kangaroo, 70 High Street. Tel: 01273 478554 Mastercard/Visa Mail Order

West Sussex

Arundle–Rowan at David's Needle-Art, 37 Tarrant Street. Tel: 01903 882761

Burgess Hill–The Fabric Shop, 29 The Martlets–Tel: 01444 236688 Mail Order Mastercard/Visa

Chichester–C & H Fabrics, 33/34 North Street. Tel: 01243 783300

Horsham–The Fabric Shop c/o Chart & Lawrence Ltd–Tel: 01403 217945 Mail Order Mastercard/Visa

Hove–The Fabric Shop, 77 Boundary Road–Tel: 01273 419358 Mail Order Mastercard/Visa

Seaford–The Fabric Shop, 30 Broad Street–Tel: 01323 891011 Mail Order Mastercard/Visa

Shoreham By Sea–Rowan at Shoreham Knitting, 19 East Street. Tel: 01273 461029 Mail Order Email: skn@sure-employ.demon.co.uk

Worthing–The Fabric Shop, 1 Guildbourne Centre. Tel: 01903 207389 Mail Order Mastercard/Visa

Teeside

Guisborough–Leven Crafts, Chaloner Mews, Chaloner Street. Tel: 01287 610207

Hartlepool–Bobby Davison, 101 Park Road. Tel: 01429 861300

Tyne & Wear

Gateshead–Rowan at House of Fraser, Metro Centre. Tel: 0191 493 2424 Mail Order Mastercard/Visa

Newcastel Upon Tyne–Rowan at Bainbridge, Eldon Square. Tel: 0191 232 5000

Warwickshire

Studley–Clare–28 High Street. Tel: 01527 854441

Warwick–Warwick Wools, 17 Market Place. Tel: 01926 492853

West Midlands

Birmingham–Rowan at Rackhams, Corporation Street. Tel: 0121 236 3333 Mail Order Mastercard/Visa

Solihull–Stitches, 355 Warwick Road, Olton. Tel: 0121 706 1048

Wolverhampton–Rowan at Beatties, 71-78 Victoria Street. Tel: 01902 422311 Mastercard/Visa

Wiltshire

Calne–Handi Wools, 3 Oxford Road. Tel: 01249 812081

Salisbury–Stitches, Cross Keys Chequer. Tel: 01722 411148 Mail Order

Worcestershire

Droitwich–Fil D'or, 20 High Street. Tel: 01905 776793

North Yorkshire

Helmsley–Rowan at Tapestry Garden, 2 Castlegate. Tel: 01439 771300 Mail Order Mastercard/Visa

Ripon–Rowan at Cathedral Yarns, 6 Kirkgate. Tel: 01765 604007

Settle–Ancient & Modern, Station Street. Tel: 01729 824298

Whitby–Rowan at Bobbins, Wesley Hall, Church Street. Tel: 01947 600585 Mail Order Mastercard/Visa Email: bobbins@globalnet.co.uk

York–Rowan at Craft Basics, 9 Gillygate. Tel: 01904 652840 Mail Order/Mastercard/Visa:

South Yorkshire

Sheffield–Rowan at Cole Brothers, Barkers Pool. Tel: 0114 2768511

West Yorkshire

Hebden Bridge–Rowan at Attica Fabrics, 2 Commercial Street. Tel: 01422 844327 Mail Order

Holmfirth–Rowan at Up Country, 6 Market Walk. Tel & Fax: 01484 687803 Mail Order American Express/Mastercard/Visa Email: gpaul@upco.u-net.com

Wales

Conwy–Ar-y-Gweill, 8 Heol Yr Orsaf, Llanrwst. Tel: 01492 641149

Dyfed–Wool Baa, 33 Blue Street, Carmarthen. Tel: 01267 236734

Fishguard–Melin Tregwynt, 6 High Street. Tel: 01348 872370

St Davids–Melin Tregwynt, 5 Nun Street. Tel: 01437 720386

Scotland

Aberdeen–Rowan at Harlequin, 65 Thistle Street. Tel: 01224 635716 Mail Order Mastercard/Visa

Aberdeen–John Lewis, George Street. Tel: 01224 625000

Beauly–Linda Usher, 50 High Street. Tel: 01463 783017

Castle Douglas–Needlecraft, 201 King Street. Tel: 01556 503606

Edinburgh–Rowan at John Lewis, St James Centre. Tel: 0131 556 9121

Edinburgh–Rowan at Jenners, 48 Princes Street. Tel: 0131 225 2442 Mail Order Mastercard/Visa

Edinburgh–Rowan at Wooly Mammoth, 17 Jeffrey Street, Off the Royal Mile. Tel/Fax: 0131 557 5025 Mail Order/Accepts Credit Cards Email: mammoth@ednet.co.uk

Glasgow–Rowan at Mandors, 346 Sauchiehall Street at 1 Scott Street. Tel: 0141 332 7716

Helensburgh–Rowan at Elizabeth Potterton, 42 West Clyde Street. Tel: 01436 671747 Order Mastercard/Visa

Isle of Arran–Trareoch Craft Shop, Whiting Bay. Tel: 01770 700226

Isle of Skye–Struan Craft Studio, Struan. Tel: 01470 572 284

Lanark–Strands, 8 Bloomgate. Tel: 01555 665757 Mail Order Mastercard/Visa

Longniddry–Longniddry Post Office, 29a Links Road. Tel: 01875 852894

Montrose–Mary Stuart Scott, Lumenart, 20/22 Murray Street. Tel: 01674 675502

Shetland Islands

Rowan at Wimberry, Gardens, Skeld. Tel: 01595 860371 Mail Order Mastercard/Visa

United States of America

Distributor: Westminster Fibers Inc, 5 Northern Boulevard, Amherst, New Hampshire 03031 Tel (603) 886 5041/5043 Email: wfibers@aol.com

Alabama

Birmingham–The London Knitting Company, 2531 Rocky Ridge Rd, #101, 35243 Tel (205) 822-5855

Alaska

Anchorage–Knitting Frenzy, 4240 Old Seward Hwy., #101 99503 Tel (907) 563-2717

Arizona
Tucson–Purls, 7862 North Oracle Road, 85704 Tel (520) 797-8118

California
Anaheim Hills–Rowan at Velona Needlecraft, 5753-B Santa Ana Canyon Road, 92807 Tel (714) 974-1570

Berkeley–Rowan at Straw Into Gold, 3006 San Pablo Avenue, 94702 Tel (510) 548-5243

Carmel–Rowan at Knitting by the Sea, 5th Ave & Junipero, 93921 Tel (408) 624-3189

Danville–Rowan at Filati Yarns, 125 Railroad Ave, Suite D, 94526 Tel (510) 820-6614

Glendale–Village Needleworks, 1413 1/2 W Kenneth Rd, 91201 Tel (818) 507-5990

Los Altos–Rowan at Uncommon Threads, 293 State Street, 94022 Tel (415) 941-1815

Oakland–The Knitting Basket, 2054 Mountain Blvd, 94611 Tel (800) 654-4887

San Francisco–Rowan at Yarn Garden, 545 Sutter St, Ste 202, 94102. Tel (415) 956-8830

San Francisco–Rowan at Greenwich Yarns, 2073 Greenwich Street, 94123 Tel (415) 567-2535

Santa Barbara–Santa Barbara Knitting Studio, 2253, A Las Positas Rd., 93105 Tel (805) 563-4987

Santa Maria–Betty's Fabrics, 1627 So. Broadway, 93454 Tel (805) 922-2181

Santa Monica–L'Atelier on Montana, 1202 Montana Ave 90403 Tel (310) 394-4665

Solana Beach–Common Threads, 531 Stevens Avenue, 92075 Tel (619) 481-2112

Colorado
Denver–Skyloom Fibers, 1705 S. Pearl, 80210 Tel (303) 777-2331

Connecticut
Cheshire–Have You Any Wool, 1101 S Main St, 06410 Tel (203) 699-9644

Westport–Rowan at Hook 'N' Needle, 1869 Post Rd East, 06880 Tel (203) 259-5119

Washington Depot–Featheridge Designs, 4 Green Hill Road, 06794 Tel (800) 371-1014

Illinois
Chicago–Barkim Ltd. (Mail Order Only) 47 W. Polk St., 60605 Tel (888) 548-2211 Email BarkimLtd@aol.com

Chicago–Weaving Workshop, 2218 N Lincoln Ave, 60614 Tel (773) 929-5776

Clarendon Hills–Flying Colours Inc, 154 Burlington, 60514 Tel (630) 325-0888

Elmhurst–Great Yarn Loft, 120 N York Rd, Ste 220, 60126 Tel (630) 833-7423

Evanston–Closeknit Inc, 622 Grove St. 60201 Tel (847) 328 6760

Springfield–Nancy's Knitworks, 1650 W Wabash, Ste 1, 62704 Tel (217) 546-0600

St Charles–The Fine Line Creative Arts Center, 6 N. 158 Crane Rd, 60175 Tel (630) 584-9443

Indiana
Ft. Wayne–Cass Street Depot, 1044 Cass Street, 46802 Tel (219) 420-2277

Indianapolis–Mass. Avenue Knit Shop, 521 East North Street, 46204. Tel (800) 675-8565

Kansas
Lawrence–Rowan at The Yarn Barn, 930 Massachusetts Ave, 66044 Tel (800) 468-0035

Maine
Camden–Rowan at Stitchery Square , 11 Elm St, 04843 Tel (207) 236-9773

Freeport–Rowan at Grace Robinson & Co, 231 US Rte 1 South, 04032 Tel (207) 865-6110

Maryland
Baltimore–Rowan at Woolworks, 6305 Falls Rd, 21209 Tel (410) 337-9030

Bethseda–Rowan at Needlework Attic, 4706 Bethseda Ave, 20814 Tel (800) 654-6654

Bethseda–Rowan at Yarns International, 5110 Ridgefield Road, 20816 Tel (301) 913-2980

Massachusetts
Boston–Yarnwinder, 247 Newbury St, 02116 Tel (617) 262-0028

Harvard–Bare Hill Studio/Fiber Loft, Rt. 111, P.O. Building. 01451 Tel (800) 874-9276

Lexington–Rowan at Wild & Woolly Studio, 7A Meriam St, 02173 Tel (781) 861-7717

Lenox–Rowan at Colorful Stitches, 48 Main St. 01240 Tel (800) 413-6111

Michigan
Birmingham–Knitting Room, 251 Merrill, 48009 Tel (248) 540-3623

Howell–Stitch in Time, 722 East Grand River, 48843 Tel (517) 546-0769

Menominee–Elegant Ewe, 400 First Street, 49858-3308 Tel (906) 863-2296

Traverse City–Lost Art Yarn Shoppe, 123 East Front St., 49684 Tel (616) 941-1263

Wyoming–Threadbender Yarn Shop–2767 44th St, SW, 49509 Tel (888) 531-6642

Minnesota
Minneapolis–Rowan at Linden Hills Yarn, 2720 W. 43rd St, 55410 Tel (612) 929-1255

Minnetonka–Skeins 11309 Highway 7, 55305 Tel (612) 939-4166

St Paul–Rowan at The Yarnery KMK Crafts, 840 Grand Ave. 55105 Tel 612 222 5793

White Bear Lake–Rowan at A Sheepy Yarn Shoppe, 2185 Third St, 55110 Tel (800) 480-5462

Montana
Stevensville–Wild West Wools, 3920 Suite B Highway 93N, 59870. Tel (406) 777-4114

Nebraska
Omaha–Rowan at Personal Threads Boutique, 8025 W Dodge Rd, 68114 Tel (402) 391-7733

New Hampshire
Center Harbor–Keepsake Quilting & Country Pleasures, Senter's Market, Rt. 25, 03226 Tel (800) 865-9458

Center Ossipee–Rowan at Yarn Express (Mail order only), 120 Moultonville Rd, 03814 Tel (800) 432-1886

Exeter–Charlotte's Web, Exeter Village Shops, 137 Epping Rd, Rt. 27, 03833 Tel (603) 778-1417

New Jersey
Chatham–Stitching Bee, 240A Main Street, 07928 Tel (201) 635-6691

Garwood–Knitter's Workshop Inc., 345 North Avenue, 07027 Tel (908) 789-1333

Parsippany–Creations, 177 Parsippany Road, 07054. Tel (973) 581 1998

New Mexico
Albuquerque–Village Wools, 3801 San Mateo Ave, N.E., 87110 Tel (505) 883-2919

Santa Fe–Needle's Eye, 927 Paseo de Peralta, 87501. Tel (505) 982 0706

New York
Bedford Hills–Lee's Yarn Center, 733 N Bedford Rd, 10507 Tel (914) 244-3400

Brooklyn–Rowan at Heartmade (Mail Order only), 521 Third St, 11215 Tel (800) 898-4290

Buffalo–Elmwood Yarn Shop, 1639 Hertel Ave, 14216. Tel (716) 834 7580

Commack–HappiKnits, 6333 Jericho Tpke, 11725 Tel (516) 462-5558

East Hampton–Knitlove, 42 Gingerbread Lane, 11937 Tel (516) 329-0700

Garden City–Rowan at Garden City Stitches, 725 Franklin Avenue, 11530 Tel (516) 739-5648

Great Neck–Open Door to Stitchery, 87A Middle Neck Road, 11021 Tel (516) 487-9442

Ithaca–The Homespun Boutique, On The Commons, 14850 Tel (607) 277-0954

Locust Valley–The Wool Shop, 25 The Plaza, 11560 Tel (516) 671-9722

New York City–The Yarn Company, 2274 Broadway, 10024 Tel (212) 787-7878

New York City–Rowan at Yarn Connection, 218 Madison Ave, 10016, Tel (212) 684-5099

Schenectady–Ye Olde Yarn & Gift Shoppe, 839 McClellan St., 12304 Tel (518) 393-2695

Skancatcles–Rowan at Elegant Needles, 5 Jordan St., 13152 Tel (315) 685-9276

Ohio
Aurora–Edie's Knit Shop, 215 W. Garfield Rd, 44202 Tel (216) 562-7226

Cincinnati–Rowan at Wizard Weavers, 2701 Observatory Rd, 45208 Tel (513) 871-5750

Cleveland–Fine Points, 2026 Murray Hill, 44106 Tel (216) 229-6644

Columbus–Wolfe Fiber Art, 1188 W 5th Ave, 43212 Tel (614) 487-9980

Marion–Abbey Yarns & Kits, 1512 Meyers Road, 43302 Tel (800) 999-5648

Oregon
Ashland–Web-sters, 11 North Main St, 97520 Tel (888) 482-9801

Eugene–Soft Horizons, 412 East 13th Ave, 97401 Tel (541) 343-0651

West Lynn–Molehill Farm, 1246 SW Borland Rd, 97068 Tel (503) 638-6799

Pennsylvania
Chaddsford–A Garden of Yarn, Rt. 202 & Rugg Road, Olde Ridge Village #10, 19317 Tel (610) 459-5599

Lancaster–Oh Susana, 2204 Marietta Ave, 17603 Tel (717) 393-5146

Philadelphia–Rowan at Sophie's Yarns, 2017 Locust Street, 19103 Tel (215) 977-9276

Philadelphia–Tangled Web, 7900 Germantown Ave, 19118 Tel (215) 242-1271

Sewickley–Rowan at Yarns Unlimited, 435 Beaver St, 15143 Tel (412) 741-8894

Rhode Island
Providence–Rowan at A Stitch Above Ltd, 190 Wayland Ave, 02906 Tel (800) 949-5648

Tiverton–Rowan at Sakonnet Purls, 3988 Main Rd, 02878 Tel (401) 624-9902

Texas
San Antonio–Rowan at The Yarn Barn of San Antonio, 4300 McCullough, 78212 Tel (210) 826-3679

Vermont
Middlebury–Charlotte's Collections, Merchant's Row 05753. Tel (802) 388 3895

Woodstock–Rowan at The Whippletree, 7 Central St, 05091 Tel (802) 457-1325

Virginia
Falls Church–Aylin's Woolgathercr, 7245 Arlington Blvd. #318, 22042 Tel (703) 573-1900 Fredericksburg–Rowan at Cambridge Studio, 580 Belle Plains Road, 22405 Tel (540) 373-5497

McLean–Rowan at Wooly Knits, 6728 Lowell Ave, 22101 Tel (800) 767-4036

Manassas–Old Town Needlecraft, 9774 Center Street, 20110. Tel (703) 330 1846

Middleburg–Hunt Country Yarns, 1 West Federal Street, 20118-1206. Tel (540) 687 5129

Richmond–The Knitting Basket, 5812 Grove Ave, 23226 Tel (804) 282-2909

Washington
Bellevue–Parkside Wool Company, 17 102nd Ave, NE, 98004 Tel (425) 455-2138

Poulsbo–Lauren's Wild & Wooly, 19020 Front St.,98370 Tel (360) 779-3222

Seattle–Rowan at The Weaving Works, 4717 Brooklyn Ave, N.E., 98105 Tel (888) 524-1221

Wisconsin
Appleton–Jane's Knitting Hutch, 2001 N.Appleton St, 54911. Tel (920) 954 9001

Delevan–Studio S Fiber Arts, W8903 County Hwy A, 53115 Tel (608) 883-2123

Elm Grove–The Yarn Haus, 940 Elm Grove Rd, 53122 Tel (414) 786-5660

Madison–The Knitting Tree Inc, 2614 Monroe St, 53711 Tel (608) 238 0121

Madison–Weaving Workshop, 920 E Johnson St, 53703 Tel (608) 255-1066

Waukesha–The Woolgathering (Mail Order only), 750 Calico Ct., 53186 Tel (888) 248-3225

Wausau–Rowan at The Black Purl, 300 Third St, 54403 Tel (715) 843-7875

INDEX